THE
Ms. Spent™
MONEY GUIDE

THE
Ms. Spent™
MONEY GUIDE

....

Get More of What You Want
with What You Earn

DEBORAH KNUCKEY

JOHN WILEY & SONS, INC.

New York • Chichester • Weinheim • Brisbane • Singapore • Toronto

Published by John Wiley & Sons, Inc.
Published simultaneously in Canada.

Ms. Spent is a registered trademark of Deborah Knuckey, LLC.

This publication is designed to provide accurate and authoritative information in regard to the subject matter covered. It is sold with the understanding that the publisher is not engaged in rendering professional services. If professional advice or other expert assistance is required, the services of a competent professional person should be sought.

Library of Congress Cataloging-in-Publication Data:

Knuckey, Deborah.
    The Ms. Spent money guide : get more of what you want with what you earn / Deborah Knuckey.
        p.   cm.
    Includes index.
    ISBN 0-471-39634-6 (cloth : alk. paper)
    1. Finance, Personal.   2. Money.   3. Consumer behavior.   I. Title.

HG179 .K5798 2001
332.024—dc21   00-046263

For my mother,
Donna Young,
who taught me the value of a big dream
and the value of a dollar.

Acknowledgments

Thanks to all the people who shared their stories: Your struggles and triumphs inspired me to keep writing and will inspire readers who see *their* stories in yours. Thank you for your time and your openness.

Thanks to Denise Marcil, my literary agent, who took a chance on an unpublished author, and to Debby Englander, Meredith McGinnis, and everyone at John Wiley & Sons for working with me from day one to get the message out. For everyone at FinancialFinesse.com: Thank you for giving me the opportunity to share the message.

Thanks to all the people who contributed their skills and thoughts. Special thanks to James Davies for his fabulous photography, Martin Gold and Alison Brown for their design skills, Adrienne de Kretser for her insight and logical thinking, Jodie Klein and Amy Watson for helping me get Ms. Spent into the media, and Tony Schaps for bringing Ms. Spent to life on the Web. Thanks to my personal coach, Caroline Otis, who helped me find the carrots and sticks needed to keep me writing. I appreciate the input of the academics, economists, and hands-on experts who shared ideas with me, including Dr. Dean Maki at the Federal Reserve, Nick Zwileneff at the Bureau of Labor Statistics, Sue Wilson at AllState, Eric Taylor at Federal Funding, and the helpful people at AARP, the Social Security Administration, and Sallie Mae.

To my family—Mum, Ed, Ian, Michael, Jane, Joan, my gorgeous nephews Alex and William, my beautiful goddaughter Caitlin, and my American-Mom Gena—your love and support mean so much to me. Thanks to the many friends who put up with me through chapters thick and thin. And no thanks to my cat, Cous Cous, who thinks it is more important for me to be amused than productive.

D.K.

Contents

PART THREE

Go: Becoming a Conscious Spender
205

THE
Ms. Spent™
MONEY GUIDE

Introduction

T HIS BOOK IS NOT JUST ABOUT MONEY. IT'S ABOUT YOUR LIFE. It's about how you use money to get the life you want. Money is what I'm talking about, but I could just as easily be talking about time, or relationships, or emotional energy.

This book is designed to help you have more of the life you want, not by wishing and yearning and striving and struggling, but by taking the resources that are already available to you and using them for your highest good. Too many of us have a misspent life. While a misspent youth brings images of running with the bad crowd, a misspent life is about not running at all. A misspent life happens when you forget what it is you really want, when you settle for someone else's idea of life because you are too busy to pursue your dreams.

When I started writing my Internet advice column, I chose the name Ms. Spent as a tongue-in-cheek reminder of how much of our hard-earned money is spent on stuff that is not what we truly want. The moniker may be funny, but my mission is dead serious: I want to help you get more of the life that you want.

. . . .

One day you wake up and find your fairy godmother standing by your bed. "I've come to tell you that you will receive some money

1

*every month from now until you retire. I must warn you, however,"
she continues, "you must spend it the way you really want to or it will
disappear." With that, she's gone.*

*Over the years, nothing special happens. At your retirement party,
you look through the crowd and see a familiar figure. She comes over
and says, "Well, what did you do with it?"*

*"With what?" you ask petulantly, "I just worked hard, and lived
my life. I bought a home and a car, put my kids through school,
saved for retirement, and traveled once in a while."*

"Ah, so that is what you really wanted," she interrupts.

*"Well, no. I really wanted to take my family and live on a boat for
a year. I wanted to give a gift to a poor child that would change his
life forever. I wanted to see every great show on Broadway with my
wife. I wanted to retire in style without needing to work part time.*

"What happened to that gift you promised?" you demand.

*"Gift? Oh, I was referring to your income. I guess I was right. If
you didn't spend it on what you really wanted, it would disappear."*

. . . .

What I like to call "Conscious Spending" is the art of aligning
how you use your money with what you truly value. It is an awareness that directs your spending toward your dreams. As you learn
this art, you will take charge of your financial life and move to a
place where it is shaped by your conscious, deliberate choices.

Sometimes it is hard to see your finances, or even your life, as
being largely under your control. Circumstances happen. Choices
made one year can impact the rest of your life. An unexpected crisis can turn your whole world upside down. However, at the end
of the day, you still have tremendous opportunities available to
you with the money you already have. This book helps you reclaim these opportunities.

What about the fairytale? What would your life have been like if your fairy godmother had majored in clear communication? You would have made more conscious choices with your money. Perhaps you would have taken your family to live on a boat for a month one summer and traveled to New York for a weekend of theater every so often. Remember, though, the choices would have come at a price. Perhaps you would have ended up driving an older car, brown-bagging lunch more often, and not redoing the second bathroom.

I wrote this book for your inner fairy godmother. I want you to give yourself more of the life you want with the money you have. My wish for you is that you consciously strive to make your dreams a reality. You shouldn't unconsciously accept someone else's dreams. You shouldn't stifle or put your dreams on hold until you are too old to enjoy them.

Travel, learning, fast cars, meaningful causes, high fashion, family reunions, wine collections, home, sweet home—what you get juiced by is your business. My business is to help you focus on the stuff that juices you and to give you the tools to get more of those things. I can't guarantee that you will ever get all that you want, although I strongly believe that if you want something enough you'll find a way to earn it. I can guarantee that if you use money consciously to follow your passion, you will get more pleasure for your money.

Two quick asides. First, I won't advocate penny-pinching frugality. That may be how you decide you get the most for your money, but this book is not about living frugally or stopping consumption. I'm all for spending money—on the things that you enjoy. Second, I'm not going to judge which are the "right" values or what is "good" spending. All spending puts money into the economy and keeps others gainfully employed. If spending $70 on a pair of new shoes brings you more enjoyment than giving the money to charity or completing a long-delayed repair on your home, that's fine. I don't think that makes you any better, worse, holier, or unholier than another person who makes a different decision. It just makes you *you*. And, that is what makes life interesting.

Coaching Versus Counseling: Two Ways to Change Your Relationship with Money

Money is a deeply emotional issue. That's why it is so hard to change our behavior around money even when we know that our behavior is irrational or not serving our best interests. Whether or not you're aware of the patterns that lead to your behavior around money today, those patterns probably have a strong impact on how you act around money. A number of recently published books have addressed the emotional issues surrounding money. Most books approach the issues from a typical counseling or therapy belief that you need to understand why a pattern was created before you can unhook from it and move to a healthier pattern. Such books generally start with the need to understand the assumptions made in childhood and to heal the emotional wounds that created them.

This book takes a coaching perspective rather than a therapy perspective. Coaching operates from a place of looking forward to the goals and dreams in your life and starting to move in that direction today. You may never understand the details of why you adopted the beliefs you have carried around for so long, but you can still change your behavior.

I grew up in a fairly typical middle-class family in Australia. However, my father died before I was five, leaving my mother with three young children to bring up alone. When I was eight, I romanticized the feisty parentless heroines of the novels that I read, such as Pippi Longstocking and Anne of Green Gables. I didn't know what my mother's financial situation was, but assumed that there was never a lot of spare cash around. Even though my needs were always met and my mother was generous, I decided that we were poor and I started playing the little martyr. I stoically avoided asking for what I wanted: a movie with friends, or some extra money for a Girl Scout event. I learned later that my mother owned her house outright and had enough income for us never to have to worry. However, my misplaced belief that my father's death left us financially vulnerable has played out in my behavior around money ever since. I tend to save a lot and have a level of financial security that is out of line with the likelihood of my ever ending up on the streets. Is it a logical belief? No, there were never any wolves at the door. Do I need to undo every illogical childhood assumption before being able to manage my money well? I don't think so.

Under the counseling or therapy approach, I would spend a lot of time analyzing how I felt growing up in my family circumstances. The therapy approach highlights just how much of what we *know* about the world is simply an individual interpretation: Siblings growing up in the same household with the same circumstances may have very different stories about the same events. What impacted one profoundly may have gone unnoticed by another. The self-knowledge that comes from the counseling approach may bring other gifts as well. For example, when your adult self unravels the stories your child self told you about money, it may also unravel the stories about love, being wanted, and fitting in. All interesting stuff, but for some people it may be the work of a lifetime. Psychotherapist Gay Hendricks in his book *Conscious Living* comments: "The downside of therapy is that people often remain not only focused on the past, but enthralled by it."* Another downside is that it can feel scary as you begin to dig around in the pain of dealing with past wounds.

Although the coaching approach acknowledges that there may be painful stories that have created your past behaviors, it focuses on today's behaviors and tomorrow's goals. The coaching approach is not unsympathetic, nor is it shallow. It's an approach that builds a better today and tomorrow by taking action. In the process, learning about yesterday may happen; however, it is not required before moving ahead. Some very deep "aha's" can flow from the coaching approach as people notice how their new behavior feels different from their old behavior.

By approaching money management from the coaching perspective, I give you the tools to change your actions today regardless of what stories and experiences have had an impact on your behavior in the past. As you change your actions, you may recognize and unhook past stories, and at times you may hit your old beliefs head-on and find yourself falling back into patterns that have hurt you financially in the past. This approach recognizes the way that habits can draw you back into their well-worn paths and gives you tools to stay on your newly chosen track.

A Note about the Case Studies

Throughout the book, many people share their stories of how they work with money. Some people are identified, but most are disguised. Some of the stories are about one person's experience, but many are composites of the stories of people facing similar experiences. Whatever the particulars, the case studies are intended to illustrate the issues that many of us face with money and to show

---

*Gay Hendricks, *Conscious Living: Finding Joy in the Real World* (New York: HarperCollins, 2000), p. 28.

us that we are not alone in our attempts to improve how we manage money.

A Note for International Readers

I believe that the Conscious Spending approach is relevant to all of us who spend money, regardless of whether we spend dollars, pounds, yen, marks, or rupees. The information in a couple of places refers to the United States, however the Conscious Spending philosophy holds true even if the details of your tax code or the names of your retirement planning tools differ.

PART ONE

READY TO CHANGE

Is Your Hip Pocket Off Balance?

Managing money well involves more than having the best of intentions. This book is designed to help you move from intention to implementation, to give you the tools to really change how to manage your money. The book is organized into three parts. The first part lays the groundwork for the book by introducing Conscious Spending, looking at what money is, and identifying why it is so hard to manage money well. The second part describes each of the categories of the Conscious Spending Model, and the third part guides you through the process of developing your own Conscious Spending Plan and creating the structures, systems, and habits you will need to put your plan into action.

Part One starts with a look at the choices that are open to us when we spend money and an exploration of how our values can be reflected in how we use money. Chapter 2 describes what money is, as well as the only three rules needed to manage money well. Chapter 3 then introduces the Conscious Spending Model and its seven categories. Finally, the last chapter in this section looks at all the reasons why it is hard for us to manage our money well.

You'll get the most out of the book by reading it in order and doing the exercises as you go along. However, if you like to skip around, I'd recommend reading the first three chapters before skipping on to the second or third sections.

So hang on to your wallets, and lets get started!

CHAPTER 1

....

Where Did It All Go?

The Unconscious Spending Trap

After my friends finished their slide show, we sat by the fire and reflected on the great scenes they had just shared. For two years Adrienne and Dale had lived their dream. They traveled the globe, seeing every corner of Africa and South America and parts of North America they had not visited before. While their travel style was modest— local pensions and public transportation—they experienced exactly the adventure and exposure to local cultures that they had dreamed of. They had rented out their home while they traveled, and both had taken time out from their careers. Adrienne, a freelance editor, had a good reputation in the industry—she would be remembered if she took some time off. Dale, an engineer, knew his employer valued his skills, but he was willing to risk finding there was no job to come back to after a long journey.

Back home, settled into their jobs, some of their friends who have been treated to the slide show tell Adrienne and Dale that they are lucky. "We're not lucky," Adrienne counters emphatically. "Nearly all of our friends can afford to do what we have done if they spend their money differently." While their friends were buying larger houses, Adrienne and Dale were paying off the mortgage of their nice, but modest, home. While their friends were upgrading to the latest sports utility vehicles, they were making do with their eight-year-old car that was not top of the line even when it was new. When their friends started having kids, they waited. But when it came to travel, they found plenty of money. "We are not lucky; we simply made different choices."

. . . .

Over the course of your life, you will probably earn more than a million dollars in today's terms; possibly much more. How will you spend it? Will you consciously use it to live out some of your dreams, or will you unconsciously spend it just living? Will you consciously choose your lifestyle, or will you unconsciously drift into it?

Your Money, Your Choice

Money is one of the greatest tools in life. It can buy convenience, freedom, fun experiences, memorable events, warm surroundings, and all sorts of things that make life more comfortable. But money can also be frittered away, scattered on a pile of small things that have little impact on your life or spent on big-ticket items that have small-ticket results. The way you use your money in your life is up to you.

Some of your spending will be involuntary (taxes . . .), and a lot of it will be on the very basics of life (food, shelter, getting to and fro . . .). Two choices you have already made impact how you spend a lot of your money: your residence and the car you drive probably account for about half of your total spending. Other circumstances that arise have an impact on how we spend our money or how much money we have to spend. Sometimes we are thrown curveballs that can knock out our best laid plans—divorce, illness, death of a spouse, unemployment, a sick parent, a child with special needs, a natural disaster. There are plenty of situations that can make you feel as if life doesn't offer much choice at all. However, the reality is that you have control over most of the money that goes through your hands.

This choice is an incredible luxury. We live in an era of unprecedented wealth. Incomes are high. The basics of life cost less than ever before. Despite all this wealth, many people often don't even know where their money is going and few if any are happier. If anything, catching up to ever-escalating consumer standards is costing us inner peace. And for many of us, it is also costing financial security: we are getting in debt just to keep up.

What Do You Really Want?

The key to getting more of what you want is knowing what it is that you *do* want. I know this sounds obvious, but how long has it been since you have stopped and asked yourself what you really want from life? It's very easy to be caught up in day-to-day living and never step back and take a look at all the decisions you make about how you live your life and how you spend your money. Life gets so busy, and our everyday path gets so well worn, it's easy to forget to stop and ask ourselves this critical question: What do I really want?

To help you arrive at the answer to that question, ask yourself the following three questions:

1. If you think of the last $5,000 that you earned, what did you spend it on?

2. If you were given $5,000 unexpectedly, what would you spend it on?

3. If you were given $5,000 with the express instruction that you *must* spend it on something you really enjoy, what would you spend it on?

If you are like most of the people who take my money coaching classes, your first list was probably as dull as a shopping list: the mortgage or rent, utility bills, food, a family member's birthday gift. The second list probably began to reflect some of the pent-up demand in your life: a debt to pay off, a class you want to take, an upgrade to your home you have been putting off. And the final list probably reflects some of your true passions, true ways of expressing yourself: travel to a place that fascinates you, a class that will help you change careers, a vacation with people you love, a piece of furniture that will make your home more nurturing, or an electronic system to play music that inspires you. The list could go on. My students have dreamed of everything from touring Italy's wine region to buying a specialized tool for making jigsaw puzzles.

How can you manage your money so that you have enough left after everyday spending to pursue some of your dreams? How do you keep hold of the big goals in your life when you are mired in the little everyday tasks?

Introduction to Conscious Spending

Conscious Spending is being aware of how you spend your money and how well that spending aligns with your personal values. The next sentence is the key to the rest of the book, so read it carefully. *Conscious Spending works by minimizing the money you spend on things you enjoy less, in order to free up money for things you enjoy more.* That's all Conscious Spending is: moving money from unfun things that drain your resources, and putting it in the pleasure zone. Conscious Spending is the opposite of the unaware "frittering away" of Unconscious Spending.

Why spend so much of your life working if you don't use your earnings in a way that makes you most happy? Even if you love your job, most work is simply not *that* much fun that we'd do it purely for the joy of it. So take the payment for your work and put it to your own best use. This concept is not selfish and does not mean that you are only spending money on frivolous things. Conscious Spending may include donating money to charity, holding a great party for your friends and family, going back to school purely for the joy of learning, buying a home in a neighborhood with good schools, or supporting your parents. Of course, Conscious Spending may also include traveling to the ends of the earth, buying a really flashy car, eating in the finest restaurants, or finding out whether diamonds are your best friend (I figure you have to have quite a few before you can really know). Most people end up with a mix of the heartfelt and the fun. Does this make some people good and others selfish? I don't think so. It simply means people have different values. And I'm not going to give you grief if your values are not my values, as long as you promise not to give me grief because my values are not yours. We're different, and that's what makes the tapestry of life particularly colorful.

The essence of Conscious Spending is ensuring that your money is spent in a way that supports you. What counts is congruency: whether *your* spending fits *your* wants and *your* values. Some of this involves guts. If your values are different from those of your friends, colleagues, and neighbors, then the way you use your money will differ. Driving an old car so you can travel overseas every year may feel like rebellion when all your friends are driving the latest model cars. The combination that feels right to you may be very different from some hypothetical norm that you see on television. Living in a way that truly reflects your own values—not those of your peer group, not those of your neighbors, but your own unique mix—is a radical act.

Conscious Spending is easier if you are single and making decisions for yourself than if you are in a relationship and making decisions for a household; however, the essence is the same. As a couple or a family, you may even find that the Conscious Spending approach diffuses some age-old arguments by focusing on your underlying personal values, not on the shopping lists in your head.

If your money management is not focused on getting what you really want, you are an Unconscious Spender. Unconscious Spenders are not necessarily overspenders, compulsive spenders, or irrational spenders. Some may even be great at saving money. They are simply spenders who are not really conscious of where their money goes. They don't stop to ask what they want their money to do for them today and throughout their lives. They don't actively make choices that will bring them as much happiness as possible. The result, not surprisingly, is that Unconscious Spenders don't get as much of what they want as they could.

The Cost of Unconscious Spending

So what is the cost of Unconscious Spending? There is a significant emotional cost that comes from not spending money in a way that is aligned with your true personal values. This may not be the sort of angst that keeps you awake at night, wringing your hands; it is more subtle than that. What is the cost of never having enough money to be what you would really love to be, do what you've always wanted to do, or have what you truly want? What is the cost of the energy you spend maintaining a lifestyle that does not bring you deep happiness? What is the cost of working hard but still not having what you want at the end of the day? What is the cost of not fulfilling your dreams or expressing yourself fully? What is the cost of getting some, but never enough, of what you enjoy?

Should we simply aim to earn more? The difficult part about focusing on earning is that often the goal we are aiming for moves. While singer k.d. lang's song "Constant Craving" was written about romance rather than money, the title sums up how most of us feel in a consumer-oriented society. At $35,000 a year, it seems that $45,000 a year would be enough to meet all of the unsatisfied wants. Yet when that new level is reached, there seems to be another goal that is further out. What is the emotional cost of being constantly aware of what we don't have rather than simply grateful for all we do have?

As I began teaching people about Conscious Spending, I discovered that there is a very different essence in the wanting that you feel when you are expressing your personal values and the wanting you feel when you are out of touch with your values. The wanting that comes from expressing personal values doesn't have the same level of neediness under it. It has less of the jabbing, needling quality of unaligned wants. It has the quality of a person living comfortably in his or her own skin. The wanting that is not aligned with your values has a begging five-year-old air to it, with a pout and a tantrum, demanding: "I want a bigger car. My life will not be complete without a bigger car!" It has an undercurrent of trying to fill an emotional hole.

Most of us could create a list as long as our arm of things that we would enjoy owning. Does this mean that we are all doomed to a lifetime of constantly wanting the next thing over the horizon?

Yes and no. Unconscious Spending sometimes comes from trying to fill the gaps in your sense of self with a whole pile of stuff. Conscious Spending is simply expressing your sense of self through how you use your money. The more secure you are in your sense of self, the more optional the pile of stuff becomes. It doesn't mean you won't want anything, just that having more is the icing on the cake.

Conscious Spending is about being more of who you are, honoring what you care about, taking responsibility for how you live today and how you will live tomorrow. To succeed, you need to know yourself well enough to know what will make your life rich and interesting, uniquely yours, and deeply satisfying.

Imagine feeling content, a foreign feeling for many people. Conscious Spending helps you move toward contentment. When I first started teaching this approach, I thought I was simply teaching people how to better manage their money. I was surprised how many students came back with stories of how their lives had changed when they stopped and focused on what they really wanted. They discovered what I hadn't realized: Conscious Spending is about first filling yourself from the inside, as much as it is about having nice things around you.

. . . .

As Tracy moved her spending to a more conscious place, she also realized how much her past spending had been coming from a place of gaining approval from others. "I realized I bought clothes because I was trying to impress somebody: so much of it was about how I wanted others to perceive me. I wanted them to think I look good in this. Some of that feeling is OK, but a lot of it? I don't want that feeling to be there. I want to buy stuff that I feel good in. I want to cut out that extra layer of approval and just ask: Do I like this? Do I look good in this?" It was the act of being conscious around her spending that moved her to focus on expressing herself.

. . . .

What Do You Really Want?

Becoming a Conscious Spender depends on the one critical step of getting to know what you really want. Let's look at two components of what you want: your values and your dreams.

Values are the underlying qualities that you hold sacred in your life. They are an immutable part of what makes you *you*. Your values are the list of qualities that you would use to describe who you truly are: loyal, adventurous, independent, successful, honest, fun loving, caring, connected, creative, dependable, and so on. There is no neat list to pick and choose from, and it is important not to let the words get in the way. It is more important to get clear on what small handful of values is critical to your being you.

Values are not things, but the things that you buy can express them. The way that you express your values, however, can be as complex and individual as you are. A quick look at car ads will show you how one car is designed to appeal to a person who values adventurousness, whereas another is designed to appeal to a person who values achievement. However, although one car may be designed to appeal to people who value adventurousness, all adventurous people are not going to express that value in the same way. One person may express his adventurousness with a rugged SUV that never goes off road. Another may be equally happy expressing her adventurousness through rugged travel in far corners of the world. Values are not about what you do or have, but who you are. Conscious Spending involves making choices with an awareness of what values you express through those choices. By stripping back your wants to the underlying values, you are removing the shopping list and returning to the self-expression.

Whereas values are qualities, dreams are a specific way that you would like to express a value that is very important to you. For example, a client has a very strong value around being close to her family. One specific way that she dreams of expressing that value is by having a farm in the country where her children and grand-children could spend summers and holidays with her every year. One of my top values is a love of adventure, and a dream I have is to get my pilot's license and fly all over Africa.

Exercise: Defining the Life You Want

It is very easy to get caught up in the race for new and better possessions and experiences. Yet when all is said and done, some of the most satisfying things in life come not from what you owned or what you did, but who you were.

Go to a quiet place where you won't be disturbed. Close your eyes and quiet your mind. When you are relaxed, imagine that you are at your 80th birthday party and all the people you love and care for in your life are there, along with others whose lives you have touched. Imagine the speeches that each person would make. Take 10 minutes to write everything that you would like to be remembered for by the people who you care about. Once you have the list, mark next to each item whether it is something you have (a possession), something you do (an experience), or something you are (a personality trait). For example, your list might include: being a great parent (personality trait), traveling the world (experience), and owning a beautiful home (possession). From this perspective, which items are most important? Which items most defines who you are? What do you care about more than anything else in the world? What legacy do you want to leave?

As you look at the items that are most important to you in your life, list the values that underlie them. Prioritize your values, getting clear about the top three or four. One way to get down to these core values is to take a longer list of values and ask yourself: "If I could not be _____, would I know how to be me?" It doesn't matter if you are not certain about the list. As you create your own Conscious Spending Plan following the guidance given in Chapter 12, you will choose between different things that you spend money on and as you do that, you will be able to feel out which of the values are most important to you.

. . . .

The Evolution of Values and Dreams

Do your values change over time? Generally they remain pretty fixed; they are the core of your personality, after all. However, the way you express them may evolve over time, and as you begin to satisfy one level of values, the ones below them may become more important.

. . . .

"I guess I've always valued connecting with people very highly," Sean said. "In the past that meant that I spent a lot of money on my social life. That's changed since I became involved in a serious relationship. Connecting one-on-one in a really meaningful way has satisfied much of that value. These days, I go out a lot less, although we entertain a bit and we are involved in the community. Connection is still key for me, but the way I connect has evolved." As that value has been satisfied, Sean started to become more aware of other values as

well. "As I have become more satisfied about the personal connections that I have in my life, I have also started to find the resources to focus on other values too: I have started collecting art because I love having beautiful things in my life."

. . . .

I have undergone a similar evolution. My two strongest values are security and adventure. In the past, I have expressed those both by being good at saving for my retirement and by traveling for long times to obscure parts of the world when I had the chance. I managed the inherent conflict between the two values by only traveling when I had both the spare money to do so and a great job to return to. As I began to build a solid retirement portfolio and see many places that I wanted to see, I began to move deeper into my list of values. Whereas earlier where I lived was not so important, I recently started to value having a home that felt like a sanctuary in which I can write, coach clients, and recharge between travels. To honor that value, I moved from my small inner city apartment to a quiet home opposite the woods. Would I have made that move at the cost of giving up my security or my adventure? No. Yet because I am satisfying those needs, I can move further down my wish list.

Sometimes, however, a major event may bring to light a value that was not as important previously. When Judy discovered she had breast cancer, she realized that she simply did not value being successful in her career as much as she valued being close to her friends and family. While she is still working as a successful lawyer, she has moved her priorities to honor her values around being close to people. Start Conscious Spending based on the values and dreams that are most important to you and your family today, and allow space for them to change over time.

Dreams are more likely to evolve as lifestyles change. Often getting into or out of a relationship can involve rethinking a lot of our dreams. Similarly, as we grow older, some of the dreams that seemed important when we were young may simply seem less interesting or attractive. For example, someone who values making a difference in the world may dream of living in an underdeveloped country and providing hands-on help for a village when they are young and single. As they grow older or get involved in a relationship, they may find that dream fades and a different way of expressing the values may emerge. The critical thing is to make sure that you are not creating a future of "I wish I had . . ." regrets.

Aren't We Being a Little Selfish?

Wow. Just imagine . . . it's okay to want everything that I want. Me, me, me, me, me! I can hear some of your inner judges and critics lining up for comment. "I'm being selfish." "What about the people who don't have enough?" "Who am I to want so much—there are others who count too." "I should not be spending money on trivialities when I could be giving it to charity."

Many people have been brought up to feel that there is something inherently wrong with fulfilling their values and dreams. You may have been told it is self-indulgent, selfish, greedy, or even just plain wrong. If you are a parent or in a relationship, you may feel that your wants should fall behind the wants of everyone else in the family. Perhaps you feel that you don't deserve to get what you want, or that getting what you want will somehow hurt others. Perhaps you have a values conflict, where you have not reconciled a value of contributing to society with a value of feeling comforted, or a value of putting your family first with a value of being independent.

For those engaged in this internal conflict, stop for a minute
and look at your list of values. If giving back or making a difference is one of your values, then honoring that value will involve
giving back to society in some way. Additionally, if you value connecting with people, then honoring your values may involve showing your love for the people in your life in many different ways.

Conscious Spending focuses on honoring your values throughout your lifetime. If you are in a relationship or are a parent, it is
about honoring the values and dreams that you share as a family
as well as individual values and dreams that are important to each
of you. Putting your own dreams at the bottom of the list or act-
ing in a way that is not aligned with your values does not benefit
anyone. If you are being untrue to your own values, how can you
model integrity to your family? If you are putting your own
dreams at the bottom of the list, how can you help your children
learn to honor and value their own dreams? If you are not being
true to yourself, how can you share your whole life with the person that you love? Being true to who you are and what you want
means being wholly yourself, and that is the greatest gift you can
give to the people around you.

Exercise: File of Dreams

A couple of years back, I noticed that while I was doing a lot
of things I enjoyed, there were some dreams that were no
closer to being realized. I drew up a list that I called 50 Things
to Do Before I Die, fearing that one day I would be one of
those older people who looks back and says "I always wish I
had . . ." Some are pretty mundane (grow my own tomatoes),
others rather grandiose (travel to the mountain in the Antarc-
tic named after my father), and many have nothing to do with

things that money can buy (love greatly), but the list is an important touchstone. I may not check off the whole list in my lifetime, and I may lose interest in some things, but I know I am less likely to fritter away time and money on passing hobbies at the cost of never doing what I really dream of.

In the busy-ness of life, it is easy to lose track of your dreams. Create a file of all the things you dream about being, doing, and having.

- Take half an hour to write a list of everything you would like to be, do, and have in life. Aim to make the list very meaningful for you rather than just long. These are the things that you don't want to be caught saying one day "I always wish I had . . ."

- Go back through the list and remove anything that really is not so important to you and prioritize what is left. This is a great exercise to do on a computer so that you can re-order the items based on how important they are to you (with number one being most important).

- Take action on the top five things on the list, even if they are financially out of your reach today. For example, if you have always wanted to go to Italy to see some famous pieces of art, pick up some brochures from a travel agent on tours to Italy. Even if your action is just finding out what some of your dreams cost, it brings you closer to realizing the dream. Sometimes knowing the price can help you save money because the goal is so much clearer.

- Revisit your list at least once a year to see whether your dreams are changing and how you are doing in making them come true.

. . . .

. . . .

CHAPTER 2

Conscious Spending

Honoring Your Values

CONSCIOUS SPENDERS GET MORE OF WHAT THEY WANT BECAUSE they *know* what they want. Let's look at a Conscious Spender and an Unconscious Spender. For example, let's take two people who earn the same salary and go shopping for clothes. The Conscious Spender buys clothes aware of how much she can afford over a year and what sort of clothing purchases give her most pleasure. The Unconscious Spender buys clothes with no particular budget or aim in mind. One day, they both see a jacket that is simply gorgeous. It has a nice cut, is well made, and is a color that flatters them. It is $400. The Conscious Spender knows that within the $1,500 she has set aside for clothing, she can afford one or two really good pieces and all the usual basics. This jacket meets all her criteria. It makes her heart pound (many guys won't understand this part; if so, imagine test driving a Porsche Boxster), it goes with plenty of things she already owns, and she knows she won't regret the purchase in a year. So she buys it. The Unconscious Spender also tries on the jacket. Her heart also pounds. She wrestles with herself but walks out feeling smug because she resisted the temptation. After all, $400 is a lot of money, and she could get several things for that amount of money.

At the end of the year, it turns out that they both happened to spend $1,500 on clothing. The Conscious Spender has her favorite jacket and one really stunning dress to show for her $1,500, along with the usual list of basics and work clothes. What does the Unconscious Spender have? In all probability, a long, but unremarkable, list of the usual basics and work clothes. Nothing stands out. Nothing gives her great pleasure.

Consider the scenario with a different Unconscious Spender. She also buys the jacket. At the end of the year, the Unconscious Spender does have something to show for her spending: the great jacket, a suit that is really fabulous, a nice dress for a friend's wedding, and so on. Problem is, she also ends up spending $2,300 on clothes and is carrying around a bunch of credit card debt. Not surprisingly, she has spent a whole lot not only on clothes, but also on furnishings, her social life, and so on. Consequently, she does not have enough for that vacation she really wants.

In both scenarios, the Conscious Spender gets more bang for her buck. She ends up with more satisfaction, more control over the end state, and more of what she cares about.

Ultimately, Conscious Spending is about making conscious choices among the many things each dollar could buy. Would you rather spend a lot of money on small things that really don't mean that much to you, or on a few well-chosen things that express who you are?

In Chapter 3 I introduce the Conscious Spending Model, a simple, visual tool to help you direct your money to what you want. But first, let's get clear on some definitions: what money is and the three basic rules that underlie Conscious Spending.

Money: The Tool to Get What You Want

So what exactly is money? Everyone uses it and most people want more of it than they have. The love of it has been called the root of all evil, yet it has the power to do a lot of good. It has started wars and it has paid to clean up the destruction those wars have created. Some people marry for money, yet arguments about it are the leading cause of divorce. It has been attributed to making the world go round. Money is much more than pieces of paper and coin. It is more than the numbers in your bank account. But what, exactly, is it?

In Economics 101 money is defined simply as an exchange of value. As dull as this definition is, it holds true: you exchange your hours of work for an income, you then exchange your income for food, shelter, and so on. But it is not just time you are trading. You receive money in exchange for your life energy. You exchange physical or intellectual labor, creativity, inspiration, emotional energy, and so on in return for either an income or perhaps part ownership in a company. For many of you, earning an income takes a large slice of your life energy. You probably trade 8 hours a day, 230 or so days a year, for your income. Perhaps even more: longer hours, work taken home at night, a second job to make ends meet, hours spent getting dressed for work, commuting there and back, and unwinding after a stressful day. And the amount of money you bring home is not directly proportional to the time or energy spent. It is based on how much demand there is for your skills, how the job market values your abilities, how well you sell yourself, and so on. However you earn it, what you have at the end of the day is a pile of money, small or large, that represents the life energy you exchanged to get it. (It is possible, of course, that you may have additional ways of receiving money, such as inheritances, prize money, and income generated from assets you own, such as real estate or stocks.)

That exchange, life energy in return for income, is only the first exchange. This is called earning. There is also a second exchange called spending. It involves the exchange of money you have received for goods (cars, homes, investments) or services (haircuts, education, tax preparation).

Money can also be seen as a flow. Money flows in at the pace you earn it and flows out at the pace you spend it. If you spend it faster than you earn it, you have to borrow to make up the difference. If you spend it slower than you earn it, you can build up reserves for use in the future. Managing your money is about managing that flow.

Exercise: Draw Your Money Flow
· ·

Take 5 minutes to reflect on the flow of money in your life. Using the analogy of a waterfall, create an image of what your money flow looks like. Take notes, or even draw a picture, of what you imagine (see Figure 2.1).

What does your money flow look like? Is it plentiful or running dry? Is it calm or wild? What does it sound like? Is it well directed or splashing wildly? Is it a trickle or a gush? How

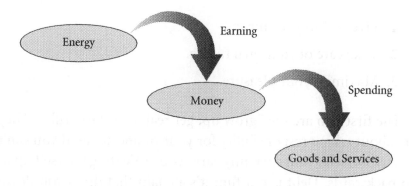

FIGURE 2.1 The flow of money in your life can be likened to a waterfall.

does the flow feel? Is it a consistent flow or does it flood, then dry up? Is it dammed in places and running on empty in others? How do you feel about your money flow? Are you scared that there is not enough or are you comfortable that there is plenty flowing in? Does the amount of money in your life seem like a fair trade for the amount of energy you put into earning it? Do you get enough of what you want for the amount of money that you spend? Does it feel in your control? What would you want to change about it?

Three Rules of Money Management

So how do you better manage the flow of money in your life? A great place to start is with the three rules of money management that underlie Conscious Spending.

Some people love rules, others hate them. For those who like rules, the good news is that if you follow these three rules, you will be well on your way to being a Conscious Spender. For those who hate rules, the three I'm about to introduce are the *only* ones in this whole book. And one of them you'll really enjoy. I promise!

The three rules that are critical to Conscious Spending are:

1. Live within your means.
2. Take care of your own future.
3. Maximize your pleasure.

The first two are the "grow up, get real, be smart" rules. They are about taking responsibility for your financial life. If you can't live within what you currently earn, you are setting yourself up to go backwards. Debt is not fun; it's a chain that drags you down and ties you to a never-ending treadmill.

. . . .

Francis arrived at the meeting sporting a fancy new watch. Flashing it around, he admitted that he had bought it with his credit card. "I've always wanted a good watch, and I didn't go overboard," he said. His watch had cost a little more than a week's salary, but the tax and interest meant it would eventually cost about half a month's income. "I'd rather have it now and enjoy it for longer than to wait until I can afford it. I know I'll be earning more in a few years time, so it's okay to live beyond my means now. I can afford the payments."

. . . .

Francis lived beyond his means as a young graduate burdened with student debt because he was looking to his future earnings. He assumed that one day his earnings would catch up with his lifestyle. However, my experience working with hundreds of people has taught me that generally this is not the case. People who cannot live within their means at $25,000 a year will probably have trouble living within their means at $50,000 a year. There is a good chance that your wants will grow at the same rate as your income. This means that if you spend 10 percent above what you earn at $25,000, you are probably likely to spend 10 percent above what you earn at $50,000. And all that buys you is a lifetime of catching up.

Except for people who really are facing hard times, living within your means is not about how much money you have; it's about your attitude toward the money you have. It's about living in the present, not mortgaging your future. Living within your means is a simple, if not particularly palatable, necessity. There are a couple of exceptions. Gaining an education often involves living beyond your means for a few years. Retirement requires redefining your means to be your income from various sources, plus perhaps a slow drawdown of your assets.

Taking care of your own future is another "get real" rule. The unpleasant fact is that Social Security will not pay enough for an average person to live on comfortably, and few employers provide fully funded pensions. Saving is not about self-deprivation, it's about preparing to spend in the future and being able to live the good life throughout your whole life. Saving for your future through an employer-matched program or other retirement savings tool is not a nice extra, it's an absolute necessity if you don't want to be old and poor one day. For women, this is even more critical, because women generally earn less, have interrupted work patterns because of time taken off to bear children, and therefore have less to save. In addition, their savings often grow more slowly because they are more conservative about their investment choices. And to top it all off, women generally live longer, making financial independence in their retirement years harder to achieve.

Rule 1 and Rule 2 are not that much fun: the "eat your veggies or you'll have no dessert" rules. Rule 3, I promise, will make up for it.

Rule 3 is dessert. Once you've done the necessary but mundane stuff in Rule 1 and Rule 2, the only other rule for managing your money is this: maximize your pleasure. That's right. Have fun. Not just some, but as much as you can afford. If you can afford a boatload of it, go right ahead. The bottom line is you don't know how long your journey on earth will be, so I believe you should have as much pleasure with your money as you can afford to have. Of course, pleasure is in the eye of the beholder. One person may maximize his pleasure by paying for the best education possible for his kids. Another may collect as many fancy high-end basketball shoes as he can. Values vary a lot, and your values are the single biggest influence on what gives you pleasure.

Of course, Rule 3 can only be followed if you know what makes you happy, that is, what you value. Once you are clear about that, you can direct your resources to those things or activities that make you happy.

Exercise: What You Are Buying
· ·

You may have played the game where you have to choose what (or whom!) you would take if you were to be stranded on a desert island or what you would save if your house were on fire. The games, though pure speculation, ask you to make a very quick, clear prioritization of what you have in your life. We'll do a similar exercise.

Take a minute to think of all the things that you spend money on today. Going down the left side of a page, list 10 things that you spend money on that most reflect who you think you are. They do not have to be the most critical (no one wants to live without a roof over his head and food on her table), but they must be the most important when it comes to expressing who you are. Then go back to each one, and list two or three values or emotions that the purchase represents. Compare this list to the list of values that you developed earlier. Which values are you honoring?

Next, list five values and emotions that you feel you do not fully honor in your life today. Next to each one, list two or three ways you could use your money to honor each value.

· ·

Becoming a Conscious Spender

Conscious Spending is a very simple approach to the very tough challenge of managing your money well. However, simple doesn't mean easy. Managing your money well is like getting fit. Getting fit is simple—you have to start working out and eating well—but that does not make it easy. It is not easy for many people because we have to motivate ourselves to take action. The Conscious Spending approach motivates you to take charge because it starts with what you want. It's easier to take actions that move you toward what you want than it is to do something solely because you think you should.

So how do you decide how best to use your money? And how do you manage the flow so that you never have a drought that will send you into bankruptcy? Those who truly master their money have it all: they live within their means, save for their future, and afford some things they truly value. Does this mean they earn a lot of money? Not necessarily. Although it's certainly easier to get the balance right if you have high earnings, there are plenty of people with high incomes but no savings or little real satisfaction with what they have in life, and some with lower incomes who find the right balance. People who are true money masters are those people who align their resources—whether they have a little or a lot—so they get what they want from their lives.

When you are a Conscious Spender, you make choices throughout your life. You know that if you consciously choose where your money is going as your earnings increase, you can satisfy more and more of your dreams and desires. Think about this for a minute. If you take one part of your spending that is really not so important to you, and keep that spending steady even when your earnings rise, you free up money for the purely self-expressive spending that reflects your values. Let's look at two colleagues who earn the same amount. One of them has always leased a car and every two or three years when the lease is up, she upgrades to a new, nicer car because she can afford to and it seems like a natural thing to do. Her colleague really doesn't care much about cars, as long as he has something safe, reliable, and reasonably comfortable. Rather than leasing, he borrowed and after a few years, owned his car outright. It never occurred to him to sell his car and buy a more expensive one because there were so many other things that he wanted to do with his money: buy an engagement ring for his honey, travel overseas, and donate some money to a favorite cause. While the first person remained tied to lease costs that were larger every time she upgraded her car, her colleague's costs were flat, and then much lower once his car was paid off. The money that he was not spending on his car, he could spend on things that brought him a lot more joy.

Finding a Way

I moved to the United States when I was 26, after growing up in Australia. I meet so many people who tell me that they've always wanted to go to Australia. Now, maybe they are being polite, but I suspect most are being honest. I don't blame them: Australia sounds exciting, wild, and friendly, rather like Colorado before the cowboys traded their leather chaps for silicon chips. Yet every time I hear it, part of me wants (but is too polite!) to ask "So why haven't you gone?" Really. Whether you dream of traveling to Australia or learning to make wine, sailing the Caribbean or competing in a triathlon in Hawaii, if it's an "always wanted to" dream, just *find a way* to do it.

Some of you may be blanching, saying that it's too expensive. And for some people, a dream that runs into thousands of dollars may be permanently out of reach. But for most of you, the simple answer is that you have not wanted it badly enough. Each year you spend tens of thousands of dollars. Every year. That's a whole lot of dollars. If you are not spending those dollars on your dreams, what are you spending them on? Your home, your car, your food . . . a whole lot of everyday things. That's true, but my question for you is: What changes are you willing to make so that you can afford more of what you really want? Some of your spending is "have to," but most of it is "want to." For example, a roof over your head is a "have to." However, a home with a yard, a garage, central air conditioning, and good neighbors is a "want to." Conscious Spending shines a spotlight on all of the "want to" decisions so you choose the combination of things that adds up to the highest value for you.

How easy it is to follow the three rules and become a Conscious Spender depends partly on how you currently behave around money. To grossly oversimplify things, there are two basic money personalities: Spenders and Savers.

Spenders and Savers

Spenders and Savers have very different personalities when it comes to money management. Spenders live in the today, and spend as if there is no tomorrow. They may not necessarily be in debt, but they have little in the way of financial security because they pretty much spend everything they have. Savers take a future-oriented approach to money, putting money away for their next big purchase or their retirement.

Spenders and Savers don't really understand each other, although they usually seem to have relationships with each other (what is it about this "opposites attract" thing?). If saving has always seemed necessary, it is hard to imagine how it feels to spend every cent today without thinking about tomorrow. If spending has always come easily, saving may seem like a discipline as difficult and self-controlled as advanced yoga. You may meet a Saver and a Spender who have very similar values; however, the one differentiator is how they think about the timeline of their money.

At the extremes of the spectrum there are Spenders who juggle 20 credit cards and end up bankrupted by the stuff they bought without thought of the long-term need to pay for it, and there are

Savers who stash so much cash for the future that they end up wealthy but too old to enjoy some of the money that could have given them pleasure throughout their lifetime. At both extremes, people are motivated by fear. Fear of missing out and not having enough today drives extreme Spenders to overconsume. Fear of being vulnerable and not having enough tomorrow drives extreme Savers to oversave. However, most people are not spendthrifts or misers; they are just somewhere in between.

Conscious Spending is about moving away from fear toward a more grounded relationship with money. Conscious Spenders ultimately operate from a place of balancing their needs today with those in the future. That balance embraces their own needs and wants and their household's needs and wants. Spending meets their basic needs and honors their values. Saving meets their future needs and supports a vision of a future that is also aligned with their values.

Exercise: Are You an Conscious Spender?
....

Look at each of the following 10 statements and choose whether it describes your behavior: *never, sometimes,* or *always.*

1. I don't know how much I have spent in a month until my credit card bill arrives.

2. I often buy things spontaneously.

3. I often say no to things that I really want because I don't think I have the money.

4. I have purchased things that I have never used.

5. I never seem to have money for what I really want even though I earn a reasonable amount.

6. If I have money in my account, I spend it.

7. I do not know the cost each year of my regular habits such as buying lunch or smoking.

8. I automatically upgrade my lifestyle when I earn more money.

9. I don't save for retirement because the future seems so far away.

10. I cannot clearly list what I value in life.

There is no simple scale to measure whether or not you are a Conscious Spender; however, Conscious Spenders are likely to answer *never* to most of the statements. But we are not aiming for perfection here, so some *sometimes* are fine. If there are any questions that you answered *always* to, ask yourself if that habit is keeping you from getting what you really want with your money.

. . . .

CHAPTER 3

Becoming Conscious

Getting More of What You Want

THE REMAINDER OF THIS BOOK PROGRESSES FROM THE THEORETICAL to the practical. It's not enough to know that you are an Unconscious Spender and understand what a Conscious Spender is. You need tools to help you become a Conscious Spender.

Why Conscious Spending Works and the "B" Word Fails

The reason why most people find money management difficult is that the old approach makes it difficult. What is the old approach? *Budgeting.* This mention is the only time you will see the "B" word in the book. The old approach starts with everything you currently spend money on and asks you to cut back. Often it asks you to cut out the most enjoyable things. It bores you with a long list of terms ordered in a way that does not make sense to the average nonaccountant.

If you read some of the personal finance books on the market, you might think that sound personal finance is a long and not very enjoyable journey of scrimping and saving and being as tight-fisted as you can be. The only time I would approve of scrimping is when someone gets a genuine kick out of being really clever by stretching a dollar as far as it can go. Or when someone hates work so much that he would rather live a tightwad's life and min-imize his time spent at work. Believe me, when it comes to buying clothes, the first category fits me to a tee. I love discount stores such as Filene's Basement and Loehmann's. The thrill of finding a great deal can be one of life's pleasures. But would I want to be a bargain hunter in every aspect of my spending? Not a chance. For those in the second category who hate their jobs, I'd rather see them find work that brings them pleasure so they can have the double delight of enjoying their money and enjoying their work.

How can you motivate yourself to change your spending pat-terns if you are being asked to focus on what you can't afford? That's just plain hard. Any money management approach based on self-torture is bound to fail for most people.

The old approach also fails because controlling your spending by counting every penny is tough. If you've ever tried to lose weight by counting calories, you know how difficult it is. We sim-ply do not think of food in terms of numbers of calories. It's the same with money. It's hard to see your overall financial plan when you are stuck in the tiny details of recording every purchase. Just as planning what you eat is easier by thinking in terms of servings (five fruit and vegetable servings a day to keep the doctor away), planning what you spend is easier if you think in terms of broader, logical categories.

To succeed, you need tools that will help you create a plan based on what you value and keep a level of consciousness as you move forward.

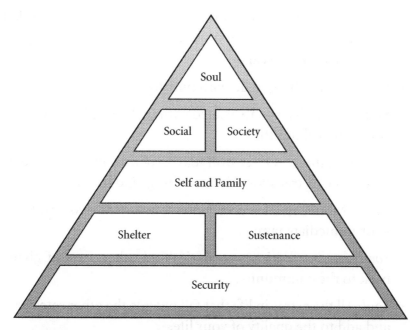

Figure 3.1   The seven categories of the Conscious
Spending Model.

The Conscious Spending Model

The Conscious Spending Model takes all the items that a typical household spends money on and organizes them into seven categories: Security, Shelter, Sustenance, Self and Family, Social, Society, and Soul (see Figure 3.1). These are not the categories that your typical accountant or personal financial planner will talk about, but I think you'll find they make a lot more sense than a long list of categories such as insurance, education, transportation, and so on. These categories reflect how we think about money. They are briefly described as follows:

- *Security*. Savings and insurance purchases that ensure that you can weather financial storms and be financially independent in your later years.

- *Shelter*. Everything to do with putting a roof over your head.

- *Sustenance*. All costs associated with fueling and maintaining your physical health.

- *Self and Family*. Other everyday expenses for your household, such as transportation, clothing, and so on.

- *Social*. Money spent in social interactions with people outside your immediate family.

- *Society*. Contributions to charity and other ways of giving back to the community.

- *Soul*. All the extras in life that fall outside the other categories and add to the quality of your life.

The Conscious Spending Model includes money that you spend as well as money that you save. (Remember that saving is really only deferred spending: putting aside money today so you can spend it in the future.) This model is a significant departure from previous money management tools because it starts with asking you to make meaningful, value-driven choices about how you spend your money.

The categories are based on the way that you think about money. If asked what proportion of your income feels right to spend on insurance, most of you would draw a blank. However, if asked the same about Shelter or Social, you could probably come up with a figure that feels right. In Part Two of the book I discuss each category in detail, giving you strategies for aligning the spending in each category with your values. Most common expenses will clearly fall into one of the seven categories, although, as you will see in Chapter 11, the top category, Soul, can at times overlap with others, depending on your values.

Let me briefly introduce the two models that inspired the Conscious Spending Model: Maslow's Hierarchy of Needs and the food pyramid.

In 1954, a researcher by the name of Abraham Maslow was observing what motivated people. He found that people have what he called a Hierarchy of Needs, that is, a ranking of things that are most important to them. His pyramid-shaped model (Figure 3.2) identifies five levels of needs, from the most basic physiological needs (food, clothing, and shelter), up to what he termed "self-actualization" (a need to follow a calling or to achieve your fullest potential).

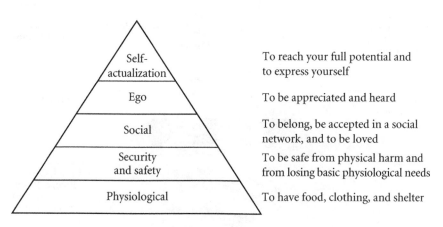

Figure 3.2   Abraham Maslow's Hierarchy of Needs.

The five layers of the model are ranked from the basic ones at the bottom of the pyramid to the most fulfilling ones at the top. For example, you can't live long without food and shelter, but it is possible to go through a lifetime without feeling you have found your vocation. In a nutshell, you don't become concerned about fulfilling a need until you have fulfilled the needs below it in the pyramid.

Another model that you may be more familiar with is the food pyramid (Figure 3.3). Using a similar concept, it prioritizes food from the most important basics at the bottom (grains, fruits, and vegetables), to the tastier but not so critical stuff at the top (sugar and fat).

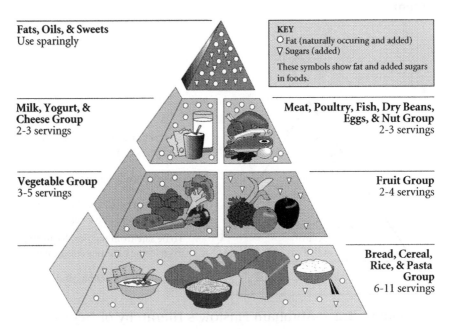

Figure 3.3   The U.S. Department of Agriculture's
food pyramid.

Again, the stuff at the bottom is fundamental to your diet, and you only get to consume the tasty stuff at the top (chocolate bars!) if you balance it with the healthy stuff at the bottom. This model is not only about prioritizing what you consume, but also about having appropriate balance between the different types of food. It simplifies managing your eating by looking at an ideal diet as a number of servings of food in each category.

Instead of talking about psychological needs or food types, the Conscious Spending Model analyzes what you spend money on. Instead of saying that you have to limit the good stuff that you get, the Conscious Spending Model gives you permission to have as much "chocolate" as you can afford, only this time the chocolate is what you value.

Just as with the food pyramid, the Conscious Spending Model looks at both priorities and proportions. The priority is represented by where the category is in the pyramid. From the base of the pyramid up, the categories are prioritized according to the order that you need to set aside money for each category. Security is at the base because unless you are having trouble affording a roof over your head or a meal on the table, your financial security is your most basic financial need. As you develop your Conscious Spending Plan in Part Three of the book, the size of the category will represent the proportion of money that you aim to spend on each category. Whereas the food pyramid recommends ideal proportions, you are the author of your own Conscious Spending Plan and you can choose what proportions work for you. Unless you are really struggling to feed, house, and clothe yourself and your family, you are likely to have enough money to meet your basic needs and afford some things in each category.

The Conscious Spending Model is used as a tool to analyze how money is currently spent and, more importantly, to plan how to use money in the future to get more of what you value. The model works because it enables you to focus your resources on what you care about. It does this by identifying the areas where you have been Unconsciously Spending more than you want to, and redirecting that money to the areas from which you derive most satisfaction. In Part Three of the book I give you detailed instructions about how to use the model to analyze your current spending patterns and to create a plan that aligns with your values.

Where Money Really Goes

Looking at the seven categories, where would you guess most of your money goes? Looking at spending data from the Bureau of Labor Statistics, we can approximate the size of the categories for a typical household (this is not exact because the definitions differ somewhat). The largest category is, not surprisingly, Shelter. Most households spend approximately 30 cents of every after-tax dollar on housing and related costs. Next comes Self and Family, at a little over 25 cents, most of which is transportation. Sustenance comes in third, although it varies greatly depending on age because health-care costs rise dramatically as people age. And Soul? Only 4 to 5 cents on the dollar is spent on Soul.

As you develop your Conscious Spending Plan in Chapter 12, you will ask yourself what is most important to you and your household. What would you like your proportions to be? How important is Shelter to you? Social? Society? Which categories are less important to you and may have room to cut back so that you can spend more on what you really enjoy? Is your Security category being funded well enough to provide for your future spending and protect your financial needs today? There are no right answers, no ideal proportions. The only rules are the three that were introduced earlier: Live within your means, take care of

your future, and maximize your pleasure. How will you choose to
do that?

About Cost

As we explore each of the seven categories in Part Two, the cost of
your choices is discussed. But what is cost? Is it the amount on the
price tag? Sometimes, yes. But other times it is more. Throughout
this book, two terms that are key to using the Conscious Spending
Model are Full Cost and Lifetime Cost.

Full Cost

Full Cost takes into account every hidden cost that is related to
a purchase. The Full Cost not only includes tax and any financing costs, it also includes all the peripheral expenses related to a
purchase.

Anyone who has started a home project will have experienced
how the Full Cost adds up. Let's say you want to paint a room.
The paint costs $40 for two cans, and another $8 for the paint for
the trim. But, as they say in infomercials, that's not all! You need
brushes, roller and a roller tray, perhaps a gadget for getting the
paint looking great in the corners, tape to cover the areas you
don't want to get painted, drop cloths to protect the floor, and so
on. Quickly you are up to $100 and counting.

Often, however, the additional costs are not as obvious. Even
people who are not fashion conscious understand that buying a
new article of clothing often requires more than just the article itself. Let's say you buy a great jacket that is perfect for the office's
new casual Friday policy. It costs $120 plus tax, which you feel is
what you want to spend. You get the jacket home and realize that

it doesn't go with much in your wardrobe. The next day, you stop at the mall to get the other items you also need. These "but that's not all" needs can easily double the cost of a purchase.

By now you may have spent $200. Sure you got more than just the jacket, but all the spending happened because you bought the jacket. So is $200 the Full Cost? Not if you purchased the jacket and other items on a credit card that you don't pay off in full each month. The cost of borrowing is also included in the Full Cost of a purchase. First, there's the interest. Even if you pay off a fair amount the next month, carrying a balance means you will be charged interest from the day you purchased the items to the next billing cycle. And that can add up, particularly if you have a card with a high interest rate or carry the balance over for a couple of months. You must also add in any fees you may incur, such as late payment fees, overbalance fees, and so on. Credit card companies don't give you cards for your convenience. They make a profit on all the interest and every fee you pay. Their fine print makes their business profitable. The only way to ensure that the Full Cost of anything you buy is not inflated by the cost of borrowing is to buy only things you can afford with money you have today.

Lifetime Cost

Lifetime Cost accounts for the ongoing cost of owning a certain item or choosing a certain lifestyle. It includes the cost of either maintaining an item over the years or repeating a habit. Let's say the jacket you bought for work is dry clean only. Suddenly the Lifetime Cost is the Full Cost plus $20 in dry cleaning each year. Of course, fashions change, so you might only keep the jacket for 3 years, so now you have an outfit that costs at least $260 over its lifetime. If you really want to make getting dressed in the morning more painful, work out how much your jacket costs you per wear.

Lifetime Cost is particularly relevant for anything that is a repeated cost—even small things. While often we focus on the big purchases in life, such as houses and insurance, the little ones can be just as critical because they are so hard to see. It's like a leaking tap that ends up wasting gallons and gallons of water, one drip at a time.

For example, if you buy a gourmet coffee to beat the midafternoon sugar slump, it's only $2.75 a day, plus tax. That's not much to spend on a little pleasure . . . Oh yeah? The Lifetime Cost might put that gourmet coffee in another perspective. Assuming you average 15 lattes a month for 10 years, your latte-a-day habit is worth nearly $9,000, if your alternative is investing that money at a 10 percent return. If you are looking at 20 years, that number balloons to over $32,000! And that's not even calculating what it could be worth if you had put the money into your company's retirement plan instead.

To garner a lifelong perspective, consider my Latte and Lunch Retirement Plan. If a 25-year-old saves $3 on a latte and $5 on lunch 15 days a month by brown-bagging it and puts that money into a tax-deferred retirement plan, she will have *$1,000,000* in her retirement fund at age 65 (in today's dollars, assuming a 10 percent return above inflation). If her employer matches her contribution, she will have even more.

Women's fashion and beauty habits are classic places where one-time choices have high Lifetime Costs. I am a hands-on person and have never managed to grow elegantly long nails. Two years ago, after finishing my renovations, I decided I wanted to buy some elegance. A full set of acrylic nails later, I was looking great. They cost $70, which didn't seem too bad. Then every couple of weeks, a fill and/or a color change cost me $25. The occasional break cost another $5. After 3 months of elegance, I started counting the cost of the choice. Not only had I spent $180, but I also had to carve out one precious evening every 3 weeks to maintain this new look. Over 10 years, the nails would have cost $4,600, including interest forgone. Elegance in the form of perfectly manicured nails was just not important enough for me to commit the time and the money that it was costing. Growing them out was messy, but now I have more money and more time.

Add a couple of habits—subscribing to a newspaper you barely glance at except for Sundays, having a couple of premium cable channels, perhaps even smoking a pack of cigarettes every couple of days—and the Lifetime Cost of habits you are barely conscious of can cost you a lifetime of harder work. You're the one that has to get up in the morning to earn the cash that pays for the habits. When you are conscious about their Lifetime Cost, you can choose where your life energy is going.

None of this is meant to say that you should give up your mocha lattes or daily paper. The key to Conscious Spending is to use it to understand the Full Cost and Lifetime Cost of your spending decisions so that you can spend your money in a way that brings you as much happiness as possible throughout your life. You just have to take into account the Lifetime Cost when you *choose the habits you want to keep.*

Cost Versus Value

The cost of a purchase is not always equal to its value to you, even if you are taking the Full Cost and Lifetime Cost into account. Value is how much something is worth to you and you alone. While Full Cost and Lifetime Cost can be counted in dollars, value refers to a much less tangible measure. Value is measured in comparatives, not dollars. It is a test of whether the money you spend is getting you as much happiness or pleasure as you can get for that money. Value is about how well your spending aligns with your personal values. Every purchase you make is a choice. For example, when you choose to spend an extra $3,000 on a car with a few more features, you're also choosing not to spend the $3,000 on, say, a trip to Italy, a class you want to take, freedom from some debt, or any number of other things on the endless list of what you could buy for $3,000.

Ultimately, understanding the value of a purchase requires asking yourself if the money is being used in a way that moves you closer to your goals. Each purchase, every financial decision, is a choice between spending money now or later, between buying something basic or something that makes your soul soar. Often, the decision to spend on basics does not feel like a choice. However, if you choose to cut your spending on necessities, you are also choosing to free up more money for what you truly want.

Exercise: The True Cost of Small Habits
· ·

Take out a blank sheet of paper and divide it into five columns as shown in Table 3.1, or work on a spreadsheet program such as Microsoft Excel. All numbers used in this exercise are

Table 3.1   Figuring the True Cost of Small Habits

Item	Cost Per Year	Amount Earned to Afford It	What It Would Be Worth if Invested for 10 Years	Is It Really Worth That to Me?
Café Latte	$2.98 × 15 × 12 = $536.40	$536.40 ÷ 0.72 = $745.00	$745.60 × 14.49 = $10,803.74	*Yikes! Not really— will cut down to once a week*
Cable TV	$39.95 × 1 × 12 = $479.40	$479.40 ÷ 0.72 = $665.83	$665.83 × 14.49 = $9,647.77	*Yes—saves on movies, videos, can't live without sport channel*

in today's dollars, meaning that I have adjusted all the numbers as if inflation were zero to make it easier to understand
because you know what money is worth today. An 8 percent
return on investments is used in the exercise and is assumed
to be the return *after* inflation.

In the first column, list at least 10 things that you purchase
habitually but that are not absolute necessities. These might include a muffin and coffee on the way to work (you could
brown-bag it or eat at home), health club membership (you
could go running for free), cable TV (you could just watch network television), a café latte midafternoon (you could drink the
coffee supplied at work or just take a walk around the block for
a break), or a weekly car wash (you could do it yourself).

In the second column, write down the cost per year. This
cost is calculated by multiplying the approximate price (including tax and tip, if applicable) of each purchase, by the
number of times per month that you make the purchase by
12. The result is the amount you spend annually out of your
pay.

In the third column, divide the amount in column two by 1
minus your tax rate (so if your combined federal, state, and
local tax rate is about 28 percent, then divide column two by
$1 - 0.28 = 0.72$). This calculation gives you the amount you
have to earn before taxes to have enough money to pay for it
out of your take-home pay.

In column four, multiply column three's amount by 14.49.
This final amount shows what you would have in your retirement savings if, for 10 years, you put all the money you spend
on the habit into a tax-deferred retirement savings account
and received an 8 percent return. Even if you went back to the
habit after 10 years, the money you put away in those 10
years would continue to grow until you retire and need to
draw on it. The additional compounding, if you are young,
can make the Lifetime Cost dramatically higher. For example,
if you are 35 today and you break a habit that has the poten-

tial to save $10,000 in 10 years, by the time you need the money at age 65, it will be worth $174,494 in today's dollars. That's *without saving another cent* from age 45 to retirement. Expensive latte, isn't it?

The last column is your moment of truth. Knowing the full cost to you over a 10-year period, you're asked to look inside and find out if the habit is worth it to you. If it is not, ask yourself if you want to cut out the spending completely or just to cut back on it.

. . . .

CHAPTER 4

· ·

The Excuse File

Why Unconscious Spending Tempts

CONSCIOUS SPENDING MAKES SENSE: YOU WORK HARD SO YOU should get what is best for you and your household with the money you earn. Yet most people don't spend in a way that is in their own best interests. Why? Economists refer to people as "rational economic beings," meaning that we are supposed to make decisions that give us the greatest value. But there is nothing particularly rational in our economic behavior most of the time. Why are we irrational, uneconomic, and very human beings?

The simple fact is that it often feels easier to be an Unconscious Spender. The pressure to spend is everywhere; our whole economy revolves around it, and much of our culture does too. Also, we tend to live in the moment; it is easier to see the pleasure in a frozen yogurt on a hot day than to imagine a comfortable retirement on a day far away. Let's take a minute to look at what we are up against. There are a number of external and internal pressures that drive us to spend. You have a choice. You can use these pressures as excuses and end up bitter and twisted that you never got what you really wanted (is that violins I hear?). Or you can recognize these excuses for what they are and choose to go for what you want anyway.

External Pressures: They Want You to Spend

Although no one *makes* you spend money, a lot of time and money is spent by experts who make it hard not to spend.

They Tell You What to Want

First, there's the advertising and marketing industry. Imagine hundreds of highly paid psychologists, statisticians, filmmakers, marketers, copywriters, and artists hired to influence your buying decisions. Every ad that makes it on to the shows you watch on prime-time TV and every item that makes it to the stores where you shop is the product of years of research into what you like, what values you hold, what aspirations you have, and what emotional buttons to push to get you to make a purchase. Advertisers' and marketers' success depends on their ability to link their product with your wants, and increase the volume until you make a purchase. Think you can pit your self-will against their sophisticated marketing? It's tough.

The selling process starts before you even know what you want and continues until you make a purchase or, even better, become a loyal repeat purchaser. "What we want grows into what we *need*, at a sometimes dizzying rate," says consumption expert Juliet B. Schor in her book *The Overspent American*.* In marketers' arsenals are tools that give them a very detailed understanding of what

---

*Juliet B. Schor, *The Overspent American: Upscaling, Downshifting and the New Consumer* (New York: Basic Books, 1998), p. 6.

you value. Author Michael J. Weiss shares some of the sophisticated marketing tools used to target your household in *The Clustered World*.* He points out that marketers don't use a shotgun approach. Their messages are targeted to appeal to households with very specific sets of values and characteristics. "Forget the melting pot. America today would be better characterized by the salad bar," he writes. The salad bar consists of many distinct clusters of people with similar values and similar buying patterns. One marketing tool, known as PRIZM, identifies 62 clusters and describes their typical earnings, family makeup, buying preferences, and so on. Claritas, the owner of the PRIZM cluster system, knows the proportion of households in each cluster that live on every street in America. Cutting the data even finer, credit card companies, Internet analysts, and your grocery shopping club card provide even more information on exactly what your spending tendencies are.

The result of all their work? You are bombarded with marketing messages and offers that are designed to push your buttons. At home, the newspaper, mailbox, and TV deliver temptation almost every waking hour. As you travel, the billboards wave to you and the radio sings to your soul about what it wants. In movies, strategically placed products whisper to you. On line, carefully targeted banner ads ask you to click on them. And if they are successful, they will lead you to want something you never wanted before.

They Dangle It in Front of You

The second external pressure comes from the merchandisers, who know how to turn a browse into a buy. Experts in the field of

---

*Michael J. Weiss, *The Clustered World: How We Live, What We Buy, and What It All Means About Who We Are* (Boston: Little, Brown, 2000), p. 10.

shopping provide even more data to stack the cards against an undecided shopper. In *Why We Buy*,* Paco Underhill lets us peek into the world of retail consultants, the highly paid professionals who can boost a store's sales by determining where and how to display products, what signage to use, and how to make the transaction enjoyable. If one vital ingredient is missing, sales can be lost. Merchandisers are not confined to stores. Catalogs, the Internet, the shopping channel, and even personal contact selling schemes (Tupperware, Amway . . .) provide other channels for merchandisers to reach you so that you can make purchases.

So the marketers and merchandisers create an external pressure, and we, whom they so lovingly call "the consumers," have little chance of avoiding wanting and buying what the marketers and advertisers want us to want and buy. The good news is that all this data collected about you means that you get information about things that you are somewhat likely to want: If you're a Velveeta type of household, you get Velveeta coupons; if you're a Brie household, you get flyers from your local gourmet market. The end result is a whole lot of consumption that drives the economy. In fact, the longest economic boom in history that carried America into the new millennium is fueled by it. "If we went into stores only when we needed to buy something, and if once there we bought only what we needed, the economy would collapse, boom."† What is bad is if the marketers sleep well while you struggle to make ends meet, pay for a house full of stuff that never gets used, or face your future with little saved for a rainy day and a sunny retirement. In among all this noise, how can you know what you really want?

---

*Paco Underhill, *Why We Buy: The Science of Shopping* (New York: Simon & Schuster, 1999).
†Ibid., p. 31.

They Offer Anything You Can Think Of

The next external pressure comes from the incredible range of things to choose from. Years after the Berlin Wall had fallen and market reforms had swept Eastern Europe, I traveled across the unending expanse of Russia on the Trans Siberian. It was a very long train trip, broken only with endless bowls of cabbage soup and an overnight stay in Irkutsk, a town in Siberia where Stalin's exiles were sent. Siberia was not at all as I imagined: It was pretty, with pine forests and a town of gingerbread houses. Interrupting the beauty were monolithic Russians buildings, laden with the stale air of the humorless communist regime. One of these concrete blocks was a department store. It was not unlike the expensive stores on Fifth Avenue: rows of glass display boxes with a few items on display. But there was a catch. The sparseness was because there simply was not much to buy. The floors were scuffed linoleum tiles. The glass cabinets were cracked and the stuff behind glass was low-end, poor quality merchandise that you would be pressed to find in a five-and-dime store in America. Even with my relative wealth and desire to find something full of Siberian *je ne sais quoi*, there was nothing I wanted to buy.

Today, in most developed nations, you can buy almost anything you can imagine almost anytime of day. Whatever you want, from electronics to cheese spread, comes in a multitude of varieties. The idea of walking into a store with virtually no merchandise is something most of us will never face. And if you walk out of a store without purchasing, it is more likely to be because you are overwhelmed with the choices than because you are unable to find something suitable. Of course, all this choice means that "suitable" gets increasingly defined. A Siberian shopper may want cheese and only have a choice between a couple of types. Here, the choice is between hundreds of varieties and your refined taste may have you looking for low-fat, chive and dill cheese spread in a 16-ounce container.

Marketers are not only telling you that you want an increasingly specific product, but they are also marketing an ever-growing range of products designed to meet increasingly obscure needs. If someone imagines a need and a marketer believes that others have the same need, then there is a good chance that you will find it in a store near you one day soon. Flicking through the many catalogs that come through my door, I can find hundreds of items that I survived without for years but that clearly serve a purpose: from special clips that close bags of chips, to storage containers for all the remote controls that have flourished; from bedside sound systems that rock you to sleep with the digitized sound of waves, to alarm lights that wake you gently with a slowly brightening light. Someone buys them, proving that the wealth of the economy is being used to satisfy more and more subtle and obscure wants. The trend to spend is fueled by an economy so fat with spending options that there is always something new to add to your wish list.

They Build In Obsolescence

Another external pressure that adds to the drive to buy is that times change. A lot of what you buy becomes obsolete or out of date. Keeping up with the times can create a seemingly endless need to spend. The product life cycle—the time between when a product is first released on the market and when it goes into decline—is getting shorter. A new luxury item one year may be a standard household fixture a few years later.

Think about all the money you have invested in technologies that you no longer use. Most households harbor a museum of technologies past: a BetaMax video recorder, maybe an 8-track tape player, a computer that is more than 5 years old, a rotary phone that still works but no one has the patience to use anymore, perhaps a black and white television, or the family heirloom radio that came in a cabinet as big as a sideboard. As technology evolves more quickly and becomes more affordable, the lifespan of many household items gets shorter. People who always try the latest thing, a group that marketers call "early adopters," feel this cost more than most. They were quick to move from vinyl records to CDs, from CDs to minidiscs, and now to downloadable music players that are making minidiscs old hat. While these early adopters may be on the cutting edge, they have also spent money on more than their fair share of technological flops.

Additionally, the length of time that a durable good lasts is shrinking, redefining durable to mean "lasts until just after the warranty expires." I recently replaced a dishwasher that was installed in my 1947 home when it was built (I didn't even realize they had dishwashers then). After 53 years, it died. The installers commented that most of today's dishwashers are only 5 to 10 years old before they rinse their last rinse cycle.

Both of these factors mean that spending just to keep up with the times has grown. Rather than buying something and using it for the length of its working life, there is a good chance you will replace it well before it has finished its useful life.

They Make the Money Easy to Get

The final external pressure that fuels the trend to spend is having more access to money, whether or not it has been earned yet. Credit cards, home-equity loans, store cards, even advances on paychecks through check cashing stores allow people at most financial levels to have unprecedented access to borrowed funds. Living on debt is not just a possibility; it is a reality for many. A generation ago, having unmortgaged debt carried a stigma and declaring bankruptcy was a social embarrassment. Today debt is so normal that it is considered a little odd to be without credit cards. Bankruptcy is not exactly acceptable, but people will admit to having been bankrupt without fear of being judged stupid or irresponsible. In fact, as a result of so much concern about the number of people who turn to bankruptcy when they get into financial deep water, education programs have been designed to teach that bankruptcy should be a last resort, not a quick way out.

Internal Pressures: We Want to Buy

As nice as it would be to place the whole blame on the evil marketing industry, we, the consumers, are hardly blameless. In a day and age when a television show called *Greed* is produced, it's hardly shocking to note that most of us want more than we can afford. Many of us have unwritten shopping lists that would make Santa roll his eyes. Why?

We Want More

The fundamental challenge for most of us is that we want more than we can afford. One of the reasons is that our culture has blurred the line between wants and needs. When I said that I needed something as a kid, I remember my mother asking me: "Do you want it or need it?" Usually the answer was "want." My mother didn't mean I couldn't have it, she just wanted me to appreciate it was an optional extra. If you look at all the things you spend money on, how much is spent on things that you really need? Probably not a lot. Yes, you need a roof over your head, food on your table, a way to get to work and back, and education for your kids. But what you really need is just the basics. Chances are, most of what you spend is driven by what you want: a home that is comfortable, food that is tasty and easy to prepare, a car that has more than just four wheels and a seat, an education that will give your kids an advantage.

Part of this has occurred because we no longer keep up with the Joneses, but rather aim to keep up with a composite person who doesn't exist. "The average American is now more likely to compare his or her income to the six-figure benchmark in the office down the corridor or displayed in Tuesday evening prime time," Juliet Schor comments.* The composite picture may include the dress standards of your boss, the gardening and maintenance expenses of your neighbors, the social life of a new romantic interest, and the car of your best friend. It may also include fictional benchmarks, such as the great apartment that the characters on the TV show *Friends* live in even though they seem to barely ever work. All this ups the ante, resulting in normal people having aspirations that are far from achievable on a normal salary.

The result is that most of us have an infinite shopping list in our heads. When we manage to afford the things on the top of the list, we find that there are more wants just underneath. We end up with an internal wish list that is like a magician's unending string of scarves, with more popping up every time we think we are near the goal of feeling satisfied.

We Want What They Have

Another way that we try to fit in is by following trends.

· ·

Peter joined my class after going through a massive change in his career and lifestyle. He left a career that paid him hundreds of thou-

---

*Juliet B. Schor, *The Overspent American: Upscaling, Downshifting and the New Consumer* (New York: Basic Books, 1998), p. 13.

sands of dollars but gave him little inner satisfaction. When we spoke, he was scaling back his lifestyle so he could afford to explore other paths. "The one big expense I still have every month is the payments on my car, and I don't even like it anymore," he mused. "I bought the biggest damn SUV on the road because everyone I knew was going for the biggest and best. Now, I just wonder why."

. . . .

We have all fallen prey to it at one time or another: buying something, upgrading something, just because almost everyone we know is doing the same thing. Or just because we can afford to. Or just because. If you have ever shopped for a home or a car, you probably have had a salesperson assume that you want to spend as much as you can afford. If you qualify for a $300,000 mortgage, but choose only to go in half that deep, you are the odd man out in the home-buying world. If you can afford the "biggest damn SUV" and you choose a modest sedan that gets you from point A to point B efficiently but with much less oompf, you are a radical.

Is it wrong to want to keep up? Not at all. Wanting to fit in is a very normal human desire. Besides which, most of the stuff that we want is nice. Luxury cars are more comfortable than regular ones. Expensive clothes are usually cut better than cheap ones. Good restaurants serve tastier food than cheap ones. The problems arise, however, when we consume more than we can afford.

We Want It Now

Life is faster than it used to be, and we are used to getting what we want sooner. With easy credit and readily available goods, it is easy to act on our wish list today. For many people, waiting seems unwarranted and planning for the future unnecessary.

. . . .

Stacy, 26, recently changed jobs. "I cashed out my retirement savings because I have more need for the money now than in the future. My friends say I'm crazy and that if I left it alone, I could have a whole lot in the future, but saving for retirement now seems pessimistic." She cashed out her small retirement savings account, getting several thousand dollars after tax was deducted. "The point is that I can really use a couple of thousand now and I expect in a few years I will be earning enough that putting away a couple of thousand again will be easy."

. . . .

We Are on the Consumption Escalator

Another internal pressure arises as earnings rise. People have more money than ever before and the average household is significantly better off than a decade ago, but why don't we feel any richer? It's often because Unconscious Spenders have jumped on the consumption escalator: When their salaries increase, their lifestyles become more expensive. Remember junior high chemistry class when we learned about solids, liquids, and gases? Gases, we were told, expand to occupy the available space. Put a certain amount of gas in a small container, and it will take up that much space. Double the size of the container, and the gas will expand to fill the extra space. Money, it seems, is the same. If you have seen your pay rise over the years, you probably are having just as much (or as little) trouble living within your means at your current earnings as you did when you earned half as much.

Let's look at a fictitious person, a young accountant who has just started her first job. She earns $25,000, contributes 5 percent of her income to a retirement plan, spends $500 a month on a studio apartment, and spends another $100 a month on her social life. A few years and several promotions later, she is earning double, contributing 5 percent of her income to a retirement plan, living in a larger apartment with a garden for $1,000 a month, and spending $200 a month on her social life. Is she better off? Sure, her apartment is more spacious, and her social life is in nicer bars with more expensive drinks. But is she really better off? Maybe not. Even though her earnings have doubled, she still is getting the same thing for her money: a roof over her head, a few great nights out with friends, and money saved for her retirement.

Robert H. Frank points out in *Luxury Fever* that humans are highly adaptable and gain little ongoing satisfaction from increasing amounts of conspicuous consumption. "Once we become accustomed to the bigger TV, the more spacious refrigerator, or the better loudspeakers, their favorable features fade into the background. We are no longer conscious of them."*

What if our accountant had chosen to stay put in her studio apartment? With the $500 she would save, she could squirrel away $250 a month toward the down payment on a house and spend the rest traveling to some corner of the world every year to follow her passion for whitewater rafting. Would she be better off? She'd certainly get more for her money: all of what she originally got, *plus* some great experiences and a home down payment. By jumping off the escalator in that one area of housing, she could free up a lot of money to spend on things she really valued.

Escalating your standard of living is fine when it is a conscious choice. Unconsciously escalating your standard of living can cost you the ability to choose the life you really want.

---

*Robert H. Frank, *Luxury Fever: Why Money Fails to Satisfy in an Era of Excess* (New York: The Free Press, 1999), pp. 179–180.

Shopping Is Not Just About Shopping

As if all this temptation were not enough, shopping has moved from the realm of fulfilling basic needs to entertainment. I bet I'm not the only woman who has used "retail therapy" to get over a broken heart or gone shopping to avoid studying for exams. As Paco Underhill says, "We use shopping as therapy, reward, bribery, pastime, as an excuse to get out of the house, as a way to troll for potential loved ones, as entertainment, as a form of education or even worship, as a way to kill time."* Shopping malls have become places that are as much about socializing and entertainment as they are about shopping for many people, from the elders who use malls as indoor walking tracks, to the teens who are not old enough to hang out elsewhere. One high-end gourmet grocery chain near where I live even has singles nights, where the store stays open late and has samplings of food and various displays to break the ice among the single people who would otherwise just gaze longingly at each other over the broccolini.

. . . .

Judith knows the buzz of shopping, "I used to go shopping and get maybe $300–$400 of stuff. The act of pulling it off the shelf, trying it on, and then having them wrap it up in a package, and coming home and unwrapping it was a real charge. After that the enjoyment went down—it didn't have the same charge. I bought to make myself feel better, maybe as a social ritual or just a reward because I worked hard," Judith recalled. As a therapist, she has seen her shopping habits replicated by many of her clients, and she likens it to an addiction. "That's why people go shopping: It alters brain chemistry and you can get addicted to it. You want more, more, more because

---

*Paco Underhill, *Why We Buy: The Science of Shopping* (New York: Simon & Schuster, 1999), p. 95.

when once you get [what you bought] home, it doesn't have the same charge."

. . . .

I have to confess that I am pretty weird when it comes to shopping. I don't enjoy it. In fact, I really dislike it. I am completely missing the "is girl, likes shopping" gene. I guess it stems back to those days when it was hard to find fashionable size 10½A shoes, but shopping for the sake of shopping leaves me cold. This inclination is a great thing for my wallet. However, I know that if I spend a day wandering in a mall with no particular shopping list, by the end of the day there are a half dozen things I want that I had not even thought of wanting before.

Money Simply Evaporates

Evaporation of money is another internal pressure. Most of us simply don't like the tedious work of tracking where our money goes, and it seems to evaporate. Hundreds of insignificant purchases add up to a significant amount but do not have a significant impact on our standard of living. For some people, having cash on hand means that it simply gets spent on little things. Others find that credit cards result in the same evaporation, with a surprisingly large bill coming at the end of the month, summing up numerous small purchases that have faded into the background by the time the bill arrives. When you look at money a week at a time, a month at a time, it seems as though there's not all that much to go around. We are simply frittering away our ability to use our money to make a difference in our lives.

. . . .

"I doubled my income last year!" Frost told me as we caught up around tax time one year. He is an architect in Los Angeles whose

great work has been getting more and more attention. Frost finally had a strong flow of interesting work coming in; a couple of big design projects and the successful completion of some smaller ones. "I can see it on my tax return—I definitely earned a lot more—but I have no idea where it went. I got a better car and upgraded the house a bit, but that doesn't account for half of it. I really don't know where it all went."

. . . .

A lot of people avoid managing money because it sounds like hard work. Remember the king who was stuck in his counting house counting out the pennies? Not the person we aspired to be in our nursery rhyme days.

. . . .

Steven, a freelance computer consultant in Colorado, has tried repeatedly to manage his money. "Managing money looks like it is going to take a lot of time and then I'm not going to be able to go out with my friends." His pattern has been that he lets the paperwork pile up and lives day-to-day on whatever positive balance he has in his bank account, then periodically tries to track his money on a computer program to better understand where he stands financially. The day he starts the tracking involves hours of entering in old receipts. "When I do that, it is a self-fulfilling prophecy and I end up resenting it, so it doesn't get handled."

. . . .

Letting money just flow through our fingers feels easier than managing our money, but the problem is we end up not getting what we want. Conscious Spending is an antidote to money's tendency to evaporate because it focuses on what you want and is inherently more motivating than nickel-and-dimeing yourself to boredom.

For many people, all the external pressures encouraging us to spend and the internal ones that make resisting difficult add up to a life of Unconscious Spending. All of these pressures to spend result in a culture where many people live for today without really considering the impact on the future. This means that many people do not save enough for retirement, get into debt, and effectively work today to pay for what they consumed yesterday.

Exercise: Getting Out of Your Own Way
· ·

Take 5 minutes to make a list of all the influences on your financial life that you are most aware of. Think of where you are, who you are with, and what you are doing when you start to want something. Remember some of the unnecessary purchases you have made recently. What prompted them? How did you decide on that purchase versus everything else on your list? Where did you first hear about the product you bought? Did you make the decision alone, with other members of your household, or with the support of friends or colleagues? Do you know someone who has something similar?

Over the next few weeks, begin to watch for the triggers that start the process of wanting. What do you see and hear that impacts what you want? Who do you compare yourself to? Where is your danger zone: in front of the TV, in a mall, reading magazines, talking with friends? As you begin to understand your behavior patterns better, make some decisions that will help you become a Conscious Spender. Are there friends with whom you are better off not shopping? Are there catalogs or cable channels that lead you into temptation? Are there habits that make it harder to listen to your true wants?

· ·

PART TWO

SET TO SPEND

The Seven Conscious Spending Categories

YOU ARE WHAT YOU SPEND! IN THIS SECTION, WE LOOK IN detail at each category of the Conscious Spending Model: Security, Shelter, Sustenance, Self and Family, Social, Society, and Soul. I outline the items that make up each category and the values that may come into play. The Full Cost and Lifetime Cost of each category are examined, and specific strategies to lower the cost or get more for your money are shared.

As you read this section, you will meet more people and hear their stories. Some are Conscious Spenders, others are overspenders. Some find it hard to save, others find it hard to enjoy their money. Some are just recognizing the challenges they face, while others have been following the Conscious Spending approach for a while and have radically changed how they perceive their money and what it can do for them. You may recognize yourself in some of their stories. One thing I discovered while speaking with these people is that many of them share the challenges we face with our money.

In this section you will find tips and ideas about managing your spending. Keep a list of ideas that appeal to you and realizations that you have. Some ideas can be implemented instantly, others may take some time. When you get to Part Three, you will create your own Conscious Spending Plan, basing it on all you realized about your current spending in this section.

....

CHAPTER 5

Security

Your Financial Foundation

What Is Security?

Security is the foundation stone of your personal finances (Figure 5.1). It is at the base of the Conscious Spending Model because it is the most fundamental financial need of people in modern economies. Few people in developed countries struggle with choices about having a roof over their heads or a meal in their stomachs. I assume that if you are reading this, at least those basic needs are being met.

Security underpins all the other categories. If you look at the three rules of personal finance—live within your means, take care of your future, and maximize your pleasure—you can see there is an implicit balancing act going on. How do you fine-tune the balance between today's needs and tomorrow's needs? How can you find the right balance of spending and saving so that you are comfortable throughout life?

What springs to mind when you think about financial security? Retirement savings, probably. However, Rule 2 requires that Security be broader than just retirement savings. Taking care of

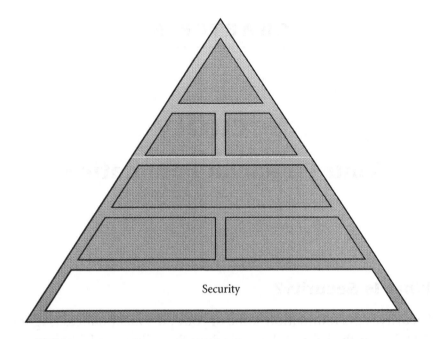

- Cash cushion
- Retirement savings
- Life insurance
- Disability insurance
- Umbrella liability insurance
- Consumer debt repayment

Figure 5.1   Security is at the base of the Conscious Spending Model because it is the foundation stone of your personal finances.

your future means putting preventive measures in place that take care of *all* aspects of your financial future. In addition to retirement savings, Security includes having a cash cushion to ensure that an unexpected bill will not knock you off the tracks; having an insurance structure that takes care of your needs and obligations in case of an accident, disability or death; and making sure your debt is managed. Why are all these important? Try as you might, there simply is a lot you cannot plan for. Having a strong Security base means you are less vulnerable to unexpected circumstances. Statistics show that most people who declare bankruptcy do so because of an unexpected event that threw them for a loop financially. Divorce, illness, unemployment, disability, business failure: None of these events are planned, but the fact is that they do happen. Security is your secret weapon to ensure that events such as these do not send you into a financial spin so severe that you end up in bankruptcy. While living in fear of one of these events does not make sense, putting in place a financial airbag to take the impact if they do occur does, and this chapter shows you how to ensure that that airbag is in place.

Security and Values

What does Security mean to you? Is it a way to sleep well at night? Is it part of being a good parent? Is it a gloomy reminder of the fact that you are aging? Is it a liberating freedom that allows you to take risks and pursue your dreams? Does planning ahead feel like you are not living for today? Does today hold more excitement and possibilities because you have handled your future? Is Security simply a part of being responsible and taking care of your obligations? Is it about taking responsibility for yourself? Is it about taking care of those you love?

I talked in Part One about Savers and Spenders. If you are a Saver, this chapter looks at the way you structure your savings and fills in some gaps that you may already be aware of. If you are a Spender, however, I can see that you are already fidgeting and planning to put the book down "just for one minute," never to re-open it. I know this because this is the part in my classes when a whole lot of people have to get up to check their voice mail, take a bathroom break, or just stretch their legs. Stick with it. Remember that this is also about spending: spending through thick and thin, and spending in your golden years.

But wait, I hear you Spenders say, didn't you talk about aligning spending with personal values? What if I don't value Security? I thought this was supposed to be fun, and you are making me save?

Don't get me wrong. I know this may be very difficult for you. However the reality is that you have to bite the bullet. Yes, you may not value Security directly. You may feel taking care of such things is stodgy and constraining and so future focused that it is taking away from your enjoyment of the day. You may value freedom and see the responsibility implicit in Security as conflicting with those values. You may value youth and action and feel that Security speaks of age and accident, scary concepts that are far removed. You may simply be so focused on other things that when you think about Security, it is an annoying mosquito of a thing, buzzing around periodically and reminding you that you have unfinished business.

You need to make a choice: Either continue to ignore or avoid Security, or reposition Security so that it does feel aligned with your values. The first choice has all those consequences that you and I know in terms of financial vulnerability and inability to have a comfortable future. The second requires some crafty playing with your values.

· ·

Maria is a free spirit with responsibilities. At 30, she left a steady job as an administrator. "I was going out of my mind because it was so boring and I knew that there were other things I needed to do in my life. I was willing to put that all on the line to go back to school and study to be an artist." She studied pottery making and now creates high-end crafts in a resort town in Canada.

"Freedom is probably my highest value," she said, "I've always had a very daring, impulsive nature. Part of what draws me to this lifestyle is the personal control I have day-to-day. I don't have to listen to anyone else's needs or wants. I'm a free agent and that's worth a huge, huge, huge amount to me." However her love of freedom has played out in her life as avoiding financial responsibility.

Now 48, married, and the mother of twin 11-year-olds, Maria has a highly unpredictable cash flow. "Because I'm a self-employed artist, my money comes in very sporadically. It's not like I get X-amount every month: I can go from zero one month to ten thousand the next month, and then only a thousand or so over the next 3 months. There is little structure to it. So much is at the whim of customers and weather and shows."

Although she and her family live a fairly modest lifestyle, the months when the cash comes in can be difficult because she has so much pent-up demand for treats. "A few years ago, I'd go to a big show in Toronto and get a few thousand dollars in my pocket in a day, and I'd go and buy a $60 pair of slippers that I normally wouldn't buy. The cash is there and I am in this fog of denial that in 3 months' time there's not going to be the money to pay the mortgage. It's a bit like a drinking binge. I hand out cash to my kids—'go buy this or that.' It goes from such a famine to such a feast."

The result has been periodic near-bankruptcy experiences. "It was pretty bad 5 years ago when I was terrified to answer the phone," she recalled, remembering the dreaded calls from creditors.

Realizing that the way that she has expressed her love of freedom resulted in worries that don't feel very freeing at all, she is changing her patterns. "My partner and I are in a transition period because we are both quite sick of being worried about money. I think the novelty has worn off. Finally, I know that I can change this if I want to. I am exploring how to get a better grip on my finances so that I do have something for the future." Maria is redefining the freedom which she values: Taking care of her finances frees her from the drama of near bankruptcy and the drudge of the part-time jobs she sometimes takes to make ends meet. For all her resolve, the change is not happening overnight. She accepts her responsibilities with some reluctance: "There is a big part of me that is a 10-year-old kid who thinks that 'Daddy' will take care of it . . . and I don't know who this 'Daddy' is."

. . . .

Security can be positioned to fit with almost any primary values. If you value freedom, Security helps you to be free to change jobs, avoid phone calls from irate creditors, and have a fabulous retirement doing whatever you please. If you value family and home, Security helps you take care of your children and parents if anything happens, not be a burden to your children when you are older, and spend your retirement flitting around the country visiting all of them. If you value looking good in others' eyes, Security protects your image if you hit a rough patch and may buy you bragging rights as people you respect chat about the stock market.

Have you ever heard a 5-year-old's reaction to being told to go to bed? "Do I have to?" Kids have an unmistakably whiney tone when they know in advance the answer is a definite, but not unsympathetic, "Yes!" There are probably a few of you out there having the same reaction to Security. "Do I have to?"

Yes, you have to!

Unless you have already handled your retirement savings, put away enough cash to handle 3 months' expenses, and have a watertight insurance plan, you have to. Whine and stamp your feet a bit if it makes you feel better. Then just do it. If it helps, think of all the good stuff you'll get out of it. You will be able to stop beating yourself up for not having handled it. You can feel smug around your friends who are still putting it off for a rainy day. You can picture a fabulous retirement without feeling like you're kidding yourself.

The bottom line is that if you can change the way you perceive Security so that you are motivated to take action on it, it will pay off for the rest of your life. It's worth it and it's necessary, so let's get down to business.

The Elements of Security

As we look at Security, remember that the Full Cost and Lifetime Cost are a little different than for most categories. The bigger question is: What is the cost of not having Security? When you develop your Conscious Spending Plan, you may spend much more on this category than you have in the past as you realize the necessity of each of the elements. However, there are still ways to ensure that you are not paying more than you need or receiving less than you should.

Cash Cushion

The first element of Security is a cash cushion. This is what you land on if you trip up financially. Your cash cushion is your CYA fund: Cover Your Assets. You do not want to be forced into selling a car, house, or investment to get through a rough patch.

There is plenty of variation in what people think is enough for a cash cushion. Most financial planners talk about having 3 to 6 months' living expenses on hand. Some people argue that having a credit card with a decent (and unused) limit is enough to tide them over most unexpected glitches. My rule of thumb is to plan for reasonably pessimistic events and hope that they never happen. Could you lose your job? Could illness take you away from your work and other responsibilities? Could accidental death wipe out much of your family's income? Could an accident leave you with expenses to cover? Could divorce leave your finances, as well as your heart, in shreds? Could a parent's illness mean you have to take time off work or cover additional elder care bills?

I'm not generally a pessimist, but every so often, I take a look at the almost-worst-case scenario and make sure I'm covering myself for that. When I was an employee, I kept 2 to 3 months' worth of expenses covered, knowing that the worst case was that I would lose my job or get sick. I had the sort of skills where I could pick up some sort of job quickly (even if I had to look around for a while for the perfect job), and I was well insured in terms of disability insurance. Now that I'm self-employed, I have a much more substantial cushion because I know that my income sources are less predictable, I do not qualify for disability insurance, and my expenses are less flexible.

If it, whatever "it" is, hits the fan, you can quickly stop all your variable spending. You can get by with no new clothes, no social life, and so forth for a while. What cannot be stopped so easily are the "fixed" costs: your rent or mortgage, your utility bills, your baseline food costs, and your transportation expenses. Some new costs might arise as well: an interview outfit and resume service if you lose your job, long distance calls and an airfare or two if a member of the family dies, a down payment on a new car if old faithful blows her gasket, or a good lawyer's fees if your honey trades you in for a new model. Another cost that may arise is an insurance deductible. If your house burns down or you are in a car accident, you may be responsible for a thousand dollars or more before you can start your claim.

Whatever amount you pick for your cash cushion, begin stashing the cash in a way that you won't be tempted to dip into it for minor emergencies. Sorry, but the goldfish dying simply doesn't qualify. Put the money in a cash account or money market account that pays some interest and is, preferably, FDIC insured. If you need a little extra discipline to keep your cushion intact, make it harder to access. An ATM card or checkbook might make it too easy to lay your hands on the cash. Think about requiring a trip to the bank if you want to touch the money. You need to be able to access the money with little or no notice or penalty, so don't tie it up in a 12-month CD or invest it in stocks that may gain or lose value. If you do dip into the cash cushion, move quickly to replenish it as soon as the crisis has passed.

To manage the Full Cost and Lifetime Cost of your cash cushion, be conscious of the return you are getting and the fees you are paying. Low interest rates or high bank charges could mean that your cash cushion is not even keeping pace with inflation. The financial services industry is so competitive these days, you should be able to find a money market account with low fees and a reasonable return.

Exercise: Sitting Pretty with Your Cash Cushion

Use the following worksheet to figure out what sort of cash cushion you need to tide you over a rough patch.

1. Identify your fixed costs by filling in your average monthly payments for the following:

   Housing (mortgage or rent plus taxes/fees)   _____

   Utilities (phone, gas, electricity, water)   _____

   Transportation (lease/loan, gas, registration)   _____

   Food (groceries only)   _____

   Other   _____

   Total monthly fixed costs   _____

2. Multiply by number of months that you want your cash cushion to cover:

Total monthly fixed costs × _____ = _____

3. Add enough to cover a large unexpected expense such as an insurance deductible or several hours of a lawyer's time:

Deductible/emergency expenses =   _____

4. Add 2 and 3 to get the size of the cash cushion you need.

_____ (from 2) + _____ (3) = _____

. . . .

Retirement Savings

When you are young and healthy and there are so many other demands for each dollar, it is easy to put off saving for retirement. Yet this step is the single most important strategy that you can use to build your financial security. There's something about being old and poor that puts a chill up the spine. Retirement savings are the antidote to that chilling picture. (Of course, no one uses the term "old" anymore, except young people who don't realize how quickly the numbers can rise even though you feel the same at 70 as at 37.)

Most people retire somewhere between the ages of 55 and 65, though more and more people are choosing to work full or part time for years after reaching retirement age. Some people are aiming to retire even earlier. Whenever you do retire, there's a good chance you will be partly or fully retired for many a long year. Medical advances mean that more and more of us are living to a grand old age, even if we have to replace half our bodies with plastic parts to get there. The question is: How are you going to support yourself? Relying on anyone or anything else to provide for your future is simply wishful thinking, unless it is solid, in writing, and backed by an institution that cannot go broke or change the rules.

Only a generation ago, most working people had a company pension plan that was their primary source of retirement savings, and at-home spouses also depended on those pension plans. Today, all the rules have changed. People are more likely to have to contribute voluntarily to a retirement fund that their employer offers, less likely to hold one job for life, and less likely to stay married to one person for life. Marriage is no longer a guarantee: Just ask any divorcee who married well in the days when a well-paying career was not deemed necessary for a woman of marriageable stock.

Generations before that, having a dozen or so hardy children was the best pension plan there was. "Honey, have us another couple of sons to take care of the farm, would you? I want to play golf when I retire." Today, with the average cost of raising a child from birth to age 18 running in the hundreds of thousands of dollars, you'd be better off having no kids and a fat retirement fund if the decision were purely about financial security.

Social Security has been another traditional source of long-term financial security in the United States. Most economists feel that the Social Security system will survive for years to come, but the amount it pays the average retiree is pretty small for most people.* An average $804 a month will not pay for the sort of retirement most people aspire to.†

---

*Log on to www.ssa.gov or contact the Social Security Administration to find out what your estimated Social Security benefits will be.
†Social Security Administration.

What if the mythical god of luck hands you the lottery? No need for all that saving and planning and being good, is there? Not true. Companies that buy out lottery winners' annuities say that fully one-half of all lottery millionaires end up in dire financial straits.[*] Curtis Sharp, Jr. could have been one of them. A maintenance worker at Bell Labs, he kept his job for 8 years after winning the lottery so that he would qualify for his pension. He did this despite winning $5 million in 1982, one of the largest jackpots in history at the time. That pension is now his main financial security: His winnings were consumed by a lavish lifestyle, poor investments, and undirected generosity.[†] People who don't buy lottery tickets probably have a hard time imagining the mindset of those who religiously spend their $1 a week or a day on a tempting morsel of hope. Fully half of all people in a study of lottery players think of their gambling as an investment.[‡] It is not an investment. It is a gamble. The chances of getting any return are uncertain and unfavorable. Putting the same amount in a tax-deferred retirement instrument is an investment.

At the same time that all of these changes have been occurring, people have started retiring younger and living longer. The resulting increase in the number of years that people are retired means that a well thought out retirement plan is more important than ever.

The old ways of providing for your future, such as marrying for money, being loyal to your boss, relying on the government, and hoping for lady luck, simply cannot be relied on anymore. Guess who that leaves?

---

[*]Jack Hitt, "The Broke Millionaire," *GQ* (April 1999): 198.
[†]Ibid., 196–203, 234.
[‡]Philip J. Cook and Charles T. Clotfelter, *Selling Hope : State Lotteries in America* (Cambridge: Harvard University Press, 1991).

If you don't take care of your future, nobody will. You are the only person you know who is *guaranteed* to be with you through thick and thin, for richer and for poorer (despite what the marriage vows said). Your spouse, kids, employer, and government may be there to help out, but do you want a "maybe" to determine the difference between a comfortable retirement or one spent balancing precariously just at the poverty line?

Excellent books about how to invest for your retirement are available and I have listed some in the bibliography and have others on my web site. Here I introduce some of the concepts you need to think about when you choose how to consciously use your resources.

How Much to Save

The amount you need to save depends on a number of things: how much you will spend a year when you are retired, what age you will retire, how long you will live, what other income sources you will have, and what return you get on your investments before and after retirement.

The way you spend money as a retiree may differ substantially from the way you spend it before you retire. Some costs will rise: health care, travel (in the years you are mobile), and leisure activities. Others will fall: clothing, work-related costs, and home payments (assuming your mortgage is close to being paid off or you downscale at some stage). Conscious Spending is relevant as you save for retirement as well as when you are retired. Aligning your spending with your values is just as important when time is scarce and money flow is strong, as when time is plentiful but your income comes from your investments.

Your retirement age may well be determined not only by when you want to retire, but also by when you can afford to retire.

Whether you leave the workforce at 50 or at 70, how long your savings need to last has no certain answer. Advances in medicine, improvements in diet and even safer cars have contributed to lengthening life spans. A male born in 1950 had an expected life span of 65.6 years, whereas a male born in 2000 is expected to live until 73.7 years of age. For females, the trend is the same, but the expected life span has risen from 71.1 years to 79.5 years.* These figures are averages, and factors such as the age at which you retire have an impact on them, so work with conservative estimates so you don't outlive your money. With longer life spans, it is quite possible that you could be retired for as many years as you worked.

Retirement is also changing. More and more retirees are not giving up the working life cold turkey. Some retirees discover that life without any sort of work to define their days and keep their mind sharp can be boring. Part-time work or second careers just for the fun of it are becoming more and more prevalent. Retirement with zero work-based income is less common, making the math of guesstimating how much you will need even more difficult.

Your ability to retire in comfort depends not only on how much you put away, but also on how you invest it. A reasonable return and a long period of time can turn even a small contribution into a sizeable nest egg. To get a reasonable return, part or all of your retirement portfolio can and should be in stocks (depending on your age). Get help if you need it in determining the right combination of large, medium, and small company stocks, the right mix of industries, and the right mix of U.S. stocks versus international stocks. Ask a financial planner or fee-based investment adviser for help. However, let me use one example to show how different investment strategies can really have an impact on

---

*Social Security Administration.

how comfortable your retirement will be. Suppose someone puts away $2,000 a year and that the stock market returns about 9 percent on average, bonds return 5 percent, and cash returns 2 percent, after inflation is taken into account. Table 5.1 shows the size of the portfolio based on different investment strategies.

Does the fact that the 100 percent stock strategy outperformed the others significantly mean that everyone should use this strategy for his or her retirement investments? For most of your working life, the answer is yes. However, as you get closer to retirement age, you will want to move some of your portfolio into bonds or cash. If the volatility of the stock market scares you, remember that you are not going to be touching the money for a long time and choosing less volatile investment vehicles that have lower returns will hurt you and mean that you need to save more.

So how much will you actually need? As you can see, there are so many variables that this is one area where all the reading you can do is not enough. You have to play with numbers on your own, and then have a certified financial planner double check your assumptions and help you structure your investment portfolio to make sure that your investments will give you the return

Table 5.1   Sample Investment Strategies and Returns

Strategy	Investment After		
	10 years ($)	25 years ($)	40 years ($)
Total invested	20,000	50,000	80,000
100% stock or stock funds	33,121	184,648	736,584
100% bonds	26,414	100,227	253,680
100% cash	22,337	65,342	123,220
80% stocks, 20% bonds	31,648	162,899	590,963
50% stocks, 30% bonds, 20% cash	28,581	123,545	364,360

that you need. Software such as Quicken and Microsoft Money have calculators that let you play with numbers. With all the assumptions, if you're going to err, err on the conservative side. Better to have your money outlast you for a few years than vice versa.

My more simple rule of thumb is to start as young as you can and put away as much as you can afford and then some. At a minimum, try to put away 10 percent of your earnings; 15 percent or more if you can afford it. However, keep a balance between enjoying today and planning for tomorrow. If you start young and get into a habit of putting the maximum contribution into the different retirement tools that are available to you, you can probably slow down your savings at a later age (just in time to pay your kids' college fees). If you are starting later and cannot afford to put away the maximum contribution, work with a financial planner to determine exactly how much you need to save. If it feels like a stretch, later chapters in this book will help you find some places where you can cut back in a relatively painless way so you can ratchet up your savings.

In my own planning, I like to be conservative in all my calculations about retirement simply because the whole "old and poor" scenario is really unappealing to me. I assume I'll live to 100 (given advances in medical science, I may even need to increase this estimate), I assume that the stock market will return 5 percent above inflation,* and I assume that my living costs will not decrease. I also assume that I will die broke, that is, use my earnings and savings for my lifetime. This sounds more appealing than working hard in my lifetime to let my heirs off easy. Two thoughts behind this: First, if I have enough to be giving it away, I'd rather see the results of my generosity while I'm alive (tell your Aunt Deborah

---

*Five percent is lower than the historic return rate, but after such a long bull market, I would rather use a very conservative estimate.

how much you really appreciate her, kids . . .). Second, I'd rather not give my heirs an incentive to want me gone. Of course, the math won't be perfect unless I plan to do a one-way bungee jump for my 100th birthday, so I have a fudge factor in there.

One thing that becomes very apparent as soon as you play with the numbers is that retiring early has a big cost. By shortening the number of years that your retirement funds can compound, you lose the chance of having your money earn a lot for you. Did you notice in Table 5.1 that the 15 years from year 10 to year 25 added about $150,000 to the 100 percent stock portfolio. The following 15 years added another $550,000. Why the difference? It's called compounding; you are earning a return on the earnings that you have already made; that is, your money is making money.

Where to Put It: Tools to Save for Retirement

Retirement savings has a language of its own. Here's a brief introduction to the tools you can use in the United States and how to prioritize them.

There are two general types of retirement savings. First are those that are exempt from income tax at the time you save the money. In effect, that means that every $1,000 you squirrel away in a tax-deferred retirement plan costs you less in terms of after-tax money. So if you are in the 28 percent tax bracket, it will take only $720 [$1,000 \times (1 - 0.28)$] out of your pay. (Of course, you should take state taxes into account, too.) In essence, the Full Cost of the $1,000 investment appears to be lower than its price tag. These retirement accounts are not taxed until you withdraw the money during retirement. The second type of account is not exempt from income tax at the time you save the money; however the earnings grow tax-free and you do not pay tax on the money you withdraw during retirement.

If you are an employee, your employer may offer a retirement plan that you pay for with pretax dollars. In the United States, the plan could be called a 401(k), 403(b), 457, SEP, Keogh, or even a pension plan, depending on the size and type of company you work for. Whatever the type of plan, your employer may match every $1 that you contribute with 50¢ or $1, up to a certain level. If so, take advantage of it—it is like getting a pay raise. Even if you are offered an employer-sponsored retirement plan, you may be able to contribute additional funds to a Roth IRA that you open for yourself. Your ability to contribute to a Roth IRA depends on your income level and your other retirement savings tools.

If you are an employee whose employer does not offer a retirement plan or if you are not working, you may be able to contribute to either an IRA or Roth IRA. Regular IRAs are tax-deductible the year that you put the money in, while Roth IRAs are not. The income from the Roth IRA is tax-free during retirement.

If you are self-employed or run a small business, you can save for your retirement with pretax dollars by opening a retirement plan such as a SEP, SIMPLE, Keogh, or IRA, depending on the structure of your business.

Visit your employer's benefits office and a branch of an investment firm to get help in deciphering the alphabet soup of retirement plans and in figuring out which ones you can put money into. The most important thing is to start saving as soon as possible, and to put away as much as possible. Once you put the money away, don't be tempted to withdraw it or borrow against it. Too many people sabotage their Security by withdrawing the money. Once the money is out, you have lost all those great advantages, and you can't put it back in. When you change jobs or retire, you can roll your retirement savings into an IRA, where you can probably choose from a wider range of investments than you are offered by your employer's fund. You can also convert money that is in a regular IRA into a Roth IRA, but get advice from a tax or financial planner before doing this.

After those options, other investments should be considered, including variable annuities and regular investments in the form of stocks, bonds, or mutual funds. Before you purchase a variable annuity, know that the investment community is really divided on these insurance/investment hybrids. The problem is that many have high commissions and penalty clauses, effectively wiping out some of the tax advantages. Some of the big investment firms have gone head-to-head with the insurance industry and the competition is driving the fees of variable annuities down, so shop around. Ask a fee-based financial advisor if this investment vehicle is right for you, and, if it is, make sure that the commission and fees you pay are as low as possible and your investment choices are broad.

Managing the Full Cost and Lifetime Cost

Retirement savings are one of the few things that may have a Full Cost that is lower than the amount you are paying, if your contributions are coming from pretax dollars, as already mentioned.

It is important with your retirement savings that you take into account the fees that are charged, as higher fees over a long period of time can have a Lifetime Cost that eats into your retirement savings. Often employers do not give much information about the fees charged by each of the investment options within your company plan. Ask to make sure that the selections you make have good returns after the fees have been taken into account. If you have an IRA that you manage yourself, such as a Rollover IRA or Roth IRA, you can also manage the Lifetime Cost by being conscious of the fees charged every time you buy or sell stocks or move your money into a new mutual fund within your IRA, as well as management fees charged by mutual fund companies.

So far we have looked at two components of Security: your cash cushion to take care of short-term bumps in the financial road and your retirement savings to take care of your retirement years. The next tool in the Security category to look at is insurance.

Exercise: Your Golden Dreams
. . . .

When financial planners estimate your retirement income, they tend to assume that your current spending will either stay the same or perhaps fall. Although that may be a useful way to start, try approaching it from what you would like to be doing. Take 10 minutes in a quiet place to imagine the sort of things you would like to be doing in your retirement during your active years. Think of all the things that you do not do today because you are busy working for a living. Often by retirement, there are a few decades of "if only I had time" fantasies. Start a list of the sort of things you would like to do and have in retirement. Which of your values are going to be expressed in different ways? Where would you like to live? What activities would you like to do? Where would you like to travel? Do you have interests that you would like to turn into a small business? Would you enjoy having a part-time job? Would you like to go back to school and learn something new? Which costs will increase? Which costs will decrease? What will you want more of? What will you want less of?

In Chapter 12, you can learn how to create a Conscious Spending Plan for your lifestyle today. Once you have finished that, create a plan for the future you imagine, ignoring inflation (a financial planner can take that into account as you develop a financial plan). Determine how much after-tax income you would need to live the retirement lifestyle that you would like in the future. When you are ready to work with a financial planner on your retirement investment strategy, use this plan to show your planner that you have thought through what your costs are likely to be after retirement.

· ·

Life, Disability, and Umbrella Liability Insurance

If money makes the world go round, insurance is what makes sure it doesn't stop if a crisis hits. A critical part of your financial security is the insurance to keep the money coming in in case of death, disability, and legal liability. Note that I discuss home insurance in the section on Shelter and health insurance in the section on Sustenance. They both are part of maintaining your financial security, but are considered as part of the total cost of owning a home and sustaining your body.

Death and taxes may be the only certainties in life, but whereas you can minimize taxes, death is pretty much an on/off switch. Life insurance takes care of your financial obligations in the sad case that the switch is thrown while others depend on you. The need for life insurance depends on whether you have obligations to other people. So parents will want to insure their lives while their children are dependents. A couple will want life insurance if either partner would have to change his or her lifestyle substantially if the other partner died. And a single person with no children may want to consider life insurance if family members or others depend on his or her financial or physical care. However, many people do not need life insurance. Singles with no dependents or couples whose retirement nest eggs are enough to see them and their spouses through may be wiser to invest (or enjoy!) the money than to pay the premiums. And you definitely don't need insurance on your kids' lives. Some aggressive salespeople peddle life insurance on kids, particularly to low-income families, claiming that the parents may need to cover their kids' funeral costs in case they die. They're trying to cash in on a parent's worst fears. Don't buy it. You're better off just investing in your cash cushion for the worst-case scenarios and slamming the door in the sharks' faces.

When you chose how much life insurance to buy, think not only in terms of covering the loss of income, but also in terms of covering the cost of the person's support. So a parent may not only be covering his or her income, which is needed to pay the bills, but also the cost of hiring people to take on some of the duties that each partner performs: housekeeper, accountant, nanny, maintenance person.

Disability insurance is another vital part of your Security. Your income depends on having an able body and mind. For younger people, disability insurance is as important and probably more important than life insurance: They are more likely to suffer a short- or long-term disability than die. Disability is also more expensive than death, simply because your living costs not only go on, they probably rise as you need additional care. While health insurance should cover many of the medical and care costs, there are all sorts of additional costs that you would face if your body or brain were damaged and you were unable to work.

Unlike life insurance, you cannot just pick a number that you think you need. Disability insurance pays a percentage of your current income, usually around two-thirds of your current income. Disability insurance comes in two flavors: short- and long-term. The former covers you for the first short period that you are disabled, usually 3 months and often is provided as part of an employer's benefits package. Long-term disability generally covers you from a few months after you are disabled until you get better or reach retirement age. (Here's another argument for starting retirement savings early: How will you save for retirement if you are unable to work and are living on a fraction of your former income?)

The final type of insurance that I discuss is umbrella liability. This protects you from everything from being sued because someone tripped and hurt themself on your property, to the excess costs that you may face if you injure someone in a car accident. Umbrella liability insurance is relatively affordable, and the increasingly litigious world we live in makes it more and more attractive. For example, recently a woman in my area drove around a corner without looking properly and hit Peter, who was walking across a pedestrian crossing. His knee was damaged, he lost 6 weeks of work, and had to have surgery twice. Although he can walk, he will never fully recover from the accident, and there is a good chance that the settlement on the case may run to a million dollars or more. If the driver does not have umbrella liability insurance and the court rules in Peter's favor, the driver will be held liable for the court costs as well as the damages awarded. Her car insurance probably only pays for $100,000 of bodily injury, so the rest will come from her personal assets and she may be paying the balance of the claim out of her income every month for the rest of her life. If the driver had, say, a $1 million umbrella liability policy, her auto insurance would pay for the first $100,000 and the balance of the settlement up to $1 million would be paid out of her umbrella liability policy, which would also pick up the court costs. This scenario is not uncommon.

Even if you have few assets, you will be well served by having umbrella liability insurance because it also protects your future income stream. When people are injured (physically, emotionally, or financially), they are likely to sue to cover their costs and the intangible cost of the pain and suffering caused by the injury. Whether it is a friend whose eye is permanently damaged by your enthusiastic puppy, or a stranger whom you hit in a car accident, they have a good incentive to take legal action. While losing a friend or hurting someone is upsetting, adding a major financial loss that impacts you for life compounds it. If you have assets that you cannot afford to lose or income to protect, look into umbrella liability insurance.

In the short run, you can lower the Full Cost of insurance by shopping around for it and by adjusting the terms of the policies. For life insurance, your costs can change based on your age, health, habits (such as smoking), and so on. Disability insurance will vary based on your income, the percentage of your income that the policy will pay out, and the number of years for which it will provide coverage. Umbrella liability insurance varies based on the amount you are covering.

Because each of these insurance premiums is a recurring expense, the Lifetime Cost can be significant. One way to lower the Lifetime Cost is to reassess your coverage every year or two and make sure that you are not overinsured. Another way is to get most of your insurance through a single provider, as you can often receive discounts. When looking for such discounts also include your home and auto insurance, because the combination of all insurance policies may result in significant discounts.

Another important distinction when looking at the cost of your insurance is to distinguish between cheap and reliable. Although the policy being offered may look attractive, insurance companies differ widely in terms of the level of customer service they provide. I was hit by a car last year and the delaying tactics that I was subjected to and the ridiculously detailed information demanded by the other driver's insurance company cost me so much in time and stress that I have sworn off ever using that insurance firm, and I actively warn my friends away from it. Purchasing your insurance coverage through an agent may not result in the lowest price, but the increase in service, the advice that they offer, and the peace of mind of having someone to go to bat for you can be worth it. My agent has helped her clients many times when a series of claims resulted in the insurance company considering cancellation of her clients' policies. She can help the insurance company distinguish between a string of bad luck and a careless client who is a high risk. The context that she adds, such as telling the insurance company about her client's new burglar alarm system, can make the difference between being insured and not being insured. I have called on my agent for all sorts of advice, such as the time I was considering buying a dog and wanted to know which breeds would increase my home-owner's insurance considerably (insurance companies are wary about insuring people who own a dog breed that has a high track record of attacks).

Consumer Debt Repayment

For all the same reasons that a cash cushion is desirable, most debt is undesirable. Not only do the obligations raise your monthly costs and make it easier to trip up, but your ability to build your Security also is limited while you have competing demands such as paying down debt. Not all debt is bad. Mortgages are generally accepted as good debt, and school loans are valuable to the degree that they help you upgrade your skills and earn more over time. Consumer debt, meaning all unsecured debt such as credit cards and store cards, is undesirable, especially when it has arisen because you simply did not live within your means. Chapter 14 discusses debt repayment in detail; however, at this stage it is enough to know that paying down consumer debt is a critical part of building your Security.

The Full Cost and Lifetime Cost of your nonmortgage debt is something well worth looking at if you have any doubt about what it is costing you. Shopping around for a lower interest rate can lower the Full Cost, and committing to becoming consumer debt free can lower the Lifetime Cost. A relatively small interest payment on your credit card each month might not feel too painful, but if you add up all the interest and fees of all your consumer debt, it may be much more significant that you think. Even if you are only paying $30 a month in credit card interest and have no other debt, you could have almost $6,000 in 10 years if you had invested the $30 a month instead. If the money had been invested in a retirement plan with employer matching funds, you would have forgone much more.

The worst thing about debt is that you are spending money month after month on something you already have. All that interest you pay is simply for the right to spend money before you earn it. I like money for nothing; but nothing for money? No thanks.

The Last Word on Security

Okay, all you Spenders out there, the worst is past. Be assured that Security is the only section in the book where I drag you kicking and screaming to spend money on something that does not come naturally. And really, Security is just about spending money on yourself, so it's not that hard.

The ideas laid out in this chapter take more time to implement than most other suggestions in the book, but the good news is, they pay off for much longer. Whatever else you do in your financial life, if you are taking care of Security, you can be more relaxed about the rest. And all other decisions will seem much easier once you know that you have a strong financial foundation under you.

The most important thing is that you get the different elements in place: a cash cushion to help you manage bumps in the road, retirement savings to take care of your future, insurance to protect your financial future, good insurance, and no debt to drag you down. I'll leave you with a few ideas of how to strengthen your foundation, and then start on the fun stuff.

SEVEN SECURITY STRATEGIES TO STRENGTHEN
YOUR FOUNDATION

1. Pay less tax. If your employer offers a retirement plan, put money into it. By deferring tax, you are getting a great return on the money from day one. If your employer matches your contribution, even better. If your employer does not offer a plan or you are self-employed, set up an appointment at a brokerage firm to discuss how to set up your own tax-advantaged plan.

2. Contribute the maximum allowable amount. Try to max out your retirement contributions by using every tool available to you.

3. Put your money to work. Make sure that you have the right investments within your retirement account. It is not enough just to save for retirement, you must make sure your investments are earning good returns. Unless you are close to retirement, keep your savings in stock funds.

4. Take advantage of technology and set up automatic payments to put away some savings each pay period. This is a great way to ensure that your retirement savings and cash cushion are growing at a consistent pace.

5. Review your life, disability, and umbrella liability insurance policies, if you have them. If you do not have such policies, take some time to determine what you would like to be insured against, and discuss insurance options with your benefits coordinator at work and an insurance salesperson.

Remember, salespeople are paid by commission, so get a second opinion and several quotes before buying anything.

6. Knock debt on the head. If you are weighed down by debt, get into action and pay it down as fast as you can without resorting to pasta and marinara sauce six nights a week.

7. Kiss the lottery goodbye. If you want to buy hope, buy a drink at a singles bar!

CHAPTER 6

Shelter

Your Home, Sweet Home

What Is Shelter?

Home may be where the heart is, but it's also where the money goes. Renting or owning a home is the largest single cost facing most households, and over one-third of every dollar you take home is likely to be spent on putting a roof over your head. Shelter includes housing and all its related costs, such as mortgage or rent payments, insurance, and property taxes. It also includes all the costs of living in and maintaining the home: utility bills, maintenance, furnishings, and services around the home such as cleaning and gardening (Figure 6.1).

By looking at all the Shelter costs together, rather than having home owner's insurance in with other forms of insurance, utilities and maintenance separate, and so on, the Conscious Spending Model gives you a single snapshot of the total cost of your Shelter. The advantage of viewing all Shelter-related expenses together is that you get an overall picture of where your money goes and whether that spending is aligned with your values.

Shelter is such a significant amount of your spending that a small percentage decline in it can free up a significant amount of

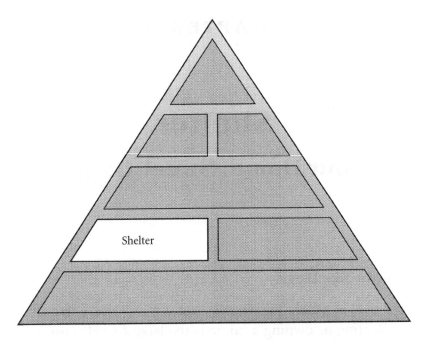

- Mortgage or rent payments
- Property tax and home-owner fees
- Home and mortgage insurance
- Household fittings and furnishings

- Household running costs
  Utilities
  House maintenance
  Mowing/gardening services
  Cleaning services
  Other

FIGURE 6.1   Shelter is one step above Security on the
pyramid in the Conscious Spending Model.

additional cash. For example, if an average family cuts its Shelter
expenses by 10 percent, it could increase its spending on clothing
and related services by 50 percent.

Shelter and Values

What does Shelter mean to you? Is it a place where you build a
strong family? Is it a nurturing touchtone in a busy life? Is it an

outer representation of your success? Does it bring an inner feeling of security or belonging? Is it a place where you celebrate your connections with friends by entertaining regularly? Does it serve a simple utilitarian function? Do you feel competent and satisfied when you renovate your home to your tastes? Does it bring you close to the pulse of a vibrant inner city? Is it a reflection of your love of solitude or nature?

Because Shelter is the biggest ticket item in the Conscious Spending Model, it is one area where your clarity about values can influence your spending by thousands or even tens of thousands of dollars a year. Home is only sweet when the resources it takes—both time and money—are aligned with the value you get from it. Aligning Shelter means taking a good look at the housing choices you have made and will make as you move forward.

· ·

Madhavi and Jonathan were sitting in the family room of their new home, an older house in a leafy suburb. "How often did we use the living room and dining room in our old house?" Madhavi mused. "If we're honest, maybe only two times in the last 3 years—those rooms were wasted." When they were moving closer to Madhavi's new job, they could easily have afforded something as large or larger than their old house, but they took the move as an opportunity to move closer to their goals.

"Having a big yard for the dogs was really important to us, but having a formal entertaining area . . . well, we'd rather have the money to travel or retire earlier," Jonathan explained.

· ·

Many people place a high value on Shelter, saying it is a source of happiness and satisfaction to them. The question I then ask is: What specifically do you value about your home? The answer will shape not only how much money you allocate to Shelter, but how you spend that money. For example, two people who both place high value on Shelter, but in different ways, will end up with two very different homes. One might value it as a retreat and aim to find a house with a large, luxurious bathroom and a spare room that can be turned into a cozy library. The other may value his home as a base for his social activities, and seek a house with a large entertaining area and a room for the kids to hang out with their friends. Their specific needs are very different and each person is aligned only when those needs are met by Consciously Spending money on Shelter in a way that brings them the satisfaction they seek.

How Much House Is Right for You?

Just as with all of the other spending decisions discussed in this book, the only answer to the question of how much house is right for you is: It depends on what you can afford and what you want. What you want comes from inside, and this answer will change throughout your life, depending on relationships, children, and your income. After getting clear on the Lifetime Cost and Full Cost of your current housing decisions, start getting clear on how this realization sits with you. If you find that you spend, say, 35 percent of your take-home pay on Shelter, look at how far into the year that spans. You are working until May 8th each year just to pay for your home. If you are spending 40 percent, May 26th is when you earn your first dollar for food, clothes, and other basics.

It can be very easy to fall into the well-worn path of buying as much home as you can afford. In these days of growing wealth, that can result in a lot of home. For you, is bigger better? In *Luxury Fever*, Robert H. Frank tells of the growing size of the average American home. In only a decade, the percentage of new houses that are more than 2,400 square feet grew from 18 percent to 30 percent: Such a leap that the people compiling the statistics had to create new categories to measure the larger houses.*

If you are living in a house that is more than 10 years old, a weekend wander through a new high-end home development is an eye opener. Huge closets, massive bathrooms, integrated security and sound systems our grandparents could not have imagined, formal living areas, casual living areas, multimedia rooms, and finished basements the size of some people's homes are the norm. These houses go on forever. I love the idea of his and her closets and his and her vanities in a master bathroom the size of many people's bedroom. It would be great to put a CD on in one room and hear it throughout the house. I'd love a kitchen full of massive professional-style appliances. If I had kids, it would be great to have a huge basement for them to mess up (and clean up?) all by themselves. The people designing these palaces have been listening to consumers' fantasy lists, and they are delivering.

The quality of homes has also risen. A couple of years ago, I volunteered at Habitat for Humanity and was surprised that the housing we were building for low-income families had central air conditioning. At the time, I lived in a trendy, inner-city area where many apartments have window units, and it had not occurred to me that central air is considered standard in most new construction. Such rises in quality can also be seen in appliances, double-glazed windows, number of bathrooms per bedroom, and so on. Some make sense from a Lifetime Cost point of view (double-glazed windows are a good investment because the energy efficiency saves on utility bills), but all add to the cost of new housing.

Paralleling this growth in the size and quality of houses, the proportion of income being spent on Shelter has slowly risen over

---

*Robert H. Frank, *Luxury Fever: Why Money Fails to Satisfy in an Era of Excess* (New York: The Free Press, 1999).

the years.* It is easier to enter the housing market as banks offer loans with less down payment, and people are buying more expensive houses. Indirect costs associated with housing have risen too: Central air and heat have pushed utility bills higher, and the amount spent on furnishings has risen as houses have grown. Even if you do not own or aspire to own one of the new "starter castles," you are probably spending a large portion of your income on housing and are likely to find that amount increasing unconsciously as your income rises. The question lies in whether you value Shelter enough to devote such a large portion of your resources to it. There's no right or wrong answer, and your answer may change over the years.

What if your current home does not align with your dreams? "I want more space . . ." Great. But first be really clear about what you want the additional space for. Take a good look at the areas in your current home that you use least and ask whether they can be better used. It's easy to set rooms aside for the life you *think* you are going to live and not use your home for how you really do live.

Dining rooms are a wasted space for many people who usually eat in the family room. Traditionally, many couples receive formal china when they get married and set up a similarly formal dining room to use this exquisite china. And then they spend decades thinking "I should entertain more." Any sentence that contains "should" or "ought" is a major warning signal. Conscious Spending means stepping back and reviewing how you use your home. As you look at your home, think about how you most enjoy using it. If you are a barbecue and brunch entertainer, then focus your space and resources on the sort of entertaining you actually do. Know that if you want to impress some friends or business con-

---

*Eva Jacobs and Stephanie Shipp, "How Family Spending Has Changed in the U.S.," *Monthly Labor Review* (March 1990): 23–25.

tacts with a more formal dinner, you can take them to a fancy restaurant. Such a dinner may cost a lot for one evening, but it will be cheaper than buying a bigger house for two dinner parties a year. If you spend an additional $20,000 to get a house with a separate dining room, it will cost you approximately $140 *every month* for the 30 years you are paying the mortgage. You can buy a few fabulously extravagant dinners in restaurants every year for that sort of money. What would give you more pleasure? Madhavi and Jonathan consciously aligned their resources with how they actually live, and kissed their formal living areas goodbye.

. . . .

"For the first 6 months we lived here, our lovely antique French dining set and Chippendale living room furniture were stored in the basement. They had been so expensive and were so lovely, they were hard to part with," Madhavi continued. *Then one day it just felt right. They knew they would not use the furniture again, and took it to a high-end furniture consignment store to sell it.* "Two days after we took it there, my mother stopped by and told me how she had seen a lovely Chippendale sofa that was just like ours at a store . . . she was shocked when we admitted it was ours."

. . . .

In the same vein, I thought I should practice yoga, and I set aside my lovely back sunroom as a yoga and meditation space. I barely used the room. Finally, I realized that having a writing space was more important. If the urge to practice yoga returns, there is enough space in my living room. The urge has not returned (yet!), and I appreciate my sunroom so much more in its current incarnation as a study and office.

By getting clear about how you actually live and using your space in a congruent way, you may just find that you already have enough space.* If not, and you have the resources and values that drive you to buy more house or move to a different neighborhood, then go for it! Get really clear about what it is you are seeking: the ideal combination of spaces, style, neighborhood personality and amenities, and so on. Then find the house that matches your wish list as closely as possible. If the house of your dreams is still outside your reach financially, prioritize your list of ideal characteristics and keep looking for a house that has as many of the important characteristics as possible. Or choose to make do with what you have until your resources are aligned with your dreams. The ideal house may not exist, so getting clear on what a house must start with and what you can customize later is important. For example, if both a great view and a fabulous country kitchen are important, and you cannot find a house with both, then go for the one with the view. You can redo a kitchen, but you are stuck with the view you buy.

As you create a vision of the house you want, think also about the work it will require. The size of the yard can have a large impact on the amount of work a house requires. Get clear on what you really value. "I like gardening . . ." So do I. But my idea of gardening is not weeding. It's planting bulbs, playing with color, discovering interesting new plants, rescuing a loved plant that was in the wrong place, and sitting with a glass of juice and admiring the flowers. A smaller yard may offer as much scope for the fun parts of gardening as a large yard, and free you up from the hassles that most large yards have. And as for lawns . . . The woman who invented lawns was probably married to the man who invented high heels. She got even!

If you do value a large yard, again get clear on what it is about a

---

*A few months after I wrote this chapter, I discovered a great book on this topic by an architect. Sarah Susanka, *The Not So Big House: A Blueprint for the Way We Really Live* (Newtown, CT: The Taunton Press, 1998).

large yard that you enjoy, and buy as much of that as you can afford. You may seek a big space for the kids to play in, privacy from the neighbors, a place to grow fresh produce, a place for the dogs to run, an area for your green thumb to transform. And again, if you cannot afford all that you want (taking into account the Lifetime Cost of caring for the yard), prioritize. You may find a great house that is opposite a park that provides the space for the kids or dogs to burn off energy.

Aligning is all about being conscious of exactly what it is that brings you pleasure and spending your resources on the things that really count. If you find that your spending is out of alignment with the value you receive, then reassess the choices you have made.

. . . .

"It's not that a nice home is not something we value—we value it a lot," Madhavi explains. *However, what they value is not a big house.* *"Home to us is having a comfortable retreat for when we get home from work, having the room to occasionally have friends over for a barbecue, and having a large yard."* *The one thing she'd change in their new home, which she calls* "the cottage," *is the storage space.* *"These older homes just don't have enough closet space."*

"Come on," Jonathan gently teases, *"How many of those purses we are making room for do you ever use? Two? Three?"*

She laughs, and admits he is right. "I guess I'd rather weed out the clutter than rebuild or move again."

. . . .

The bottom line is that Shelter is a large expense, and it is important that your spending be driven by conscious choices. Whatever your values, enjoy the well-used parts of your house fully, and find another use for the unused spaces. Make more room in your life for the fun parts of home-related activities and minimize the parts that feel like drudgery. Then your home will be a sweet home again.

Exercise: Home, Sweet Lockout

How much of your home do you really use? Imagine that you and your family are locked out of your home today. You are only allowed back into each room when you really want to use it or something in it. How long would it be until you used every room? Every piece of furniture? Every item stored in a cupboard, closet, or the basement? How much of your space is used for rooms that you rarely access? How much is used to store items you rarely use? How much is for guests who only visit occasionally?

If there are spaces or items that you would not use, or even miss, for a year, question why you have them at all. Some items are great memories (photos, childhood toys) others are just historic baggage (wedding presents you never liked, past purchases you feel you can't throw away). How many days a year are you working to pay for space that means absolutely nothing to you?

Once you are clear on how you actually use your home, sit down and plan out how you could use your space better. Could a fold-out couch convert your guest room to a reading retreat that you would use more often? Could the dining room be better used as a media room? Could a renovation turn un-used space into everyday space? Could clearing out unused furniture or belongings create the space that you need? Get clear on what's worth keeping after the imaginary lockout and have a virtual fire sale: Hold a yard sale or donate the excess to a local charity. If Aunt Maude asks what happened to that lovely tea set she gave you, tell her it's been locked up some-where safe.

The Elements of Shelter

Mortgage or Rent Payments

The single largest payment you make each month is probably your mortgage or rent, which is the cost of having a roof over your head. This cost is impacted by the choices you make based on personal values, as well as some very practical choices: whether you rent or buy, live alone or with others, live in a condo or a house, live near the city or far out in the suburbs, have a large or small space, and so forth. In addition, costs vary significantly from city to city.

If you are a home owner, your mortgage payments vary substantially, not only by the cost of the home you live in, but by how long you have held the mortgage and what interest rates were when you financed or refinanced your home. What can feel like a crippling expense when you first get a mortgage, may seem like a bargain 5 years down the road when you are either earning more or simply have 5 years of inflation making your payments seem smaller. Mortgages come in a number of flavors: fixed or adjustable rate, 15-, 30-, or 40-year term, FHA, VA, jumbo, and so on. They also come in a number of sizes: 80 percent of the house's value (known as "loan to value"), 90 percent, even over 100 percent. How high and how predictable your mortgage payments are will vary based on the mortgage you choose. I do not go into the details of mortgage financing in this book; however, if you suspect that you are paying more than you need to, shop around to see if you can save money.

For home owners, the Full Cost of a house is more than just the sticker price. Anyone who has purchased a house knows that there are dozens of small (and not so small) costs associated with buying a house. The settlement sheet contains many lines of costs both small (termite inspection) and large (title insurance). The closing costs add up to a significant amount and need to be factored in as you work out how much you can afford as a down payment.

Understanding the Lifetime Cost of a house involves looking at more than the sticker price of the house. The biggest cost is the stream of payments over the length of the mortgage, plus the many related costs that we look at later. The cost of the mortgage is effectively lowered because mortgage interest is tax deductible under U.S. tax law; however, it is still a substantial expense for most households. Ensuring that you have a competitively priced and well-structured mortgage can lower the Lifetime Cost of your house. A lower interest rate can have a big impact. For example, payments on a $200,000 mortgage rise by $35 a month if the interest rate rises from 8 percent to 8.25 percent. Saving that $35 a month on your mortgage can result in a nest egg of nearly $50,000 (in today's terms) in 30 years time. However, this does not mean that you should try to pay off your mortgage early: You are better off to invest any extra money that you have available rather than to repay your mortgage early.* When you buy a house, spend time with a knowledgeable banker or mortgage broker who can help you determine which mortgage will be best for you. Some of the things that will impact the answer are unknowns, such as whether interest rates will rise or fall. Others can be guessed, such as whether you plan to live in the house for 5 years, 10 years, or longer.

Upgrading your house has a Full Cost as well as a Lifetime Cost that goes far beyond just the cost of the new house. Perhaps this is why wealthy people studied in *The Millionaire Mind*† generally live in good neighborhoods in homes that they have owned for

---

*If you have any doubts about this at all, Ric Edelman, *The New Rules of Money: 88 Simple Strategies for Financial Success Today* (New York: HarperCollins, 1998), pp. 53–62.
†Thomas J. Stanley, *The Millionaire Mind* (Kansas City, MO: Andrews McMeel Publishing, 2000).

many years. By choosing not to move to larger houses and newer neighborhoods, the millionaires studied saved not only on their house, but also on many related costs. Think about how you live now: the furniture you have, the car you drive, the perfection (or lack thereof) of your lawn, and even the clothes you wear. Now imagine upgrading to a house in a neighborhood that is several rungs up the socioeconomic ladder in your town. Even if you could afford the house, you may find that there are many other costs that come with the neighborhood. Would your car look shabbier? Would your furniture not fit with your house? Would a perfect lawn suddenly seem like the minimum required? Would you even feel you should dress a little better for your weekly trip to the supermarket? It's not shallow to want to fit in. It's human. The question is: Where do you choose to fit in? Upscaling a house is rarely done in a vacuum. And it's all the other costs that are easy to forget when the first decision is made.

A larger house means a lifetime of "more." Some of the "mores" are great, but others, well . . . more vacuuming, more maintenance, more utility bills, more places to misplace things, more temptation to keep a whole pile of stuff you no longer need in all those extra closets. A larger yard means a lifetime of more lawns to mow, more leaves to rake, more weeds to kill, and so on. Or paying someone else to do it. Remember, the Lifetime Cost banishes your argument of "It's only $20 to get a kid to take care of the lawn." Spending $20 a month for a lawn service adds up to almost $4,000 over 10 years if that $20 were invested instead. If you add up the Lifetime Cost of all of the extras involved in a house, it might make the simplicity of a mobile home look attractive! When choosing to move to a larger house, make sure you understand all of the "mores" that you are buying with the house.

What if you want and can afford a house that is, say, worth 50 percent more than the one you own now? For easy math, let's say you are in a house worth $200,000 now, and can afford the $700 a month of additional mortgage payments it will take to fund an extra $100,000 and upgrade to a $300,000 house. If you can afford that, why not? Because it's not $700 a month, that's why. You have all the transaction costs associated with changing homes: commission on the house you are selling (probably $12,000), closing costs on the house you are buying (the additional money down, plus probably $9,000 in one-time costs and points), some local taxes, moving costs, and the many settling-in costs. You have to be able to afford *everything* that falls into the Full Cost category before you consider moving.

For renters, monthly rent payments vary based on the area and type of housing you are renting, as well as whether the rent includes amenities, utility costs, and so on. Flexibility costs more as well, with most landlords charging a substantial premium for rental periods of less than one year.

Renters face similar costs as do home owners, assuming that the landlord is making money on the property and is able to roll the property's expenses into the rent. What renters don't have, however, is a long-term commitment and the large amount that arises from closing costs. They also don't have the maintenance costs that we talk about soon, although again a landlord will hope to cover those costs in the rent. On the down side, renters don't have the mortgage interest deduction that makes a mortgage seem so much more affordable in the United States, and, rent is likely to keep pace with inflation as rent is reassessed each year, unlike a mortgage payment, which does not vary with inflation (though it may rise as interest rates change). Also, renters don't have an asset that may be gaining in value (nor do they risk losing money if the property market declines). However, renters often still come out ahead financially compared to buying a place that they don't live in for at least 5 years.

Property Tax and Home-Owner Fees

Property tax and home-owner association fees, which are usually based on an assessment of the market value of the house, add thousands of dollars a year to the cost of owning a home. Condo owners and people living in a development with shared amenities may pay a home owners association or condo fee, either in addition to the tax, or with the tax included in it. It is usually a monthly expense and may include utilities such as water or heat, external maintenance, and other shared resources. Unlike a mortgage, these costs increase with inflation and association fees are not tax deductible in the United States.

Once you have purchased a house or condo, there is little you can do to manage these costs, so do your homework well at the time of purchase. Being active on your home owner association board will ensure that you understand why costs may rise and have a say in the decisions that will impact the association fee. If your property taxes are reassessed at a higher rate, it may pay to challenge the reassessment. Be careful, however, in a hot market. I know someone who challenged a significant increase in the valuation that her property taxes were based on, the tax assessor researched the valuation and came back with a figure that was higher still! Unfortunately, the market had been rising so quickly, the assessor had ample proof that the first assessment had been too low, even though it was almost double what the property had been assessed at 3 years earlier.

Home and Mortgage Insurance

You may have one or more types of insurance related to your Shelter: home owner's, mortgage, or renters. Home-owner's insurance covers the structure of your house and its contents. Often there is little relation between the market value of your house and the amount that you need to insure. For example, a small wooden Victorian house in a less expensive inner-city neighborhood of Washington, D.C., may cost $150,000 to rebuild if it burned down, but it may be worth only $80,000 if it were sold today. A similar structure in a smart inner-city neighborhood such as Georgetown may cost just a little more to rebuild (assuming a higher standard of finishes) but may be valued at $500,000 or more on the market. There is no need to insure the value of the land, because even if the structure is completely destroyed, it is rare to lose the land (though you do see homes and plots of lands lost to landslides on the news at times. If you are in an area that is at risk for such hazards, talk to your insurance agent). In addition to the structure itself, home owners need to insure the contents of their home. Contents coverage covers theft and many forms of loss, but it is also important to know what it does not cover. Most insurance policies have a cap on the amount the company will pay for any one item, so you may need to add insurance to cover some big-ticket items such as your computer system or valuable pieces of jewelry. Additionally, many home owners don't discover that their insurance excludes certain circumstances such as a flood until after a disaster strikes.

Mortgage insurance insures a portion of your mortgage in case you go into foreclosure. It is often required by lenders if they are lending more than 80 percent of the value of the house; however, many mortgage brokers and financial institutions can structure mortgages in a way that avoids it. For example, if you borrow 90 percent of the value of your house in a single loan, you will probably be required to have private mortgage insurance (known as PMI) until you own a full 20 percent of its value. However, if you have two loans that include an 80 percent regular mortgage and a 10 percent second mortgage (known as a second trust), you can avoid PMI. The second trust may be at a higher rate than the first trust, and you will be making two separate payments each month, yet the savings can be considerable.

Renters can purchase insurance to cover their personal contents. Landlords generally don't carry insurance that covers tenants' contents and are not liable for damage unless the landlord is negligent in some way. It is important to note if you are in a shared household and everyone's personal effects are covered by a single policy, the primary policyholder's ability to get insurance in the future will be impacted not only by claims he or she makes, but also by claims that his or her roommates make.

Like all recurring payments, the Lifetime Cost of these insurance premiums can add up, and a little work today can pay off for months and years to come. Home owners insurance can be reduced by shopping for a good rate and having more than one type of insurance (home, auto, umbrella liability, and so forth) with a single company to get a discount. Consider increasing your deductible to $500 or $1,000, which lowers the Lifetime Cost, but do this only if you have a cash cushion that will easily cover the deductible if you need to make a claim.

Household Fittings and Furnishings

A roof over your head is just the beginning. It's easy to focus mainly on the mortgage or rent payments when looking at what sort of house you can afford and forget about the large number of related costs. Last year I moved out of a small apartment into a house that was more than double the size of the apartment. For a while I convinced myself that I liked minimalism, but after a while I had to admit that there is a difference between modernly minimal and simply unfurnished. Furniture, appliances, window dressings, and soft furnishings such as linens are part of Shelter. Some items such as refrigerators and laundry equipment may come with your home, but there are a lot of additional items for your house that you accrue or upgrade over a lifetime. I'm sure that I'm not the only home owner who was so excited about spending the first night in my home that I forgot that the windows needed covering. Some sheets and a few nails later, privacy was restored.

In my grandparents' era, furniture was bought to last a lifetime. Fashions moved so slowly that the term "home fashions" hadn't been invented. Today, catalogs of national chains such as Pottery Barn and Crate and Barrel show that home furnishing trends are beginning to move as fast as fashion trends. Add to that the Martha Stewart-esque trend of spending time and money redecorating for the seasons and holidays, and furnishing your home is not a one-time exercise.

The Full Cost of furnishing a house is impacted by its size, your taste and the brands you choose, and the quality you buy. Most of us do not furnish a house overnight, so these costs are spread out over years as we accumulate more things to hang on the walls, extra side tables, more storage pieces to store other stuff we have accumulated, and so on. The Full Cost of furnishings can be lowered by shopping smart: shopping around, waiting for sales, choosing standard fabrics, waiting until the larger chains do reasonable copies of the latest furniture trends. Starting out with a good plan can save a lot of money and effort over a lifetime, so consider using a design service to help you plan your purchases if you don't have a great eye. Avoiding one badly bought piece of furniture may pay for your investment in a few hours of a designer's time.

As for the Lifetime Cost, buying high-quality pieces will make your furniture last longer, and you may find a few good pieces result in a better look than more lower quality pieces. As with clothes, choosing classic designs and good quality means that the furniture you buy will look good longer. Taking care of your furniture, from treating it with stain-resistant coatings when it's new to having it cleaned periodically, will make it last longer. And if you have bought good-quality furniture, paying to have it re-upholstered every decade or so will still be cheaper than buying lower quality furniture that needs to be replaced after 10 years.

When it comes to buying appliances, find the right combination of price and quality—one repair can turn the cheapest appliance into a bad buy. Consumer magazines often test and rate major appliance brands. Also look at the energy efficiency of the appliance, particularly if you use it all the time. Low energy light bulbs (also called "green," referring to their environmental benefit, not the color of the light) that use significantly less energy, may seem expensive up front, but over their lifetime, they actually save you money. An energy efficient refrigerator, heating system, washing machine, and so on can cut your utility bills, making their Lifetime Cost lower than a brand that seems more expensive up front. Which brings us to . . .

Household Running Costs

Another major set of costs that you may face related to Shelter are running costs, which include utilities, maintenance, repairs, and home services such as mowing the lawn or having a cleaning service.

Whether you value Shelter a little or a lot, beware of wasting money on your home. Because a house is large and complex, the potential for "leakage"—small costs that add up to a high Lifetime Cost—is substantial. Drafts cause higher utility bills, a dripping tap is water down the drain, a poorly maintained electrical system can start a fire, gardens require ongoing maintenance, and so on. The running costs can be interlinked, for example, poor maintenance may lead to higher utility costs and unforeseen repairs. Also, maintenance involves buying (or hiring someone who has) the right equipment, whether a lawnmower or a ladder. The size and age of the house can have a major bearing on how significant the running costs will be, and the climate of the area can have a big impact too. Growing up in Australia where most of the trees are evergreen, I always thought that raking large piles of leaves was a charming tradition up there with apple pie. Now I own a house surrounded by huge old oaks and think raking leaves is just hard work. Same goes for snow shoveling. I'm tempted to do a Huckleberry Finn and invite my Australian friends over in fall and winter to experience the charm themselves.

Utility bills are one area where you have a reasonable amount of control over the Lifetime Costs. To lower utility bills, you can practice simple habits such as turning off lights when you leave a room, keeping the air conditioning and heating systems a few degrees higher/lower, and showering once a week. Okay, so perhaps we'll stick to habits that are not offensive to those around us. Ongoing maintenance can also lower the Lifetime Cost: Fixing dripping faucets, ensuring that windows and doors have good weather stripping, and changing the filters in heating and air conditioning systems all lower costs. Some very small investments can also pay off over a lifetime, such as timed or motion-sensing light switches, a programmable thermostat for your heating and air conditioning system, and a showerhead that allows you to use less water. If you renovate, extend, or replace appliances and systems, using energy efficient materials and products may raise your Full Cost of the work today, but substantially lower the Lifetime Cost of utilities going forward.

Maintenance is another ongoing expense that can have a high Lifetime Cost. In my recent move, I was surprised to find a number of maintenance expenses that had simply never occurred to me when I lived in an inner-city condo. Within months of moving in, my phone list expanded to include the numbers of a gutter cleaner, chimney sweep, lawn care specialist, tree specialist, and garage door specialist, among others. Condo dwellers have few maintenance costs compared to home owners with a yard. Maintenance of a garden is another cost to consider. It will vary based on the size, design, yard, and so on, and can cost not only a lot of money, but also your weekends.

SEVEN SHELTER STRATEGIES FOR YOUR HOME, SWEET HOME

1. **Don't flush money down the drain.** Semiannual maintenance to stop the drips and drafts can pay for itself many times over in terms of lower utility bills. And regularly maintained heating and cooling systems last years longer than those that rot under a layer of dust. Also, buy programmable thermostats. By reducing the heating or cooling during your working and sleeping hours, you will cut utility bills.

2. **Raise the deductible on your insurance.** Chances are, you'll rarely make a claim, and the lower premiums will soon cover the additional $250 or $500 that you will pay if you make a claim. However, only do this if you have a cash cushion that can handle the cost if you need to pay the deductible.

3. **If you are thinking of moving, think twice:**
   - The closing costs alone will probably cover the cost of a new kitchen or bath. Building on often is more cost-effective and less stressful.
   - Get friendly with a local hotel or guest house. It's often cheaper—and again less stressful—to pay for guests to stay nearby than to pay thousands more to live in a place with a spare room.
   - Reassess how much space you need. If you rarely entertain formally, rethink your need for a formal dining room and convert the space, if you have it, to something

you will use. You may find you have a big enough house if you use your space well.

- Cut the clutter. If you are devoting rooms, garages, or attic space to saving old furniture, give yourself more space and a tax deduction by asking a charity to pick it up. Chances are, your kids won't be caught dead with it in their first home.

4. Less is definitely more when it comes to decorating. Your home will feel larger if you selectively display your art and knickknacks. Rotate what's on display when you feel the urge for a change. If you really want a change, rearrange your furniture.

5. Protect your family and your investment. Working smoke and carbon monoxide detectors, fire extinguishers, secure locks, and so on can save more than money. They can save your life.

6. Buy once and buy well. At the lower-priced end of the scale, you get what you pay for when it comes to furniture. Buy well-constructed pieces with a timeless design to get years more out of your furnishings. Before buying new furniture or decorations at all, see what a well-chosen color can do to give your room a lift. Paint is the cheapest makeover for a room.

7. Invest a weekend in the little chores that have been distracting you. Hang pictures, oil hinges, fix the toilet roll holder in the spare bathroom. If your time is valuable and money is available, hire someone to stop by every 6 months to handle the little things. Your house will feel more like a home if the small distractions are managed.

. . . .

CHAPTER 7

Sustenance

Feeding Your Body

What Is Sustenance?

The next building block in the Conscious Spending Model, Sustenance, covers the most basic human needs along with Shelter. The Sustenance category includes all costs related to fueling and sustaining the body: from putting food in, to keeping it healthy, to providing the medical care it needs. This category is more complete than older models of personal finance that looked at each element separately because Sustenance acknowledges the interactions between the categories, for example, a gym membership may decrease medical costs (Figure 7.1).

Fifty years ago, food made up nearly a third of household spending.* Today, it has fallen to about 20 percent. At the same time, health-care costs rose above 5 percent for a while as expensive machinery and processes that deliver care became widely used, but then declined as health-care organizations changed the way they manage their finances. Health care now has fallen to 4 percent.

---

*Eva Jacobs and Stephanie Shipp, "How Family Spending Has Changed in the U.S." *Monthly Labor Review* (March 1990): 22–23.

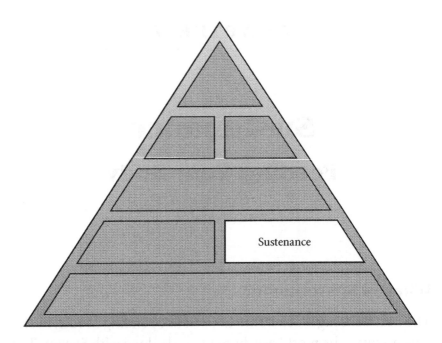

- Groceries and household supplies
- Takeout and nonsocial meals out
- Health care
  Health insurance
  Unreimbursed health expenses
  Dietary supplements
- Fitness
  Gym membership
  Fitness equipment
- Pet food and pet health care

Figure 7.1   Sustenance, covering the most basic human needs, is on the same level as Shelter in the Conscious Spending Model.

Note that there can be an overlap between this category and Social when it comes to eating out. As a rule of thumb, eating out with friends or family where the aim is primarily social is counted as Social. Eating out as a convenience in lieu of cooking is counted as Sustenance.

Sustenance and Values

What does Sustenance mean to you? Is it a reflection of your love of health and the desire to treat your body well? Is it a comfort that you indulge in when you need nurturing? Is it a reflection of your refined taste or varied interests? Is it simply about refueling so that you can get through a day? Do you value convenience? Is Sustenance about connecting with friends or showing your love for your family? Is it about looking good and being admired? Do you work out so that you can have energy to get more done or so that you can relax more easily? Does a pantry stocked with basics provide a feeling of security? Is it about having the strength to take on the adventures that call you? Is it about looking young and vigorous well past the age when many give up?

. . . .

At 60, Marcia looks as if she is in her late 40s. Her kids are grown and have left home, and her life is more active than ever. "I play sports with friends twice a week, and go to the gym at least three times. I eat very healthy food and really focus on being as healthy as I can," she told me. A businesswoman with a busy schedule, she always finds time for physical activity. "I simply see health as a necessity. It is my most important commodity, one that no one can take from me." She spends more on her health care than many people, partly because she has medical expenses that are not covered by insurance. "I spend a lot on alternative medicine, which I feel is more natural, though I probably spend less on food than some. It's simply cheaper to buy fruit, vegetables, and grains and cook them up than to buy prepared food." She sees health as the linchpin that holds everything else together. "It's my highest value because without health, you have nothing."

....

What you spend on Sustenance, more than any other category, reflects the day-to-day level of self-care that you practice. If you are what you eat, then values should come into play in the way you spend money in this category. If you've ever been a supermarket voyeur and peered into other's baskets, you know that what they purchase says much about them. A basket full of frozen, canned, and semiprepared foods? She values convenience. Fresh produce, bags of nuts, tofu? He's into health. Lots of packaged deli goods, imported crackers, obscure vegetables? A gourmet or adventurous palette. Fat-free milk, Coco Krispies, Lean Cuisine, chunky chocolate chip cookies? That basket full of contradictions is me at my PMS-y worst.

If you could peek inside people's kitchens you'd see even more. Open my refrigerator and you'll see a values battle in full fight. There's the part of me that values being smart with my cash: that's the chicken breasts bought in bulk at Costco and the bag of potatoes waiting to be microwaved in their jackets (yes, I know they shouldn't be kept in the fridge, but at least I can see when they start growing . . .). Then there are the cheeses and olives that sate my appetite for giving myself a little treat with luxury food. There is the crunchy-granola healthy me: tofu, low salt soy, and other food that found its way to the back corner of the fridge and stayed there because I was kidding myself the day that I bought it (I see the "use by" date, but which millennium is that?). My high expectations of myself are also seen in the crisper: Why else would there be so many vegetables past their prime that were bought thinking that I would take the time to cook a meal from scratch? In the freezer, the part of me that values convenience and having more time for fun is reflected in the neat stacks of Lean Cuisines— the savior of the single woman's diet.

My mother's fridge reflects a whole different sense of values. When Mum (as it is spelled in Australia) cooks, it is a reflection of pure love. When I was a kid, scrounging around the pantry for home-baked cookies was such a habit and yielded such delicious bounties, that, even as an adult, it takes me less than 5 minutes in my mother's home to find my way to the food. As she has developed a deep love of the people and culture of Thailand, the ingredients in her cupboards have grown ever more exotic. For my mother, the kitchen is where the expression of love happens. Guests are treated to elaborate meals made from scratch and even everyday meals are better cooked than your average restaurant— I don't think she's ever bought a frozen meal in her life. Clearly, the high value she places on connection with her family and friends overrides any desire for convenience.

Groceries are not the only place where values come into play. Sometimes spending on Sustenance can be an indication of habits that you have embraced or intentions you have broken. For every active member of a gym, there are probably several who started with good intentions and then hoped the rest of the year would fade away without too much guilt. And for those who spend on regular, preventive medical care, there are more who put it off until there is an expensive emergency to deal with. Health insurance often comes as a work benefit, but one that is embraced for the security that it offers. For the uninsured, the lack of insurance can reflect a battle between wanting to take care of everyday needs and planning for potential future needs—and the high cost of insurance means some families are forced to just take care of today and hold their breath that they don't need medical care tomorrow.

Exercise: The Cost of Convenience

For one week, jot down every cent you spend on food and make a note of what it was. Divide the list into groups: groceries, snacks on the run, everyday lunches, takeout/phone-in food to avoid cooking, social eating. What proportion of your food spending do you spend on each? What surprises you? Do you spend more when you are busy or when you have spare time? Do you spend more when you are at the office, on the road, or at home? Do you plan your eating ahead or get food as you need it? Is there a time of day when you are most likely to spend? Is what you eat aligned with what you intend to eat? If you are buying more than you expected, are you more concerned with excess calories or excess dollars?

If there are any groups of food that you want to spend less on, notice the triggers that set off the spending. For example, if you take a break from your afternoon work by walking out to get a gourmet coffee, ask yourself if there are other habits that would achieve the same aim of getting a break from your work. If you buy takeout meals when you are tired, ask yourself if there's another way to have convenient food without spending as much or eating as unhealthily.

The Elements of Sustenance

Groceries and Household Supplies

The first subcategory is your grocery spending. Whether you buy in bulk from warehouse stores, or stop in to grab dinner ingredients on the way home from work, if you are like most American families, you will have found your grocery bill has been shrinking over the years. It's not that the food and other things that you buy are any cheaper, it's that you are probably eating out more often. Counterbalancing this, the food that you buy at the supermarket is more likely to be partially or fully prepared, adding to the cost per meal.

For the sake of simplicity in record keeping, I include all household supplies that are part of grocery shopping in the grocery store, including everything from cleaning products to supermarket-bought personal-care items. And it is not only the human members of a household that are included: The food and health care costs of pets are included.

We all eat—Sustenance is in the lower level of the Conscious Spending Model because it is not an optional category—but there are many ways to manage the Full Cost and Lifetime Cost of our food habits. If you spend more on food that you want to, then lower the cost of food with some of the following strategies. First, buy in bulk. Warehouse stores are great places to stock up on basics that you use a lot. Just don't fall into the common trap of buying much more than you need or picking up food you otherwise would not buy. The last time I was in the checkout line at Costco, the woman in front of me said that she was buying the smoked trout in a five pack because it was so cheap. Compared to what? Would she normally buy even one at full price at the local deli? I know I have on occasion bought enough broccoli for a family of five and found myself throwing away most of it. I'm not alone in wasting food: A study found that about 12 percent of groceries are thrown away, often because they were bought for an event that was canceled. Surprisingly, though, impulse buys were rarely thrown away (Are those candy wrappers in your car?).

Another way to save money on groceries is to buy items on sale or get discounts by using coupons or a supermarket's club card. However, beware of spending a lot of extra time to gain a small discount, by either traveling further than you usually would or spending a significant amount of time clipping coupons and reading advertising flyers.

You can also manage food costs by buying fewer processed foods. A real live potato is just as easy to cook, much healthier, and considerably lower in cost than a bag of frozen potato gems. A chicken breast with a squeeze of lemon or a splash of marinade is cheaper than premarinated chicken breasts. Use convenience food only when it really saves time. Generic brands and supermarket or drugstore quality personal-care products often offer great value. Cutting back on meat, cheese, and other expensive ingredients can also help cut costs. Cooking double quantities when you do cook and freezing what's left can be a great time and money saver. Finally, limiting your spending on sodas and snacks can help your bottom line . . . both literally and figuratively.

If great food is way up there on your enjoyment list and aligned with your values, take a close look at what you enjoy so you can better align your spending. I know that great cheese is one of the true epicurean delights in my life. Knowing this, I don't buy average cheese often, I buy very good cheese once in a while, and usually when I can sit down with one or two friends and a good bottle of wine to fully appreciate it. I get more joy (and fewer calories) out of that monthly indulgence than I would out of having average cheese much more often.

Takeout and Nonsocial Meals Out

As time becomes more scarce than money, more and more people value convenience highly. In Sustenance, this value shows up as more takeout and nonsocial restaurant meals (meaning that the primary driver to eat out is to avoid cooking rather than to connect socially). Yet eating out is another way many of us blow out our food budget faster than our hips. Picking up a coffee here and a sandwich there can have a significant Lifetime Cost. Add in some takeout food and a meal or two a week in an average restaurant, and your total food bill can be surprisingly large.

· ·

When Margaret and Peter started discussing their values, family rated highly. "I'd just really love to have enough money to fly down to see my mother in Florida more often," Margaret said. A week later, Margaret came to the phone excited. "Do you know how much we spend on just everyday food? Between a muffin and coffee in the morning, picking up lunch, and grabbing a mocha once or twice a day, I'm spending almost $20 a day—more if I eat out with friends at lunchtime. Peter's about the same. And dinner—don't even ask!" She realized that much of her $100-a-week habit was avoidable with just a little effort. "I can easily have muffins at home and make coffee—if I eat in the car that will also save me 10 minutes. I don't want to take a whole lot of time making sandwiches everyday, but maybe if once a week I pack lunches that I can microwave, like pasta with sauce or soup, and stock up on fruit and protein bars, then brown bagging won't feel like such an effort. It's not free, but I can spend much less." She still eats out with friends at times, but her takeout costs dropped dramatically. "If I had been told that I should cut back, I wouldn't have done it. I wanted to do this, though, because I simply value seeing my family more than I value eating low-end takeout."

· ·

Your work environment and the habits of coworkers can have a significant impact on your daily spending and your habits. The corporate cultures at the many companies I have worked for or consulted to vary widely, and those variations are reflected in the eating habits at work. One company had a canteen with great, low-priced meals. Many of the single people working there used the canteen's subsidized food as their primary meal of the day and we would linger over meals while solving the company's problems. Another place had a culture of working nonstop and eating at your desk. At lunchtime you'd see people huddled in front of their monitors, trying not to drip their takeout Chinese into the keyboard. Another more social environment found me going out with a group for a sandwich daily and a restaurant meal at least once a week. My spending on everyday food fluctuated wildly with the different corporate cultures.

Habitual snacking generally has a high Lifetime Cost. Small habits can really add up, even though it may only be 50 cents at a time. When I worked in an office where the soda machine was only a few feet away from my desk, I went from someone who never touches sodas to a three-Cokes-a-day drinker. It was "only" $1.50 a day, but that's $360 over a work year and, more shockingly, over 100,000 calories! If you pick up any drink that has an Italian sounding name every workday, you are probably feeding a habit that runs to almost $100 a month.

If you value great food or feeling pampered, eating out less often but at better restaurants is a great way to get more of what you value without necessarily spending any more, as one couple discovered.

. . . .

Ravi and Rena had fallen into a habit that is typical of young professional couples. "At least three times a week, we arrive home and head out to a local eatery for a basic meal because we are too exhausted to be bothered cooking," Rena explained. As they did the math, they realized that the visits to moderate restaurants were costing them a sum that could in no way be described as moderate.

They made some fast decisions. "We are going to trade our three nights a week at average restaurants for one night a week at an aver-

age restaurant and one night at a really good restaurant every second week," Ravi explained.

"We want to lower the amount we spend, and get back to appreciating a really good meal when we have it," Rena agreed. "The indulgent night will give us more memories as well as more money, and we can pick up more ready-prepared food so that we can deal with those nights when we come home too tired to do anything more than microwave a meal. Also, when we cook up a big meal on the weekends, we can just make some more and eat leftovers one night, perhaps even make enough to freeze for a couple of meals."

· ·

To manage the cost of takeout and nonsocial meals out, also look at what you are ordering. Remember that the Full Cost of restaurant meals includes not only the price on the menu, but also the tax, tip, and travel costs, which often makes ordering food in or picking up takeout a more affordable option on nights when cooking seems too tough. As more and more restaurants try to give better value, servings are growing from big to huge, so consider sharing them or taking some home to be tomorrow's meal. Choosing a cheaper main course, skipping the appetizer, or having water instead of iced tea can also cut the cost. However, if you are trimming out the extras and bingeing on the bread, make sure that you tip the wait staff well.

Health Care

Health care is another major cost in Sustenance. This category includes health insurance, medical costs not covered by health insurance, dietary supplements, and non-prescription pharmaceuticals. In the United States, employers often provide health insurance, and employees don't have that much say in the cost or the benefits offered. Some employers may offer a choice of plans at different costs, and households with two working adults may be able to choose between different employers' health insurance offerings. Some employers also offer flexible spending plans that enable you to pay for your out-of-pocket medical expenses with pretax dollars. Select the amount carefully, though, as you will need to use the full amount in the calendar year or you will lose the balance. If you are not covered by an employer's health insurance plan, look into groups that you can join to get affordable health-care coverage. For example, as a writer and member of the Washington Independent Writers, I can buy health insurance through them at a rate lower than I could get it otherwise, even after adding in the annual membership fee for the group. If you are self-employed, talk to your accountant about the options available to you. You may be able to lower your Full Cost substantially by setting up a plan that allows you to use pretax money to pay for most of your health-care costs.

Another type of health insurance that you need to consider as you grow older is long-term care insurance. While health insurance covers your medical costs, long-term care insurance may be needed to cover in-home care or a stay in a nursing home. Long-term care policies are expensive, and the premiums rise as you age, so look into a policy in your fifties.

One of the best ways to keep the Lifetime Cost of health care down is simply to be healthy. Illness is expensive, even if you are insured. Eating well, taking appropriate dietary supplements, staying fit, and having regular check-ups may save you a fortune—and your life—in the long run. If you eat a high fat diet, smoke a pack of cigarettes a day, or substitute channel surfing for real exercise, you are at a higher risk of developing a preventable disease. Of course, it is great to change those habits simply so that you feel better, so let the cost be one more reason. The same goes for dental care: Regular cleaning and flossing can keep your dental costs lower.

The Full Cost of health care can be managed by trying to stay within your health insurance plan's guidelines. Often a visit to a health-care provider out of plan will be only partially covered or not covered at all. If you have a choice between a couple of health-care plans, look at whether any of them cover the doctors you currently see and additional services that you use such as chiropractors or other alternative health-care specialists. However, this choice is not just about money. Sometimes going out of plan is worth it for peace of mind. When I changed health plans, I found that my dermatologist who has been checking out my skin every year for some time was not covered by the new plan. Rather than find a new dermatologist and bring him or her up to speed on my and my family's history, I chose to bear the extra cost so that I would have continuity.

Other ways to lower the cost of health care include asking your doctor or pharmacist for generic prescription drugs, asking your medical or dental provider questions about any additional charges you may face before agreeing to the work (this is particularly important when only reasonable and customary charges are covered), and taking advantage of services that may be offered to you, such as annual flu shots.

Fitness

The final element of Sustenance is your fitness-related costs. These costs include gym memberships, workout classes, videos and fitness equipment, and the gear that goes along with it all. In some of my classes, students have argued that this element should be part of the Soul category as it is something that is done purely for pleasure. I disagree because money spent on fitness directly impacts other costs in Sustenance. I know when I work out, I eat healthier food and have fewer illnesses. Having a personal trainer may be an optional extra, but everyday fitness costs are part of your basic Sustenance cost.

. . . .

Darian decided to get fit, again. "I used to be fit, but long hours at work and meals on the run meant I just didn't have time to work out. I did not realize how heavy I was getting until I had to exchange a pair of jeans that my mother gave me for my birthday and found I was two sizes larger than the last time she had bought me clothes." He had been a member of a gym in the past. "My pattern was to join a gym, work out five times a week for the first month, then have to travel for work and simply drop it completely. Each month when I got my credit card bill with the charge on it, I'd swear that I'd get back into it, but life just took over. I hate that guilty feeling of wasting the money." This time, he's taken up running. "I didn't even need to spend money on running shoes: I found three perfectly good pairs in the back of my closet. I know this will be harder once winter hits. If I am still running 4 days a week by winter, I might let myself join a gym. But only if I really know that this time I can make it a habit, not a passing phase."

. . . .

The challenge with fitness costs is in getting the bang for the bucks you are spending. Many a yard sale has featured barely used stationary bikes, dusty Thigh Masters, and other fitness gadgets that got little use. Gym memberships have a similar tendency to collect dust, except the only way you can see it is in the decrease in the number of people trying to get on the stair climber at the gym in March compared to January.

You can manage the Full Cost of fitness equipment by only buying items that you really know you will use. If you have old equipment that is sitting and gathering dust, clean it up and give it a whirl before parting with more cash for the newest thigh-cutting, buttocks-firming fad machine. If you decide to buy equipment, check out the classifieds for preowned items. Cheaper still, find a workout that requires very little equipment, such as a videotape or pair of shoes, like Darian did. If you are buying new, check out the discount sports store chains. They often have great prices because they buy in bulk, although sometimes they have lower quality and less reliable equipment. For fitness clothing and accessories, try factory stores for discounts on up-to-date styles, but don't assume everything there is a bargain.

If you join a gym, do your homework first. Many have a 1-year commitment, and that's a long time if you don't like the gym, can't find parking nearby, or simply have a 1-month span of attention. Often special deals can be found if you look around— anything from having a free 1-week trial of the gym, to having the initiation fee waived. As you do your homework, check out the gyms on your short list at the times when you would use them. A gym that seems peaceful midmorning might be a zoo at 5.30 P.M. with long waiting lists for popular machines and crowded aerobics classes.

Pet Food and Pet Health Care

The costs of keeping the animal members of your family fed and healthy are also included in Sustenance. Some households treat animals like animals, others treat them like pampered guests. The Full Cost and Lifetime Cost of having a pet can vary greatly depending on what type of animal you have and how you take care of it. The Full Cost includes the purchase of the pet and all the equipment that you need. A pedigreed pup or kitten of noble bloodlines can cost hundreds or even thousands of dollars, especially for a rare breed. An adopted mixed breed can cost little or nothing. The equipment can vary greatly too, depending on whether your taste and budget run to a simple plastic litter tray and nondescript collar or to a chi chi bed and designer doggies duds. Don't forget to figure in the cost of reupholstering shredded chairs, cleaning soiled carpet, and replacing chewed shoes if you get a young or untrained animal. You can keep the Full Cost low by opening your home and heart to a housebroken animal that is low cost or free and requires little in the way of expensive equipment.

The Lifetime Cost of your pet includes the cost of food and health care. Most brands of pet food provide basic nutritional requirements, and there seems to be no harm in managing the cost of pet ownership by choosing brands of food available in the supermarket. There is probably less variation in the cost of your pet's health care, however you may at times need to choose whether to perform expensive medical procedures on your pet, particularly as it ages. Because the bond with an animal can be so strong, it can be difficult to say no, therefore you may want to set a limit ahead of time on how much you are willing to spend on a single procedure.

SEVEN SUSTENANCE STRATEGIES FOR WEIGHT LOSS FOR
YOUR HIP POCKET

1. Your body is your temple; take care of it. Cut its maintenance costs by eating well, staying fit, and keeping up with preventive medical care. Such lifestyle changes will lead to lower medical bills in the long run and less time off from work due to illness. If you smoke, try to give it up simply for the sake of saving medical bills and insurance costs.

2. Insure your financial health. Illness or accident can wipe you out financially if you do not have adequate health insurance or long-term care insurance. At the very minimum, carry health insurance that covers catastrophic events.

3. An old adage, but true: never shop when you are hungry. If you're inclined to impulse buy, take a list to the grocery store and stick to it, and, if you can, leave your kids at home.

4. Return to real food once in a while. Cooking from scratch costs significantly less, and simple meals don't have to take much longer to prepare than convenience food. A microwave-baked potato takes no longer than Tater Tots, is better for you, and costs a fraction of prepared alternatives.

5. Bag it. Bagged lunches can save significantly. Besides, no one makes peanut butter and jelly sandwiches better than you do.

6. Feed Fido basic brands. Read consumer magazines' periodic studies on pet food: They generally show that the fancy brands offer your furry friend little more in the way of nutrition than the supermarket brands.

7. Know thyself! Before joining a gym, take an honest look at your past fitness fads. If you don't think you'll stick with it for more than a couple of months, look for a gym with low membership fees and a short commitment. Better still, find one where you can pay per use. Even cheaper, get out the running shoes and take to the streets.

CHAPTER 8

....

Self and Family

Everyday Expenses

What Is Self and Family?

Self and Family, the next category in the Conscious Spending Model, looks at the balance of everyday household costs that you face. So far I have discussed Security, which is the foundation that secures your spending, and Shelter and Sustenance, which are the two most basic costs your household faces: a roof over your head and food on the table. Self and Family looks at the other regular costs that your household faces, including transportation, clothes, basic personal care, work and education costs (Figure 8.1).

This category is significant because it includes one subcategory that is very expensive for many households—transportation— and another that is a source of a lot of temptation for many over-spenders—clothing.

Self, Family, and Values

What do you value about the elements of Self and Family? Is transportation about convenience? Is it about comfort? Do you

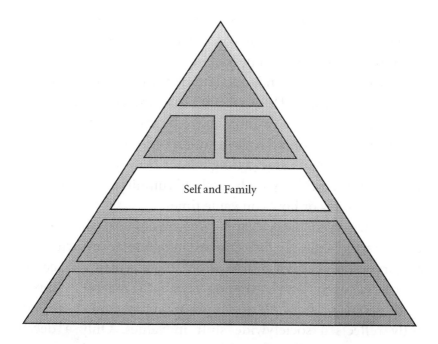

- Transportation
  Vehicle
  Auto insurance
  Gasoline
  Maintenance
  Taxis and public transportation
- Clothing
- Personal care
  Haircuts
  Personal care products
  Dry cleaning

- Education and work-related costs
- Allowances
- Other household costs
  Tax preparer
  Bank charges
  Other

Figure 8.1   Moving up the Conscious Spending Model pyramid, the Self and Family category includes everyday expenses over and above Shelter and Sustenance.

value safety above adventure? Style above environmental impact? Do your choices reflect that you value being smart concerning your money? Or do you value looking smart on the street? Is personal grooming about individuality or fitting in? Do you value beauty and elegance? Do you value ease and comfort? Do you value style above cost? Fashion above function? How does your family's spending on education and work-related costs reflect your values? Do you value getting ahead? Do you value a top education at any cost? Do your household running costs reflect how you value money or how you value time?

This category includes a variety of everyday costs that a household faces, so values can be expressed in different ways within the category. It only takes a couple of car advertisements to see how advertisers depend on positioning a car in the market by appealing to people's values. Personal grooming is similar, and currently reflects a societywide shift in values. Only a decade ago, most white-collar workplaces were home to suits and ties. Today, more and more workplaces are casual—casual on Fridays, casual during summer—even the stuffiest Wall Street banks are beginning to loosen the tie. Is it because we value success less? I would say no. People are working longer hours, after all, and more and more people are putting their short-term earnings on the line for longer-term success in companies that offer stock options. Although we still value success, it appears that we also value balance. Most of us do not have a more balanced life. Yet as a society, we are more aware of the value of balance, and employers have learned that outwardly supporting a balanced life by loosening dress codes helps them to attract and retain staff.

Exercise: Wearing Your Self on Your Sleeve
· ·

Take a piece of paper and write down 10 to 20 words that you would use to describe your personality. When you start running short of adjectives, get creative. What color best describes you? What animal is most like you? What sort of sport fits best with your personality?

Then take that piece of paper and open your closet doors. How well is your personality reflected in your clothes? Do your favorite clothes fit your personality as well as they fit your body? Are there clothes that you never wear because they simply don't fit who you are? Are there clothes that you bought in a certain mood that bring back that mood? Now take a look at your vehicle. What parts of your personality are reflected in your vehicle choice? Within the range of vehicles in a similar price bracket, which are closest to reflecting your personality and which are furthest away? Begin noticing what you assume about people's values and personalities when you see how they dress or what they drive. When you shop for clothes or your next car, run through the list in your mind before you make purchases.

· ·

The Elements of Self and Family

Transportation

One of the largest costs that a household faces after Shelter is Transportation. Transportation expenses add up to over one quarter of the average household budget, almost double what it was in 1950.* A little of that spending goes to public transport and

---

*Eva Jacobs and Stephanie Shipp, "How Family Spending Has Changed in the U.S." *Monthly Labor Review* (March 1990): 25.

taxis; however, nearly all goes toward purchasing or leasing, insuring, running, and maintaining a car, or two, or more.

Most of you probably are very car dependent. In the United States, there are an average of 1.1 licensed drivers to every residential vehicle,* and 90 percent of all short distance trips are taken in a car.† Getting from point A to point B and back again could be a fairly low-cost matter. However, today cars have become a surrogate living room and office for many of us. We eat meals, take and make phone calls, do a little personal grooming, store a change of clothes, and catch up on the news . . . perhaps by reading the paper, but hopefully by listening to the radio. Parents use cars as portable family rooms, shuttling kids between events, classes, and a myriad of other activities. Today's vehicle design acknowledges the roles that a vehicle plays, with cup holders for every occupant, mirrors for both the driver and passenger, hooks to hang dry cleaning, and storage compartments for all those bits and pieces that take up permanent residence in your car. Some new generation vehicles designed specifically for parents even include the ultimate passive child restraint system: a video player! The good news is that while we are spending more on cars, we are getting more safety, comfort, and luxury for our dollar. And if you don't want to spend so much? There are plenty of low-priced, highly reliable cars available.

Your vehicle may be the most public way that you express your values. As are your clothes, your vehicle choice is seen by the people who know you as well as those who don't. And although your clothes may say something about your desire to be fashionable, your taste, and how successful you are, your vehicle very clearly says that and more. No other possession has such a clear price tag for the world to see.

---

*Energy Information Administration, Department of Energy.
†Department of Transportation.

. . . .

"I really love my car. It may sound shallow, but I really love it," Vic admitted. His Volvo C70 convertible "is much more than I need, but I spend a lot of time in it. I wasn't completely frivolous: I bought this one because it is a large four seater, so I can easily pick up the kids from school. They know that there's no food, no mess, and no mud in my car, so we use the minivan for most running around with them." He bought the car the day after his youngest was out of the child carrier. "Annet and I fell in love because we shared an adventurous streak. Somehow we got so sensible with kids and a mortgage and everything. She was very cool when I told her I needed to reclaim that part of me. We shopped together and her only proviso was that we could fit the whole family in. She even upgraded the stereo as a birthday surprise. I didn't find out until I went in to pick up the car."

The car was more expensive than they initially thought they could afford. "We realized that renovating the basement could wait, and decided to hang on to the minivan a few more years. I can renovate when I'm old. I really want the wind in my hair while I still have hair!" he joked.

Annet chimed in, "At first I resisted: there were already so many demands on every dollar. Then I realized that our kids have toys that they love, but we had stopped playing. We want to model a balanced life by having some fun too. He gets the car. I get a massage and pedicure once a month. And the basement can wait forever as far as I'm concerned."

. . . .

Carmakers know that their products are a very public way of expressing values. A quick glance at car ads shows that what you drive is supposed to show whether you're successful, practical, a nonconformist, socially responsible, safety conscious, an outdoorsy type, and so on. If I created a little puzzle where you had to draw a line matching each of six different vehicles to six people whose values you knew, most of you would score very high. Add details such as whether there is a political or environmental sticker on the back, a kid's car seat in it, or a bike rack or trailer pull attached, and your score would probably be 100 percent. This close association of values and the type of car that is driven is clear in a marketing tool called PRIZM, which is discussed in Chapter 4.* Marketers use this model, which divides people into 62 clusters of shared values and spending patterns, to help them sell their products to their target consumers. The description of each cluster contains a list of the vehicles each group is most likely to buy. Even when the median income does not vary greatly, the vehicles chosen do. For example, the *bohemian mix* cluster contains young, college-educated, inner-city singles and the *gray power* cluster contains college-educated, affluent retirees. Their median incomes are similar, as are their home values. Guess which group buys the Cadillac deVilles, Lincoln Continentals, and Infiniti Q45s and which buys the Alfa Romeos, Volkswagens, and Audi 900s? It's not hard. And the difficulty of parking in the inner city isn't the only reason.

If your household is average, 25 cents in every dollar you spend goes to transportation. That means if you cut transportation costs by 20 percent, you can almost double—yes, double—the amount you spend on entertainment. That's very significant, and for many households, quite possible.

The Full Cost and Lifetime Cost of a car are primarily influenced by what sort of vehicle you buy, whether you buy new or used, and how long you keep it. The Full Cost includes the up-

---

*Michael J. Weiss, *The Clustered World: How We Live, What We Buy, and What It All Means About Who We Are* (Boston: Little, Brown, 2000), pp. 213, 289.

front cost of the vehicle, and the Lifetime Cost includes all the costs over time, including depreciation, interest, gasoline, maintenance, and insurance.

You can lower the Full Cost of an automobile at the time of purchase. As we saw earlier, the sort of vehicle you buy is largely impacted by your values. However, there are a number of vehicles targeted for every value set, so there is a range to select from. You can lower the Full Cost by buying a vehicle that is cheaper, buying a used vehicle, or simply keeping your current vehicle a few years longer.

To buy a vehicle that is cheaper, start by honestly assessing how much you want to spend. Then cut the cost of the vehicle you want by eliminating optional extras that are not worthwhile; you may have to insist on it, the salespeople have a strong incentive to sell high profit-margin extras such as paint coatings, logo carpets, and mudflaps. Lower the cost further by getting well educated about the dealer invoice price and how much above or below that you should be able to get the vehicle for. Find that information in an unbiased (no advertising) magazine that assesses vehicles. *Consumer Reports* is my vehicle-buying bible, and there are other good publications and websites too. The Full Cost of a car is influenced not only by the make and model that you buy, but also by your negotiating skills. If you are a lousy negotiator, use a car-buying service. My most recent car purchase was done through the warehouse store Costco, which arranged for me to get a small, set markup over invoice. I simply walked into the dealership, found a vehicle with the exact features I wanted, looked at the invoice (not the manufacturer's suggested retail price) and bought it for $100 over invoice. Is a lower price possible? Often. Invoices are becoming less meaningful, and the dealer and salesperson still get a good slice from the manufacturer. *Consumer Reports* has started estimating the dealer wholesale price, which is a better base to begin from. Invest some time in reading consumer publications on what you should pay and then be willing to walk away from a dealership if they won't sell you the vehicle for a fair price.

A vehicle that is 2 or 3 years old may sell for three-quarters to one-half of its original price. If you can find one that has been well maintained, you are well on the way to cutting your transportation expenses significantly. The great news is that someone else has taken the brunt of the depreciation for you, and with car warranties sometimes running up to 5 years, you may even find a car that still has several years under warranty. Buying a used car, however, involves a higher risk of performance problems. If you are looking for a used vehicle, read up on reliability records and get a mechanic to check vehicles over if you are unsure.

Finally, simply keeping the vehicle you have a few years longer can save you thousands. This is a great strategy if you have a reliable vehicle that has good safety features.

The Lifetime Cost can be cut dramatically by owning a vehicle that does not depreciate too quickly and by avoiding interest by paying cash if you can. Some consumer magazines estimate depreciation, that is, how quickly the value of the vehicle declines. At the time of purchase, you choose how you will finance the vehicle. Clearly, not borrowing lowers the Lifetime Cost considerably, even with some loans and leases running at very low interest rates. I dislike leasing for two simple reasons: First, it is easier to fall into the trap of automatically upgrading your vehicle when the lease is up, and second, there is uncertainty about the ultimate amount you pay. You pay more if you drive more miles than you estimate, but don't get anything back if you drive fewer miles. Additionally, if you simply hand the car back to the dealer at the end of the lease, you are getting the equivalent of a very low trade-in value.

Confession time: Although you'll never find grease under my fingernails, I am, by many women's standards, a bit of a car nut.

That led me to make the dumbest financial decision in my life. In 1999, I had just been transferred back to the mainland United States, and found myself with no car and not much need for one. I decided to forgo a car initially. That decision lasted about 3 months, and my itch to be free to travel when and where I liked needed scratching. I walked to work, so I figured I could go for a fun car. I overdid it. Listening to the part of me that values freedom, individuality, beauty, and fun, I bought a convertible MG from the mid-1970s. She was beautiful—sexy lines that you don't find in anything but a sports car, originality that is not of this day and age, and three tiny windshield wipers side by side on the tiny windshield sold me. While her soft top had been damaged in a hailstorm, the rest of her body had been restored meticulously. I was in love.

The good news is that she was relatively inexpensive. The bad news is that I spent almost as much on repairs in the first 6 months of owning the car as I did to buy her (doubled the Full Cost!). I knew I was in trouble when my mechanic not only knew my name, but also smiled when he saw me. If I wanted to sell the car, I'd be lucky to get back a third of what I had spent on repairs. Of course, I have kept her rather than take a loss and admit that I had made a big mistake. (Psst, wanna buy a cute MG? Special price . . .) And I have bought a second reliable car because I now have clients all over the city and have to value reliability and comfort.

The moral of this story (and when I waste that much money, I hope I have the right to draw a moral from the experience) is that the Lifetime Cost of a car can be a doozy. Beware: Sometimes you get what you pay for, and if all you can afford in a car is trouble, that's what you'll get.

To keep the Lifetime Cost of an automobile manageable, look for decent mileage per gallon, good reliability records, and readily available parts, which is not to say that you'd be silly to buy something with lousy mileage, a high likelihood of being described by traffic reporters as "the disabled vehicle in the right lane," or expensive parts. You'd just be paying for other values that the car fulfills, such as more safety, individuality, or luxury. And that's fine, as long as you're doing it consciously. (Of course, there are plenty of people who feel that choosing a gas-guzzler is not okay because of the environmental impact, but I know many SUV drivers who make their choice based on the perception of being safer than in a regular car).

So far we've looked at the most common transportation cost: the vehicles that you own or lease. For many people, other transportation costs are also significant. For some households, the other costs are in addition to owning and operating a car. For others, they are an alternative to a car or a second vehicle. Given the very high cost of owning and operating a vehicle, public transport, supplemented by the occasional taxi and car rental, may be a viable alternative to owning a second vehicle or any vehicle at all. For some older or less able people, taxis may be the primary way of getting around. Yet it's strange how taxis seem like a luxury. It is easy for many households to pay out hundreds of dollars every month to own and operate a second car, yet paying the same amount for taxis each month to eliminate the need for a second car would seem extravagant. The psychology of handing over the cash makes taxis feel expensive. Merging your car expenses in with all your other monthly bills can hide how much you are spending. If you put the Full Cost of every trip into a piggy bank in your car, taxis may suddenly seem affordable.

Public transport has a lot of advantages beyond the cost savings. Going to work on the metro, trolley, or bus gives you uninterrupted time to read and, if you live in an area with a strong public transportation infrastructure or bad traffic, it may be more convenient than driving. Even better, live near your work. I did this for a couple of years in downtown Washington, D.C., where there are nice residential areas near office areas. The money I saved by walking easily made up for the higher rent. With more cities encouraging residential development in or near downtown, walking to work is becoming a real possibility. The next time you move, you may want to take into account public transportation and proximity to your workplace. As companies look to make work life more flexible and as traffic gets worse in some areas, telecommuting is another real possibility for some workers, whether every day or just occasionally.

If public transport, taxis, and car rentals are a significant expense for you, decreasing the cost may involve tactics such as purchasing monthly or bulk tickets that discount public transport costs, exploring a van service or other alternative to taxis, using on-line shopping to decrease your need to travel, staying at home and embracing hermithood. Okay, the last one only works for writers who are naturally inclined that way, but there really are ways to manage your costs, especially if taxis are a significant cost and there are alternatives to the convenience they offer.

In summary, if your household is typical, 25 cents in every dollar you spend is on your transportation. That's a huge amount, so anything that you can do to decrease your spending by a couple of percentage points will free up a significant amount to spend on other things. Some costs may be cut by changing your behavior today, but, just as with housing, a lot of the cost cutting will happen over time as you choose whether to replace your car or hang on to what you have for a few more years.

SEVEN SELF AND FAMILY STRATEGIES TO CUT THE COST OF CAR OWNERSHIP

1. Keep the car you have as long as it is reliable. Upgrading your car regularly really adds up.

2. Let someone else pay for your car's depreciation. When you buy, buy a used vehicle. Most of the depreciation of a car happens as soon as it is no longer new—and buying a used car that is still under warranty means you can get the quality of a new car at a much lower price, without running the risk of being stuck with someone else's problems.

3. Go for reliability. Repair costs can really add up, so choose a make and model not likely to put you on a first-name basis with a mechanic.

4. Maintain your car by the book. Oil changes every 3,000 miles and scheduled maintenance go a long way toward making your car last the distance and preserving its resale value.

5. Drive safely. A small accident, such as rear-ending a car at slow speed, will not only cost a surprisingly large amount to repair (at minimum your insurance deductible and higher premiums for years), but will also take a significant amount off your car's resale value.

6. Shop for insurance. It's easy to pay too much for insurance, though some insurers who charge less save their money by providing lousy customer service. See if you can get a discount by bundling your auto insurance with your homeowner's policy. Also consider raising your deductible from $500 to $1,000, which means $500 more out of pocket if you are in an accident, but the premiums saved may make it worthwhile.

7. Think twice about letting the kids drive. Insurance companies know that teen drivers have more accidents. Limiting who drives which car can cut your insurance costs if you have younger drivers in the household.

Clothing

While clothes may make the man, they can also ruin the wallet. Of all the subcategories we have looked at so far, I would bet that clothing is the one where there is most variation from person to person, household to household. Even within a peer group where people may wear similar styles, one person may be a bargain hunter who shops at discount stores such as Marshall's and the other may pay full price at name brand stores. The big exception is probably teenagers: They flock together to the degree that variation in brand name and purchase price rarely happens.

Where I grew up, school uniforms were mandatory and I loved it. Some really wealthy kids attended my school, but with everyone in blue plaid and navy sweaters, socioeconomic differences were not so obvious. For many people, the workplace is a similar environment. Some employees have a uniform that defines their role, whether UPS driver or airline pilot. But even in un-uniformed jobs, a pseudouniform usually exists. A midlevel executive in a grey pinstripe suit, white shirt, and colorful tie doesn't look as though he is earning a tenth of what the CEO earns, even if it is true. And in high tech companies where the CEO shops at the Gap, everyone can look the part without parting with lots of cash. However, uniformity can add to costs when we look at fashions.

Somewhere in Milan, Paris, or New York, a group of designers conspire to make everything in a fashionable person's wardrobe look as hideously out of fashion as it possibly can. Unlike washing machines that seem to be designed to stop working after 5 years, clothes reach planned obsolescence after 1 year. If blue is *in* this year, it will be *out* next. These changes keep the fashion industry rich and the average Jo who wants to look fashionable scrambling to keep up. Women are more likely than men to listen to the fashion industry's dictums and to spend large amounts of money and emotional energy trying to feel that they look okay (which often means also trying to feel okay). Such lavish spending hurts their pocketbooks, particularly because women need to spend more on appearance in the first place with makeup, hosiery, underwear, and shoes. Women's clothes often have a higher maintenance cost and shorter shelf life. Sure it costs more to dry clean a garment with frills, but there is no excuse for the blatant sexism of cleaners who charge women more to get a basic shirt cleaned. Men are more likely to have simple styles of clothing, and women can learn a lot from them. Many men have a wardrobe of staples—jeans, trousers, jackets, and suits—that are neutral in color and relatively timeless. Their explorations into fashion may be limited to relatively cheap items such as shirts or ties.

For woman and men who try to keep up, clothing becomes a big expense, and an ongoing temptation as new fashions continually hit the stores. Many people stop running so hard on that treadmill at some age and start buying clothes that have a longer shelf life.

. . . .

Judith, a therapist, changed how she bought clothes when she cut her income as part of a career change. "I still spend money on clothes, but it's very considered. Instead of thinking 'Gee, I like that, it's cute, I'll take it' and then finding it doesn't match and it's not a good use of money, I think about what the real cost is. I may think it's cute now on the rack, but will I think it's cute in 2 weeks or 2 months or a year?" she asked. As her disposable income decreased, she became a more creative shopper. "In the fall I went shopping with some friends. I was having fun just being with them while they shopped, and wasn't missing trying stuff on or buying. Then we went to a store that had this huge rack of little bitty scarves at $5 a piece: So I got four of them and I love them! The colors grabbed me, and it was a cheap,

cheap way of altering an outfit. I've had lots of fun with them and people always comment on them. They have personality."

She gets greater enjoyment from the little spending she does. *"Clearly I don't need more clothes—I have been buying clothes for so long—but when I bought the scarves, it was for Soul."* The reason she shops has also changed. *"Before, I bought things to make myself feel better, to be part of a social ritual, or sometimes just as a reward because I worked hard. Before it was a bandaid, now it is a definite treat."* As her career progresses, she expects her earnings to rise, but *"hopefully the new habits will stay."*

. . . .

The Full Cost of clothes depends a lot on how you shop. Someone who shops from emotion and buys clothing that doesn't go with anything he or she already owns will have a higher Full Cost than someone who plans ahead or limits buying to pieces that go with some of what he or she already owns. To manage the Full Cost of clothing and still stay fashionable, do it with little accents. As I write this, blue-dyed snakeskin jackets dominate women's magazines. Last year there was not a blue snake in sight. Next year there won't be either. Rather than fork out big bucks for a jacket that will scream "Summer 2000" the second it is over, get one lower-priced piece that follows the trend—a shirt, a hairband— preferably a mass-market copy. At the end of the season, kiss it goodbye faster than the fashionistas can say passé. Save the big bucks for good quality staples that will look good for years.

A couple of years back, I decided to buy only clothes that go with black accessories. My closet was home to a number of purses that I never used, and I hated moving my stuff from one purse to another just to look color coordinated. My hard to fit size $10\frac{1}{2}$A feet gave me another incentive to minimize the accessory shopping each season. Now all I own is one black purse for daytime use and one fancy one for evenings, a range of black shoes, and a couple of black belts, plus a few random things from my old wardrobe that have not died yet. It may not work for many people, but for me, it makes shopping easier and cheaper, and when shoe fashions suddenly change from square toed to pointed, I only have to get two pairs to look reasonably fashionable.

The money you spend on clothing includes all the bits that go under clothing. Whether you are sporting Fruit of the Loom or Calvin Klein, there's a good chance that underwear, socks, hosiery and the like adds up each year. Managing the cost of those basics means shopping when things are on sale or at discount stores, or going for a more basic brand when the outside world cannot see.

The Lifetime Cost of your clothing choices is influenced by how long you use the clothes that you have and how well you maintain them. For example, if you follow fashions, you are more likely to use things for a shorter amount of time, so the Lifetime Cost may be spread out over only one or two seasons. Conversely, clothes that are more neutral and of classic design last for more seasons and are effectively cheaper per wear. Keeping something that you don't wear stuffed in the back corner of the closet does not count toward lowering the Lifetime Cost! If you buy fabrics that require dry cleaning, the Lifetime Cost will rise. If you are diligent about repairing clothes, the Lifetime Cost will fall (all of you with shirts that have not been worn for a year or so because of a few missing buttons, stand up and be counted).

SEVEN SELF AND FAMILY STRATEGIES TO CUT YOUR CLOTHING COSTS

1. Coordinate and simplify. Pick one basic color (black? brown?) to underpin your wardrobe, so you can simplify

your accessories. Laugh hollowly when the fashion magazines tell you that you have to trade all your black shoes for grey, gold and so forth. Then ignore them.

2. Be selective about trends. Neutral clothes last seasons longer. Patterns become passé more quickly. If you want to wear the season's latest trend, limit yourself to a few bold pieces and wear them to death in that season. Then empty your closet of guilt by giving them to charity.

3. Know your weakness. For Imelda, it is shoes, for Madonna, lingerie. Know what you are most likely to splurge on and carve out some cash for the fashion you find fun.

4. Invest in some great pieces. A smart outfit for dressy parties, a perfect interview outfit, a top quality winter coat—there are some pieces that can last for years and it's worth spending extra to get quality that will wear with time.

5. Turn shopping into a sport. If you really enjoy clothes shopping, change your aim. Rather than looking for the coolest things, focus on getting the one *in* thing at the best price in town. Even *Vogue* editors shop at the Gap when they offer good versions of the season's fashion necessity.

6. Repair, reheel. I always procrastinate when it comes to sewing on buttons and adjusting waistbands, but making a good piece of clothing last a little longer is worthwhile, even if it means spending a few dollars to get someone else to do it.

7. Cut the clutter. A thorough closet clean out, even just to get rid of all those empty wire coat hangers, is a must twice a year. Anything that you haven't worn in 2 years, don't feel great in, or don't have the right accessories to wear with,

should go. The great stuff goes to consignment shops or friends, the rest to charity.

Personal Care

While I'm on the topic of looking fabulous, there are some other costs I need to touch on. Personal care includes the basics of looking your best: haircuts, grooming products, dry cleaning, and any other day-to-day personal care costs. Some of these may be more optional than others, so when you create your own Conscious Spending Plan later in the book, think twice about where you draw the line between personal care and self-nurturing. For some people, a manicure is a basic cost of looking well groomed. For others, it is about the feeling of indulgence as the manicure takes place.

. . . .

Jamie's hair doesn't look like it's cut at the $12-a-cut chain store. "The key is to find a cutter who works here because of the hours or benefits. You'd be surprised how many are really good cutters who could easily charge three times as much in any other salon," she said. "I first came in when my partner was getting a cut and decided to get my bangs trimmed. Sue did such a good job, I was back a month later for a trim. I've been coming to Sue ever since, though I have to be a bit directive about the style; she simply doesn't go to the shows in New York like my old stylist." Jamie's haircutting costs fell from over $500 a year to about $150. "I wasn't at a really chi chi salon before, but a $45 cut with tax and tip every 5 weeks added up. Very few people would guess I go here. If it ever starts to show, I'll go back. Meanwhile, it's giving me a little more for my retirement savings."

. . . .

This is another area where women generally spend more than men. Managing personal care costs involves choosing habits with a full awareness of the Lifetime Cost. A man who chooses to have all his business shirts professionally laundered is choosing a weekly habit that adds up (though compared to the time taken to wash and iron the shirts at home, it is probably a great use of the money). A woman who chooses to be a blonde even though mother nature blessed her with brunette hair is choosing a habit that can add up to enormous amounts over the years. You can also lower the cost of personal care by buying supermarket brands of personal care products, finding a store that always has good prices for habitual purchases such as dry cleaning, and staying away from the most expensive salons.

Quick shortcut: if you buy grooming products as part of your groceries, just throw the cost in with Sustenance. There's no need to complicate the accounting.

Education and Work-Related Costs

The costs of getting smart and staying smart also fall into the Self and Family category. If you are an employee, you may pay some business-related expenses out of your own pocket. If you are self-employed or run your own business, business-related expenses will all go on your business books and not on your household plan. These expenses may include classes and courses that improve your earning ability, association or membership dues that provide a network or other benefits, publications that keep you up-to-date on the industry you are in, and every so often, job-changing costs such as resume services, travel to interviews, and so on.

If you have a home computer primarily for work or education reasons, include it here. The Full Cost of a home computer is determined by what brand you buy and how fast and well equipped it is, and the Lifetime Cost depends on how long you keep it and what your Internet service, if you have it, costs.

If you have children in the household, the cost of their education also falls into Self and Family. This may include tuition, books and supplies, living costs if they are at college, and other sundry costs. If you educate your children at a private school or a private or out of state college, these costs will be significantly higher than if you use the public education system and your state college system. The cost of education can also rise significantly if you incur interest through a student loan. Managing that cost may involve starting to save for your children's education when they are young, managing your assets so that your children qualify for financial aid, expecting them to pick up part of the cost of their education, and selecting colleges carefully. Even if you value being a good or generous parent above security, fund your own retirement first. Your retirement savings may not count in the calculations for financial aid, and you need all the years of compounding that you can get.

Allowances

If your household includes children or young adults, their living costs are included in the preceding categories and their allowance is also a part of Self and Family. I'll skip the bit about the Full Cost and Lifetime Cost of having kids: If you already have had children, you know this and it's too late to change your mind! However, if you are thinking about starting a family, think about the financial implications as well.

It's tough being a kid. Unless your child is the richest one in his or her class, he or she probably feels that his or her allowance is too meager. The pressure to keep up with the expensive fads that sweep schools is difficult. As did all 15-year-old girls of my era, I wanted a certain designer label brand of jeans that the rich girls at school wore but that my parents felt was unnecessary (fairly, in retrospect). I started part-time work at a local supermarket to pay my way to fashion nirvana and soon discovered that my weekend job barely covered the cost of my coveted jeans. It was a great way to learn the value of a dollar, although in these days of highly scheduled outside activities, it is not always a feasible way to help your kids learn about money.

How your kids value money will be largely influenced by how much money your household has. If your family struggles to make ends meet, your kids may learn a lot about the need to earn and take care of money without overt lessons. If, however, your family has a high income, you may need to be more deliberate in your lessons. If you are comfortably off, it's easy to have your kids exposed only to other kids of well-off families. One way to expose your kids to a wider range of possibilities is to give, say, a day a month to a nonprofit that works with people who struggle for the basics of life. If you are a member of a church, temple, or mosque, you will probably hear of opportunities to volunteer, or you can log on to www.volunteermatch.org to find a family-oriented opportunity in your area. Don't reward your kids for volunteer work; treat it as a basic obligation of being financially comfortable.

Kids are also influenced by your habits with money. If you treat credit cards as though they are free money and then struggle to keep up with payments, you are modeling that behavior to your kids. If you live in a boom and bust cycle, that is the mindset they will learn. If you consistently save a portion of your income (and they are aware of it), they may pick up your good habits.

If you have kids and want to help them be money conscious, start talking to them about money at a young age, and let them make decisions about their own money as they begin to grow up. Manage the cost of their allowance by talking with other parents that you are close to about what a reasonable allowance is, and give your children an opportunity to earn additional money by doing additional, more demanding chores.

Other Household Costs

Other household costs that don't fall into the Shelter or Sustenance categories and aren't in the realm of pure pleasure are included in Self and Family. These may include tax preparation service and bank charges. Bank charges can add up, so pay attention to your habits in using ATMs and running up late fees or over-limit fees on your credit cards.

CHAPTER 9

Social

Connecting with Others

What Is Social?

So far, we have looked at the cost of taking care of your future (Security) and your household's day-to-day expenses (Shelter, Sustenance, and Self and Family). Now we turn outside your household to look at the costs of connecting with others. The Social category includes all spending that arises from your social connections. The people you connect with include your friends, teammates, and members of clubs you are in, new people that you meet, and your family members who live under a different roof. All your social activities, communication costs arising from keeping in touch with people, and gifts that you give your friends and family are counted here (Figure 9.1).

Social and Values

What does Social mean to you? Is it about connecting with your roots? Is it about meeting new people? Do you enjoy it for the

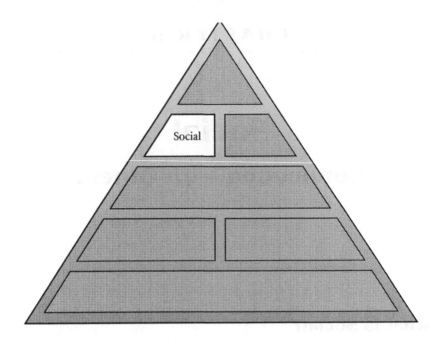

• Outings, events, and restaurants
• Group and team activities
• Communication
• Gifts

Figure 9.1   The Social category in the Conscious Spending
Model includes all expenses related to connecting with your
friends, family, teammates, and coworkers.

adventure? Do the activities draw you in? Is it about your strong
love of family? Is it about meeting strangers with common interests? Is it a reflection of your curiosity and desire to try new
things? Do you enjoy receiving the gifts that friendship offers? Do
you feel more fulfilled when you help the people you know? Does
it give you an opportunity for a deep level of connection that you
value? Do you gain a sense of accomplishment with a given activity or team?

People often enjoy spending money on the Social category because it is strongly linked with values about connecting with other people, feeling loved and accepted, being a friend, feeling as if they are a part of a team or community, and so on—all pretty warm and fuzzy values. At times there are also components of feeling as though you have made it ("I am a member of the country club. I am the man!"), are appreciated ("Hey, gorgeous. Do you come here often?"), are being self-nurturing ("I want to have someone take care of me"), are successful in competition ("I'm the best player on the tennis team"), and other values. And once in a while it may be driven by a grudging "should" perhaps because you are reciprocating a favor or politely going along with a friend's plans that do not interest you.

As I go through each of the elements of Social, remain aware of your underlying values. It's easy to assume that this is an area where cutting back means cutting off from other people. However, that doesn't have to be the case. If you need to manage your costs in this area, focus on what you value and ensure that you are cutting back on the cost, not the essence of enjoyment.

Exercise: For a Good Time . . .

Take 10 minutes and a piece of paper and list the 10 best times you have had socially in the last 5 years. The list can include specific activities or events, or the names of people that you always have fun with. Then expand the list by reminiscing about when you were a kid. List 10 of the favorite things that you enjoyed doing as a kid or the people you enjoyed being with. Once your list is complete, look for the common threads. What most influences how much fun you have; what you are doing or who you are with? Do you enjoy being with groups or with just one or two close friends? Do you enjoy being with old friends or meeting new people? Are there some people in your life that you always have fun with? Are there places or activities that are always fun? Which of the fun things gives you the biggest bang for the buck? Which of the activities that you most enjoyed as a kid have your carried through in some form to today?

. . . .

The Elements of Social

Outings, Events, and Restaurants

The first thing most people think of in the Social category is the direct cost of social life. These costs can be as varied as your interests: restaurant meals, concert tickets, a day at the races, a night at a dance, a game of cards with friends, a family outing to a theme park, a school reunion.

. . . .

Soo refused at first to add up her Social spending. "I just know I'll bug out if I see the whole amount in one place. I know it is too much; much more than I can afford," she admitted. "The tough part is that, because I went into the nonprofit field, I earn less than most of my friends from college but I spend like I earn the same amount as them. It's not all my fault—I tried to do the salad and water thing to keep my dinner costs down, but when the bill came, they just split it evenly. I would have felt like I was being cheap if I had objected. The next time I simply ordered the same as everyone." At 24, Soo cuts back in other places, sharing a house with other young professionals in her field, and brown-bagging every day. "It's getting easier as I get more friends in the nonprofit field; we know how to have fun without spending much. I want to stay in touch with my college friends, but not at the cost of ruining my finances." Soo came up with some *strategies to try: organizing dinners at lower-priced restaurants and activities such as bike riding and picnics, joining the group later so she skipped the expensive predinner drinks, and occasionally stating ahead of time that she had only $20 for dinner and would get just pasta. "At the end of the month, I felt okay about admitting I was down on cash, and if I said it before dinner and put the cash in as soon as the bill came, it sidestepped the issue. One friend even admitted to me that she wished they had cheaper nights out too, and she earns almost 50 percent more than me."*

· ·

The Full Cost of your social life can add up, especially if you are single and go out with groups of friends or date a lot, or you are retired and have a lot of leisure time. Even a basic night out with a couple of drinks at a bar and then a meal at a moderate restaurant adds up to no small amount, especially once you add in taxes, tips, and perhaps parking or cabs. If you go to events that require a certain dress code, whether nightclub sleek or black-tie fancy, your Full Cost is higher still.

Although this category can add up, some people realize they value what they get from their Social spending so much that they want to make more room for it in their plan. Events and outings are a relatively small portion of your total spending compared to Shelter, and some smart cutting back on the necessities such as utilities can free up some money to use in more fulfilling ways.

· ·

After Juan and Molly had a second child, their Social spending fell dramatically. "It's not that we were planning to cut back, we just seemed to have no time and no money to spare," Juan explained. They were conscious of rising costs because it was no longer just the two of them. "If we want a night out, we are up for an extra $50 or *so for a baby sitter and a whole lot more coordination. And family events tend to add up because it's now four of us. Most of our social life is casual meals with other couples with kids."*

Molly described the balance they are trying to find. "We want to have an active life and give our kids great memories, but we are also conscious that if we spend $100 going to a water park for a day, that's $100 not put into their college funds or our retirement. It's hard to get the right balance, though when we are just plain tired, it's easy simply to have a cheap night at home with a video." Recently they increased their Social spending because they were aware that they were not getting enough quality time as a couple. "It was as if our whole life was about the kids. We have started making sure that we have a date at least once a month. Yes, it's costing us a bit, but I think we are better parents when we get out together, even if it's just to an average restaurant."

Juan smiled, "If you had told us 5 years ago that we'd spend this much time at home with the kids, we would not have believed you. But your priorities change, and suddenly the nights out are less important than the time together as a family."

. . . .

Plenty of people love company but want to manage their spending on their social life. If you need to manage the cost of your social life, see if there is a pattern that adds to the Full Cost of your social activities: Is it the drinks, meals, or events that add up? Are there some friends who have more extravagant lifestyles and always lead you to bust the bank? Would it be harder to go out less often or to spend less each time you go out? If you want to cut back, try some selective trimming. "Sorry, I have an aerobics class after work; can I meet you at the restaurant later?" "I can make it for drinks, but I'll have to skip out after that." "Gee, I'd love to come to Le Cirque's menu-tasting fiesta, but I'm washing my hair; what about a film and coffee on Sunday afternoon instead?" Like Soo, you can also take the lead in organizing social events, get creative about low cost ways to have fun, or start the evening out with a strict cash budget and no credit card on hand. Also, off hours often mean big savings. Movies and plays are often cheaper at the matinee sessions, and restaurants' lunch menus offer similar food for a lower price.

When you have children, as do Molly and Juan, you can find other creative ways to stretch your social dollar.

. . . .

"We have some great friends in the area whose kids are about the same age as ours. Sometimes we share a babysitter, though four kids is a handful if we are away too long," Juan explained. "We've also talked about giving each other a night off once a month by having the kids sleep over at each other's place as soon as the little ones are old enough. I'm sure the night we have their kids will be a zoo, but it will be worth it to have a whole night alone in return."

. . . .

The Lifetime Cost of your Social spending is influenced not only by the Full Cost of each activity, but also by how often you are involved. A person who goes out regularly but only spends $25 on a night out may spend a lot more than someone who goes out less often but spends $75 on a night out. As Soo found out, habitually spending a little more than you can afford quickly adds up to be an unsustainable habit.

Group and Team Activities

Another part of the Social category is the group and team activities in which you are involved. These activities may range from playing a sport with a team, to taking classes that have a strong social element. When I was new to Washington, D.C., I took classes at the Smithsonian in everything from photography to presidential politics. Although I loved what I learned, the primary reason I took the classes was to meet like-minded people in the area. Because of that underlying reason, I count those expenses in Social. It differs from the personal growth classes that were primarily for my own growth and count as Soul.

As with social outings, group and team activities can be a source of great satisfaction and one where you may be very comfortable with your spending or you may want to find more money so you can really follow your passions. However, if you want to cut back, there are plenty of ways to manage the cost of these events.

The Full Cost of the team sports and activities in which you participate includes the direct fees and any memberships related to the sport, the clothing and equipment you need for it, as well as the cost of lessons, team dues, special travel, and so on.

It is easy to spend a lot on the hobby of the year. Whether your passion is fishing or furniture refinishing, bowling or playing in a band, there's a good chance that there are equipment and supplies, the cost of which adds up. It's easy to get caught up in an activity and suddenly *need* to have the latest and greatest equipment. It doesn't take too long flicking through a catalog or magazine about your hobby to see what the top of the line supplies are. Yet there are many people whose equipment well surpasses their skills: professional quality cameras owned by those who will never be more than pretty good amateur photographers and near *Tour de France*-quality bicycles owned by people who are far from competitive cyclists.

I often have a couple of social sports that I am involved with at any time, as do many active people, such as bicycling, in-line skating, skiing, diving, and others that change depending on my friends and relationships. My closets are relatively full of stuff that goes along with the pastimes and would be even fuller if I bought the equipment for everything I try. Ever since my golf clubs sat gathering dust for several years, I have spent a season getting clear on how much I like a new activity (and whether I have any talent for it!) before I put money into it. For me, it is not worth investing in equipment for activities such as skiing or diving, where that equipment requires significant maintenance, becomes outdated relatively quickly, or takes up a lot of space. Apart from my snorkel and mask and my ski boots, I rent equipment when I go diving or skiing with friends. I get my own equipment for activities such as cycling that I am likely to enjoy for years.

For parents whose kids take on new sports each school year or who grow out of their clothes and equipment well before they're worn out, finding the right combination of quality and cost can make a significant difference. Often there is a good market in second-hand gear, whether it's a casual handing on of soccer shoes between parents of kids on the same team or an organized swap shop run by the school.

The Lifetime Cost of group events and activities depends greatly on how expensive the activity is. There are plenty of activities that require little or no equipment. If you enjoy day hiking, choral singing, Internet chat rooms, or book clubs, you would be hard pressed to spend even a fraction of what someone who is into fly fishing, bicycle racing, photography, or cross-country skiing spends. If you are a dabbler as I am and you know it, manage the Lifetime Cost by limiting spending on passing fads. If you have a handful of activities that you are committed to for a long time, manage the Lifetime Cost by realistically assessing when to stop accumulating the latest and greatest equipment, and sell off your older equipment through your group or through newspaper or Internet classifieds.

Communication

Communication costs are probably growing at a faster rate than any other costs in most households. Not too long ago, this subcategory only included your telephone bill with local calls and the occasional long distance call, and some postage stamps. There were many households that thought twice before calling across country. Today the cost of communication is much higher. Even though competition has driven the cost of each call down, the number of calls has risen for most households. Of more importance, the number of ways that we communicate has rapidly expanded. Today, communication charges may also include a cell phone; calling card; Internet service provider's fee; and second phone line for your computer, fax machine, or kids. If you are really connected, you may have cell phones for each member of the family, a website that you pay to have hosted, and perhaps a special high-volume line for your computer (such as DSL, ISDN, or cable modem). And there's still the need for some postage stamps.

As the complexity of communications has risen, so has the need to regularly update your communication equipment, whether it means buying a faster modem for your computer or purchasing a home phone that handles two lines. I had the disconcerting experience recently of trying to dial an old fashioned telephone with a circular dial; my fingers and brain found the dialing completely foreign even though that was what I had grown up with. If you use your home computer primarily for social interaction, it makes sense to include its cost in this category. For other people, it may be better counted as entertainment (part of Soul) or as a work-related expense (part of Self and Family).

Anyone who has looked closely at his or her phone bill lately knows that the Full Cost of communication includes a myriad of mandated charges that range from fees to cover the cost of infrastructure built in the days of a monopoly to taxes that pay for special services for those who need them.

Communication costs can have a high Lifetime Cost because most recur monthly. As I was writing this chapter, I stopped and added up the monthly minimum commitments that I have with two phone lines, a cell phone, and an Internet service provider. Before I make my first long distance call, I'm up for well over $100 a month and average much more. Only a few years ago, before my cell phone and Internet days, my baseline cost was only $30 or so. My situation isn't unusual. Today there are fewer households with a single telephone line and without Internet access. Managing the Lifetime Cost of communication involves both choosing services with competitive rates and only paying for services that really bring you value.

If you want to reduce communication costs, shop around. If you don't have a discount long distance plan, you are paying too much for long distance calls, and if you are using the 10-10 services that sound like a bargain, make sure you read the fine print. Many will give you a great rate if you make, say, a 20-minute call, but will charge you the same amount if you make a 1-minute call; so that the rate for that minute is effectively 20 times higher. Others have monthly fees that you get charged even if you only make one call.

With the major phone companies in such hot competition, there is a good chance that a major company has a plan that is attractive and has little in the way of fees. Also explore services that enable you to dial long distance via the Internet for little or no cost. For cell phones, shopping around can save money. Rates are constantly falling, and it's getting easier to find a competitive plan that doesn't have a long-term commitment attached to it. Finally, Internet service providers are competing so fiercely for your business that some have reduced the price to zero. Before you disconnect from your current provider for a free service, however, give the free service a test run: You may get what you pay for. My only experience with a free service was that getting connected was difficult and disconnects happened often. They are said to be improving, so try them out. A quick glance at advertisements from stores that sell computers shows that a lot of computers come with a rebate of $400 or so if you sign for a multiyear contract with an Internet service provider. Do the math: The bird in the hand might have a higher Lifetime Cost than another provider offers.

Gifts

Gifts include all that is given to loved ones, family, friends, and colleagues for holidays; birthdays; celebrations of milestones such as weddings, graduation, anniversaries; and support when times are tough or friends are ill.

Ah, the joy of giving. If it's so joyous, why do the holidays seem stressful, the bride and groom have to tell you exactly what they want, and birthdays feel like just another thing to remember? For many people the joy has faded into the chore of giving. Whether a 99-cent card or an expensive gift, the thrill of finding the perfect something for that certain someone is often overshadowed by feeling overstretched in terms of time, resources, and creativity. Some people even find receiving adds stress to their lives.

. . . .

"I like to think of myself as gracious," Maria confided, "but I just had trouble sounding thrilled about another serving bowl. I've tried to tell

my mother that I really don't need anything for the house, but she feels she must give a gift and I then have the struggle of finding something to get out of the cupboards to have room for it all. I know she will notice if I don't use it the next time she is over." Maria was winding down after the holidays, which had been particularly stressful as she had hosted the family holiday meal this year. *"I sometimes think that if we could pull the plug and just give gifts to the kids, we'd all end up better off. I really don't care about what I get, what I want is to show my love and know that I am loved."*

She calculated what she and her husband spent on gifts for friends and family for the year. *"It's not that I can't afford the gifts, but it's as if we take money that could be used to replace our old dishwasher and spend it on coffee mugs for colleagues, and books and CDs for the family. At the end of the day, we probably have a pile of things valued at about the same amount as a new dishwasher, but it's not what we would have chosen to spend the money on at all. And it all took hours and hours to find. I find the shopping so stressful because I worry whether they will like what I buy."* She thought about all she had received and mused, *"I love the gift from my husband; he's not very expressive and this is his way of saying what he doesn't say out loud. And the other really precious gift is the one from my 6-year-old nephew: It's this great kiddy picture and he wrote 'to my favoritist aunt.' You know, if we slowed down the spending and really told people how much we loved each other, it would mean so much more."*

....

The Full Cost of gifts is determined by how many people you buy for and what you spend on each gift. Some stages of life result in extra gift buying, such as when many of your friends are getting married or having kids. If gift giving is adding up to more than you want to spend, manage the Full Cost of gift giving by being creative about what you give or who you give to. Because there are many gifts that may become an annual event, such as birthday and holiday gifts, the Lifetime Cost can be managed by choosing what events are celebrated with gifts.

I know some families manage holiday gift spending by each drawing a name out of a hat and giving only one larger gift to whomever they drew, or only giving gifts to the kids and sharing in their enjoyment. There are also opportunities to just stop giving gifts. I have some girlfriends whose friendship I value; however, I have enough stuff in my home and they have enough stuff in theirs, so we celebrate each other's birthday by taking each other out to a nice meal. We end up spending money that we would spend on our social life anyway, but we consciously celebrate each other's ability to age gracefully without cluttering our home. If you are concerned about raising the gift-giving issue with your family, find someone who feels the same as you do. It's easier for two of you to raise the issue with the family. In the office, simply raise the topic over lunch one day, well in advance of the holidays. Plenty of people are just as happy with a great meal out together or with a card-only policy.

As people's lives get more and more full, gifts that don't add to clutter are increasingly appreciated. Some ideas: services, such as a massage or pedicure; subscriptions, to bring a year of interesting ideas; consumables, such as a cheese basket or bottle of great wine; or even caregiving, such as a night of babysitting or a home-cooked meal monthly. Another way to simplify the process and perhaps cut the cost is to give uniform gifts. For example, give everyone in your family a matching shirt from the Gap, in a different color for each person, or find a small gift at a warehouse store that is appropriate for all of your colleagues. Better still, if you see a good, standard gift on sale, stock up so you avoid shopping every time you need a gift. I'm at that age where if I have a pile of baby gifts on hand, it is not long before there is a baby or three to send a gift to. Buying on sale doesn't have to mean saving some cash, it's also a great way to give more for your money.

Another way to manage your spending on gifts is to give goods or services that you make or provide. For example, if you have a skill, you can give a painting or poem that you created, a day of house painting, or a plate of homemade baked goodies or home-smoked meats. The key is to creatively balance your desire to celebrate with those you love, and to do it in a way that does not break your bottom line.

SEVEN SOCIAL STRATEGIES FOR SAVVY OUTINGS THAT COST NOTHING BUT FUN

1. **Get cultured.** Museums, zoos, and theaters have loads of freebies, from tours to classes. Local parks may also have family-oriented activities on weekends. And top live theaters may seek ushers and let you sit in on the performance for free.

2. **Take a hike.** You don't need the latest high-tech in-line skates to get some fresh air and see some greenery. Next time the sun is out, grab a friend, a water bottle, and a map of walking paths and go.

3. **Cheer.** Little Johnny may not be as skilled an athlete as those overpaid professionals on TV, but he'll appreciate your attendance more. If you don't have kids or grandkids, give a neighbor a Saturday morning off and play chauffeur and number 1 fan for her kids.

4. **Be cheered.** Take up a group activity needing no equipment, whether joining a chess team or a book club. If you're theatrically oriented, local choral societies, theater groups, and comedy troupes want your skill, from writing flyers, to operating lights, to being up on stage.

5. Give back. Volunteering, whether for a one-time project or an ongoing cause, can be a rewarding way to spend evenings or weekends. You can learn new skills or use existing ones, bring along old friends or meet new ones.

6. Star gaze. Find a cloudless night, grab some blankets and binoculars, and drive far enough out of town to get away from the bright sky. Gaze away and make up stories to rival those of the ancient Greeks.

7. Dust off the board games. Grab some friends, a few snacks, and that Scrabble, Monopoly, Pictionary, or Twister game you loved as a kid. Play. Laugh. Repeat.

CHAPTER 10

··

Society

Giving Back

What Is Society?

In the Social category we looked at how we interact with our circle of friends and our own community. In the Society category we turn our attention to the rest of the world. Charity, contribution, giving back, whichever term you prefer, Society is about making an impact on the world or helping out someone in need of a hand. This category includes not only charitable giving and donations of goods and services, but also "helping gifts" that may include financial gifts to help the lives of relatives, godchildren, and other special people (Figure 10.1).

Society and Values

What does Society mean to you? Is it making a difference in the world? Is it correcting an injustice and making the world a fairer place? Is it supporting a friend who is taking on a task such as a marathon or cookie sale? Is it preserving something you think is precious and endangered? Is it giving thanks and at the same time

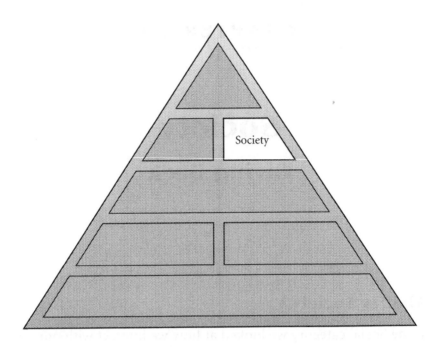

- Charitable contributions
- Helping gifts
- Donated goods and services

Figure 10.1   The Society category of the Conscious
Spending Model includes charitable contributions, lending
a helping hand, and donating goods and services.

getting recognition for the success you have had in life? Is it helping people who are facing situations you have faced or are grateful never to have faced? Is it honoring the memory of someone
that you loved? Is it expressing gratitude for what you have? Is it
habitual donating because the plate is passed to your hands? Is it
what you feel you owe?

This category is where you get to play fairy godmother to the
world. If you could wave a magic wand and change something
about the world, what would you change?

We are asked to wave our wand by so many organizations: from the priest buttonholing us in the airport for coins to help orphaned kids, to the pledge drive on public television, from the plate passed in the weekly service, to the politician's solicitation that comes in our mail. They may try to appeal to our values through guilt (pictures of kids with pleading eyes), optimism (hope-filled stories), or persistence (endless phone calls asking to donate used cars; do I look like I have a bunch of used cars sitting around?). How do we choose from among all the well-meaning causes?

Many people never choose. Instead of using their wand to make a single impact, they scatter fairy dust around a lot of causes. They give a little help to the causes that are most present: the neighbor's Girl Scout cookie drive, the friend's fund-raising marathon, the donation at the church, mosque, or temple that they visit. Some of their choices may stem from values pertaining to giving back, but some choices may also come from values about supporting friends, being loyal to their alma mater, being accepted in a community, and so on. And some of the choices may come from the fact that it is simply so hard to choose. A little in a lot of places may feel like the only way to make everyone happy. I choose to focus most of my resources on a single cause and keep a little extra to support the friends who are so passionate about their chosen causes that they put themselves through grueling physical feats to raise money (though it only encourages the behavior!), and to feed my love of Girl Scout cookies (a good cause wrapped in chocolate).

Values and spending interact strongly in the area of Society. Aligning your values with how you manage your spending in Society can be very deeply satisfying. For some people, making a difference or giving back is their highest value and becomes a vocation. Living in Washington, D.C., I meet many people whose commitment to giving back has led them to work for a cause they strongly believe in. Thanks to the many thousands of people working in the nonprofit field, being a fairy godmother does not have to be a full-time job for the rest of us who don't have it as our highest value or choose to find other ways of contributing. Without devoting your life to a cause, you can still make an impact by giving back in a way that fits with your values and your available resources, if you choose. Money or time is all it takes to start to change the world.

Although for most of us, making a difference is not necessarily at the top of our values list, for some it may not make the list at all. Many personal finance books promote a strong belief that you should give back. I prefer to remove the "should" and let you decide whether this is important to you and how much you want to give. If there are other values that you want to honor more or if you are not in the financial situation to be giving to others because you have important unmet needs within your family, then do what you feel is right. The bottom line is that your own values should lead you to a decision about how (and if) you contribute to Society. Other people's judgments about how much is *enough* and what is *right* are just that: their own judgments that they can choose to live by. Do what's right for you at your stage in life.

How much you give is a very personal choice. You may be a member of a religion or group that advocates tithing, giving away 10 percent of your income. You may give with no particular plan at all, with the amount varying based on how often you are asked. You may give through donating time because either you don't have money or you want a hands-on impact. You may have a certain percentage you always give. You may not give because you have so little that you are not far from the receiving end of charity. You may not give because it is not something that you feel is important. To give or not to give: it's your choice. You must be true to your own values.

· ·

Malcolm admitted he gave to charity in an unplanned way. "I just give a bit if a friend is in the AIDS Ride or if my kids' school is doing a fund-raiser, as well as some in the plate at church every week. My divorce hit my finances hard, so I give less than I used to." At 32, he is busy building a career and funding his retirement. "To be honest, I'm trying to put away as much money as I can afford to now. I still want to contribute to society, but there's not a lot to play with." As he started looking at how much he was giving, he was surprised. "It actually adds up to more than I thought," he told me. "And I simply don't keep records for most of it. It just drifts away." After an "imagining" process such as the one I'm about to share with you, he gained clarity. "You know, the biggest thing I would like to do is help kids who are less well off than my two girls. I really am who I am today because of the Boys' Club I was involved with as a kid. The guys there were my role models when I didn't have a dad around. I really want to help the kids in my city who don't have the advantages of my two girls, who are lucky."

· ·

Exercise: Imagine There's No . . .
· ·

Set yourself up with a pen and paper in a quiet place and become still and meditative. Close your eyes and imagine yourself looking down on the Earth from a distance. Imagine that you have been granted the power to change one thing in the world. You can change anything about the world that you want, but the end result has to be that you make the world a better place. Begin to picture yourself moving closer and closer to the Earth, and noticing all that needs changing: the pollution, the hunger, the natural disasters, the substandard education of many children, the endangered animals and places, the wars, the diseases, the violence, the unhappiness. As you get closer and closer in, know that to make the biggest impact on any of these problems, you need to choose the one cause that is closest to your heart. Feel which one of the problems is calling to you for your help, which one you feel most connected with. What is the difference that you would like to make? Who or what would be impacted and how? Would you like to make a difference locally, nationally, or internationally? Take a few minutes to jot down what you were most drawn to.

Then research the organizations that do work in the field in which you are interested. You may already know about some organizations that focus on your area of interest. If so, call or visit the website of each one to find out more about what they do. If you don't know who is doing work in your area of interest, try searching on the Web, looking in the Yellow Pages, or asking organizations that do similar work. If you were not strongly drawn to any one specific issue, look at organizations that work on broad issues, such as the World Wildlife Fund, which works with many endangered species and the lands they live in, or United Way, which works with a wide range of social, medical, and disaster-relief issues.

. . . .

The Elements of Society

If your values and resources allow you to donate money to Society, there are ways of doing it that are smarter and help your dollars make a bigger impact on the world or a smaller impact on your financial resources. There are many ways that people contribute to Society. Here, however, I look at only those that have a bottom-line impact on your Conscious Spending Plan.

Charitable Contributions

The most common spending on Society is through cash donations to charities and causes. Managing your spending in the category of Society involves being clear on how much you choose to contribute and making sure that you are making the impact that you want to make with the money that you have to contribute. While the "how much" question is answered by looking at your values, the "impact" question involves looking at the Full Cost. Charitable contributions are generally tax deductible, which means that for every dollar you give, it actually costs you less than a dollar—so the Full Cost is lower than the actual cost. Whether it is a few dollars in the plate at a religious service or membership in your local public radio station, all cash contributions are fully tax deductible if you itemize. If your donation is tied in with an item of value (such as a dinner for an organization or an incentive gift for supporting your local public television station), only the amount in excess of the fair market value of what you received is deductible, which means that you need to be diligent with your record keeping so you can get the appropriate deduction. Remember, the less tax you pay, the more money you have to use for yourself or to help others—so taking tax deductions makes everyone better off. If, however, you don't itemize your tax deductions, you do not receive a tax benefit.

If you are giving small amounts to a lot of causes, it is easy to lose track of exactly how much you have given: $1 here and $10 there can easily slip through the cracks and never end up being deducted at tax time. Set up systems that support you in record keeping. For example, if you usually put $10 a week in the plate at your religious service, you may be able to set up a monthly contribution that is paid by direct debit or charged to your credit card. This arrangement will help you track your donations so that you can deduct them fully. One habit that I have that helps with my record keeping is to simply say no to the many random requests for a few dollars; from people who collect at traffic lights to the many solicitations that I get in the mail. It is easier to track your donations if you give larger amounts to fewer charities.

If you are planning on making a large contribution to charity, talk with an accountant, estate planner, or tax adviser about how to do it most effectively. For example, if you usually do not have enough deductions to itemize on your tax return, you may benefit from donating a larger amount every couple of years so that you can itemize in those years rather than when you donate a smaller amount each year. If you donate some stock that has appreciated in value, you can deduct the value of the stock at the time you donated it, avoiding capital gains tax on the increase in the stock's value since you bought it. For people with a lot to donate either in their lifetime or through their will, various types of trusts such as a charitable remainder trust can also provide tax advantages.

Helping Gifts

The second type of giving is significant gifts that are designed to help out. The reason that "helping gifts" to relatives and friends are included in Society is because charity begins at home. The sort of gifts I am talking about are ones made to help out a family member, friend, or person in your community who would otherwise need to turn to others for help or would not be able to afford something that you see as important. I'm not talking about giving money to kids with the main purpose being to avoid estate taxes.

Although that can be a very good financial strategy for people with significant assets, its purpose does not fit in Society. Helping gifts look very different in every family and community. Examples I've seen include putting a little away every month to build an education fund for a relative's young child, helping an elderly relative with her elder-care bills so that she can stay in her home for a few more years, and buying paintings from the struggling artist up the street out of love for the person as well as his or her paintings.

· ·

Growing up, RaiShaun dreamed that she had a rich aunt who would come and give her a wonderful gift. "I daydreamed that some aunt who everyone had forgotten about would fly in and take a shine to me. I imagined she'd fly me to New York for my birthday or buy me clothes and books so I would fit in on my first day at college, or pay some tuition so I wouldn't have to apply for every bit of financial aid and still work part time." Of course, the rich aunt never materialized. Today, RaiShaun is a successful engineer and earning more than anyone in her family has earned before. Although she one day hopes to have kids of her own, she has started a "rich aunt" fund for her sibling's kids. "It's more comfortable than helping out my sisters and brother directly. I put away $20 a month each for my seven nieces and nephews in a special college fund." She knows that her siblings don't have the income to put their kids through college themselves. "I'd love my siblings to be more career-oriented—they all have the ability to earn more—but I can't change them. What I can change is the opportunity that their babies have. College completely changed my world and I want them to have that too." Today her daydream is different. "They are such great kids, it's fun to imagine surprising them with this when they are older."

· ·

Helping gifts are not tax deductible, although the recipient doesn't have to pay tax on the gift if you give him or her $10,000 or less in a year. However, there may be ways of structuring your helping gifts so that they have tax advantages and lower the Full Cost. For example, you may be able to set up an Education IRA for a relative whom you would like to support in her college years, or you may be able to put the money in the child's name when the child earns so little that he is exempt from paying tax on the income the investment earns. Again, for larger amounts, talk to a financial advisor who can help you determine if you can use trusts or other financial structures to hand the money on in the most efficient way.

Donated Goods and Services

The final element of Society is donating that involves giving time or goods and services. This can be a great way of contributing when you have more spare time or spare stuff than spare money.

Donating time can be enjoyable: a great way to meet like-minded people, as well as a way to get a real understanding of issues. Many studies have shown that people who donate time or money to a cause also feel better about themselves when they do it. If that's not a win-win situation, what is? Working hands-on with a nonprofit group may involve an ongoing commitment or just a one-time event. Another great thing about donating time is that you may get to practice or learn a skill that you would otherwise not learn. When I was about to buy my first home, I had a lot to learn about renovating. By spending every Saturday for several months at a Habitat for Humanity site, I learned how to hang and finish drywall, and they received hours of free labor. Another win-win situation.

Giving goods and services can be fulfilling too, especially when it has the side benefit of cutting the clutter in your home. Again, keep receipts for what you donate and remember that you may need to list everything so that you can estimate the fair value of the donations. Take a photo or write a detailed list before you bag it and ship it off to a charity.

If you itemize your tax deductions, keep good records because you can get a write-off for costs associated with donating time, such as parking and mileage (at a lower rate than the business mileage deduction).

SEVEN SOCIETY STRATEGIES FOR MAKING MORE OF A DIFFERENCE

1. Focus your resources. Get clear on the one difference you would like to make in the world and donate your resources to a nonprofit organization that is trying to solve the problem. You'll make more of an impact that way. If you have children, get them involved. Selecting one charity for them to support can help them develop an understanding of how fortunate they are.

2. Develop an annual plan. Determine up front how much you want to give and where you would like it to go.

3. Set up an automatic payment plan. When a bowl is being passed around, it is easy to feel embarrassed to let it pass without contributing; however, it is easier and better for tax records to simply set up a monthly contribution to be debited directly from your bank account or charged to your credit card (if you pay it off in full each month).

4. Beat Uncle Sam. If you plan to leave a significant amount in your will to charity, talk to an estate planner to determine

how to structure your will or trust to make sure your money makes the impact you would like. Charitable remainder or charitable lead trusts can be used to ensure that your charitable giving is balanced with your need for income. If you have an unexpectedly high income for one year, create a charitable gift account to get the full deduction in that year and disburse the funds as you want in the future.

5. Beat Uncle Sam, part 2. If you have stocks or other valuables that have made significant capital gains, you can donate them and get a write-off based on the appreciated value without having to pay the capital gains tax.

6. Donate your time. Giving of yourself is just as valuable as giving of your money. Find the combination that works best for you.

7. Give your clutter. The clothes, furniture, appliances, computers, and even vehicles that are cluttering your life may be of great value to others. In most areas, the Salvation Army or a similar charity will come and pick up your bulkier donations. You feel better, have more space, help others, and get a tax write-off. What a winning combination.

CHAPTER 11

....

Soul

Expressing Your Higher Purpose

What Is Soul?

Ahh, now we get to the really fun stuff! At the very peak of the Conscious Spending Model sits Soul. Soul is all the optional spending that fulfills Rule 3: maximize your pleasure (Figure 11.1).

Why the name "Soul"? I played with a lot of options for the name of this category. Nothing seemed to get to the heart of it as well as Soul. Satisfaction is too bland, silly money too frivolous, stuff that makes me smile too inane, self-actualization* too impersonal. The name Soul was ultimately chosen because this category consists of all the spending in your life that is strongly aligned with your core personal values, your very essence.

Unlike the other categories, Soul is not a completely separate category. For example, while Shelter can be neatly defined as all

---

*Abraham Maslow, the creator of the Hierarchy of Needs, used the term self-actualization to refer to people's ultimate need to express themselves and live to their highest purpose. These are the needs that surface after only more basic needs such as food, shelter, and social interaction have been met.

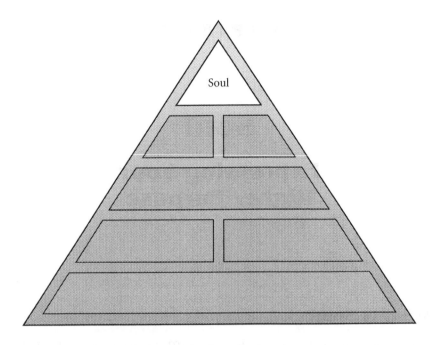

- Travel and vacation home
- Cable, books, periodicals, and music
- Hobbies, classes, sports, and toys
- Electronic equipment
- All the rest
    Body indulgences (such as massages, manicures, a personal trainer)
    Jewelry
    Art and collectibles
    Soul components of all other categories

Figure 11.1   The Soul category of the Conscious Spending
Model is at the peak of the pyramid for good reason: It
includes all the optional spending that maximizes
your pleasure.

the types of spending listed in that category alone, Soul really is best seen as a category as well as an overlay for the whole model. Some types of spending such as for travel or art fit in Soul alone. However, pieces of other categories also have a strong Soul component. For example, if you value family highly and feel your home represents that value because the family's interactions take place there, your Shelter spending will have a component of Soul. Another person may see giving back to society as a core value, and see his or her Society category as being largely Soul. To simplify the accounting, items are counted in their primary category even when Soul is the motivator behind a purchase. So the two examples mentioned would be counted in the Shelter and Society categories, respectively.

. . . .

"My home definitely has a Soul component," Ruben said. "I come from a family that is very, very close knit, and I see my home as the center stage for our relationship." He lives in an inviting brownstone, dominated by a large dining room. "This has to be the best-used dining room on the street. We have about 12 people for dinner most Friday nights, and on holidays—well, the whole house gets taken over." Early in his married life, Ruben and his wife lived in a smaller apartment. "In those days, my mother's house was the center of the gatherings, but she is getting on now and it is too much for her to do all the entertaining. I am the eldest in the family, so it seemed natural to start hosting holiday dinners. When Devorah and I were ready to buy a house, the first priority was to have a large entertaining space." He knows that he spends a larger amount on Shelter than most of his friends and family. "We are all close, but I'm the one who has my relationship with my family as my very highest value. This is what I live for. As far as the accounting goes, it's all in Shelter, but as far

as how we choose to spend our money, it's definitely influenced by Soul."

....

Soul and Values

So what does Soul mean for you? Is it connecting deeply with people? Is it being independent? Is it having adventures? Is it about being comfortable and nurtured? Is it success and all its trimmings? Is it a feeling of accomplishment? Is it fitting in? Is it standing out? Is it making a difference in the world? Is it taking care of yourself? Is it being in a strong relationship? Is it a spiritual connection? Is it helping others? Is it standing on your own two feet? Is it beauty? Is it fairness? Is it truth?

As we explored earlier in the book, values are a complex web of what we care about and what we believe. Probably the answer to a number of the questions regarding Soul was a clear "Yes!" to you, whereas others were not important. Being clear on what your core values are is a key step in Conscious Spending; however, if you cannot develop a clear list of your most important values, don't worry. Just being aware of some of the key ones will help you become a more Conscious Spender. As you move forward with managing your spending this way, you will begin to notice which sorts of spending give you the most satisfaction. Over time, you can finesse your list of values. Sometimes, it is not even important to be able to explain your values precisely. If, for example, you know that you love listening to music more than anything, does it matter if you cannot explain exactly what values your love of music fulfills? Not really. What matters is that you really know what things resonate deeply for you so that you can choose between the many things that you could be spending money on. If you are getting tangled up in trying to define your values, just ask yourself: What makes me feel most myself? What do I most deeply care about? Use the answers to these questions when developing your Conscious Spending Plan in Chapter 12.

Soul is where your personal values come into play most strongly. There are probably quite a few things on your internal shopping list that reflect your values in an obvious way, and a handful that reflect them in a way that is individual and perhaps quirky. Look back to the answer to one of the first questions in the book: If you were given $5,000 today to spend on something you love, what would you spend it on? In the group coaching classes that I run, the answers have run the gamut from the obvious— travel for someone who valued adventure—to the obscure—a saw to make jigsaw puzzles for someone who valued creative expression. The items on your list are a completely personal expression of your values.

Where Soul is an overlay on other categories, it can be valuable to be more conscious of the extra spending that you are choosing to do for Soul. For example, a basic car that gets you from point A to point B may cost, let's say, around $300 a month. For that you could get something perfectly functional; something a few years old that's reliable and comfortable. If, however, you are choosing to spend double that so that you have the latest model convertible that reflects your values of fun and adventure, or triple that amount on a high-end import that reflects your values of success and recognition, then be aware of the choices that you are making driven by Soul and not simply by need. Often when people first try to get a handle on their spending they are unconscious of these choices. By being more conscious of them, you can begin to make sure that you are reflecting those values in a way that gives you the most joy. Often when I work with couples, I find that moving the conversation away from what things they want to what values they want to honor diffuses otherwise volatile disagreements.

. . . .

"I just did not get why my wife wanted a luxury car. To me, it is simply a waste of money," Peter recollected. "It was only when we started talking about what we really valued that I began to appreciate how important looking successful is to Susan. She grew up pretty poor, so a nice car makes her feel like she's moved way beyond that." Susan's car is nice, and Peter's is a well-kept but older "bread and butter" car. "I have a pretty ordinary car because it's not so important to me, but I can appreciate her desire for a nicer car in the context of her values. Really, her desire for a nice car is no more or less frivolous than my desire for a great home theater system. By being aware of how much of our purchase is Soul, we can more equitably make sure that we both get some of what we love despite not having that much spare cash."

. . . .

Although the link may or may not be obvious to other people, I bet there is a pretty strong link for you between what you count as Soul and what your values are. Someone whose primary value is love and connection is likely to have a very different idea of what Soul is than someone whose primary value is independence. Even if they both see travel as Soul spending, one may travel to connect with people while the other travels to get away from it all.

. . . .

For Donna, taking care of herself with occasional manicures, pedicures, or massages helps her recharge after a long work week. "I enjoy spending a little money on the luxuries that relax me or make me content enough to continue doing what I do to be successful and happy: a productive citizen as well as a great Momma." After a brush with debt problems a few years ago, she learned how to nurture herself more consciously. "Probably a lot of my old overspending came from trying to get the same effect: feeling like I was taking care of myself. Now, I spend much less, but I really am aware why I am spending it and I really do feel like I have taken care of myself."

· ·

It is important to restate here what I said very early in the book: values differ and what one person values may be very different from what another values. The key to Conscious Spending is being true to your own values. Sometimes, Soul is very inwardly focused, and at other times it may be focused on your friends and family or on the community. One client commented that she would walk a mile each day to save $1 on public transport, but wouldn't think twice about giving $200 to charity. Clearly, she values her contribution to society more than comfort and convenience.

The list of things that qualify as Soul can vary widely, and I cover only the most common ones here. In addition, often the aim is to find more money for these items rather than to cut the cost of them. If you can save a little by shopping around and get more of what you want, that's great. However, for some of the items on your list, the aim is to just enjoy them, not save as much as you can on them.

The Elements of Soul

Travel and Vacation Home

Vacation may represent different values for different people. It may be about nurturing and recharging, escaping from work, learning and experiencing new things, connecting with family and loved ones, communing with nature, soaking up new cultures or journeying within. For some it may be about outward appearances: going to the "in" resort or sporting a tan in the middle of winter. Perhaps for others it may be about achieving a goal of traveling to every continent, climbing every 24,000-foot peak, or collecting an exotic array of passport stamps (I'll admit that I'm disappointed that so many countries don't bother to stamp passports anymore!). Whether you are vacationing at a weekend home or traveling to the far corners of the world, there are ways to align your vacation spending so it really is fulfilling to you.

You can lower the Full Cost of travel by shopping around for special fares and being flexible on your travel dates. The Internet has made shopping for competitive fares very easy, and there are even services where either you can be e-mailed as fares change or you can put in a request for a certain destination and dates and have airlines bid for your business. Sometimes moving a vacation a week can result in a significant saving on your airfare. However, remember that the idea is to really enjoy your vacation, so if the off-season package tour saves dollars but means that you are in the midst of the mosquito season, the savings are not worth it. When you book your trip also impacts the amount you pay. Booking too early often means that discounted fares are not offered, and booking at the last minute can cost you a lot more. Some last-minute bookings, however, can save you money if the travel company offers discounts to keep their trips full. Airlines also charge significantly less for trips that include a Saturday night stay-over. Another way to lower the cost of travel is to use frequent flyer programs. I have had many free trips because I have accumulated air miles by using an airline credit card that I pay off in full every month. Remember that credit cards that offer frequent flyer miles often have very high interest rates, so your miles are far from free if you carry a balance.

If you have a vacation home, the costs can be managed in many of the same ways as your primary shelter. In addition, you may be able to offset some of the costs by renting out your vacation home when you are not using it. If you are considering a second home, get very clear about the Lifetime Cost and extra responsibility it involves: Often it is cheaper and less stressful in the long run to have a standing rental in an area you enjoy or to use hotels when you travel.

Cable, Books, Periodicals, and Music

The many ways you entertain yourself and your family at home are a part of Soul as well. Unlike the Social category, which is about how you relax with others, the Soul category includes entertainment and recreation alone and with your family. Some of this spending may be so habitual you don't even think of it: Cable and newspaper subscriptions are often thought of as a typical household expense rather than Soul. However, by categorizing these expenses as Soul, I am asking you to consider them alongside other completely optional spending such as for books, CDs, and magazines.

If you want to lower the Full Cost of these items, look around for ways you can access them for little or no money. Many newspapers offer their content for free on the Internet or may be available at your workplace. Most communities have libraries with a good range of books, music, and magazines that can be borrowed for free. Renting versus buying can also lower the Full Cost. If you are unlikely to watch a video more than once or twice, rent it rather than buy it. Also consider pooling some of these costs with friends. I am an avid book buyer, but I can take months to get around to finishing a book and like to turn the corners of the pages down, so I don't use the library. Apart from reference books that I may use over the years, I am unlikely to ever open a book again after reading it. I get more value from the books that I buy by handing them on to friends who will enjoy them after I have finished. My friends do the same, so we all lower our Full Cost of book buying. Some secondhand bookstores will also buy books, and many charities will accept them too. I recently sent all my old management textbooks off to Ghana where they will be a lot more useful than in my basement. Handing them on keeps the books in circulation and keeps my home less cluttered.

The Lifetime Cost of subscriptions such as cable, newspapers, and magazines adds up as you pay for them monthly or annually. You can manage the cost by being selective about what you are buying and quickly canceling services that you don't get full value from. It is very easy just to keep renewing subscriptions to things you rarely use, especially if the payment is automatically charged to your credit card. For example, if you find you really don't watch the premium cable channels very often, lower the Lifetime Cost by moving to a basic cable subscription and using your local video store more often. If you don't get your 50-cents worth out of your daily paper, stop buying it. The same with magazines that you just flick through. Cancel your membership in book or music clubs that automatically send an unwanted selection of the month if you forget to reply.

Direct marketers cash in on people's tendency not to cancel subscriptions. Every time you receive a free trial offer for a magazine or some marginally useful service such as a travel planning service that is linked to your credit card, the sellers are banking on your trying it and never getting around to canceling it. You can save money as well as time and effort by never trying such offers in the first place. My rule of thumb is that unless I have been hoping that such a service/product/magazine exists, then I won't try it.

Hobbies, Classes, Sports, and Toys

What you do in your spare time probably is very strongly related to your values. Sometimes the primary goal may be connecting with the people who share in the activity with you, and other times it may be the activity itself that appeals. In the first case, count it as Social, and in the latter case, count it as Soul. Whether you are working alone at china painting or taking part in a team sport, take a look at the section on team activities in Chapter 9 on the Social category for some ideas on how to manage the Full Cost and Lifetime Cost of your leisure-time activities.

. . . .

"When I started doing my Conscious Spending Plan, I was pretty surprised by how much I spent on all the personal growth classes I do," Suzannah said. "The classes really resonate with my love of learning and my desire for spiritual growth and real relationships, so it is clearly Soul. Still, as much as I love the classes and what I learn about relationships and myself, I found I was spending way more than I could afford. It's like there's a group of class junkies who get so into the bond that they make, that they keep taking more classes. I put myself on a 'budget' where I would only take two classes a year unless I felt I really was putting into practice all the great stuff I was learning. That's helped me focus on my long-term growth, not just the short-term buzz I get from interacting with cool people."

Suzannah still takes a number of courses but is clear now about the value she gets from them. "Last year there was an extra class that I wanted to do just to be with a great group of people, so I did it but

202 The Ms. Spent Money Guide

counted it as Social. I also worked as an assistant on another course. They didn't pay me, but it reinforced what I had learned the first time I did the class, and I got to meet some more interesting people."

. . . .

Electronic Equipment

Whether you are looking to play some music or play a video game, the Full Cost of the equipment you buy will depend a lot on whether you want merely to get the job done or get it done in high style. True fanatics can pay a small fortune for top of the line equipment. Every time I take a shuttle flight I help myself to the many free magazines on hand, because I enjoy seeing what people are fascinated by. Recently I flicked through some of the high-end stereo magazines and was stunned to see what the best of the best goes for. There are some speakers that cost more than my car!

The very top-end equipment may be hard to find a deal on, but for more common brands, the Full Cost of electronic toys can be managed by shopping around. The Internet has made comparison shopping easier, and you can quickly get the best price. Also educate yourself about where the money being spent actually makes a difference. For example, with stereos, you are likely to get a big bang for the buck by purchasing good speakers, but you may be unable to hear the difference created by more expensive speaker cables. Another way to lower the Full Cost is to buy secondhand products. Again, the Internet helps with on-line auction services making the market place easier to access.

The Lifetime Cost can be managed by only jumping on trends once they are established. There are still a few households with

BETA video players, a good technology that was marketed poorly compared to VHS video players. By waiting a year or so after a technology comes out, you have a better chance of getting it at a better price and avoiding buying a technology dud. The speed at which the technology is evolving will impact the Lifetime Cost. For example, a computer may be hopelessly out of date in a couple of years, but an established item such as a CD player is likely to remain useful for a longer time.

All the Rest

With all the other things that you may want in your Soul category, the Full Cost and Lifetime Cost can be managed by shopping smart, which may range from having massages at a massage school that offers discounts to buying estate jewelry at a discount. Be careful to balance your desire to manage your spending with the bigger aim of getting more of what you want. If a massage at a massage school lacks the pleasing ambiance, involves a different masseur every time, or results in a less relaxing massage, you would be better off paying full price and really enjoying what you are paying for.

SEVEN SOUL STRATEGIES FOR GETTING MORE FUN
FOR YOUR MONEY

1. Notice which parts of Soul give you more satisfaction per dollar spent. There may be some things that you do that are very aligned with your personal values that cost little or nothing. People in my classes have noticed things such as hiking, meditation, and listening to a music collection they already own bring them as much pleasure as many of their more expensive pastimes.

2. Share the love around. If you have an interest that others share, see if a local community college would like you to teach a class in it. The joy of sharing your interest may increase your enjoyment of it and give you a chance to focus on it.

3. Go attic hunting. Who knows what past pleasures you packed up and forgot about. I know my attic has an embroidery I mean to complete, paints I enjoy using when I get around to it, photos that take me back to the travels I have done, and other toys that I will get around to using one day.

4. Turn a hobby into a business. If you love painting and have given every friend and relative at least one picture to hang on their walls, see if a local gallery would be interested in taking your work. You may earn enough to cover your costs and may be able to write off the materials. Just don't ever lose the fun of doing it.

5. Think in terms of Full Cost and Lifetime Cost. The equipment for cross-country skiing, for example, may cost as much as downhill skiing, but the daily cost of lift tickets quickly turns downhill skiing into a major money drain.

6. Share the cost around. Small groups of people can cut costs by sharing an expensive purchase such as a boat or weekend house. Just make sure everyone is clear on the arrangements, and you have a contingency plan in case one person wants out.

7. Shop around. Sometimes the enjoyment of whatever Soul purchase you are making can override your rationality. Whether you are buying art classes or a trip home, shopping around may save a lot of money.

PART THREE

Go

Becoming a
Conscious Spender

Now it's time to put all that you've learned into practice. In this section, you will create your Conscious Spending Plan and choose how to implement it in your life.

In Part Two, we looked at the seven categories of the Conscious Spending Model in detail, understanding the values that come into play with each category, and the Full Cost and Lifetime Cost of the decisions that you make. Ideas for cutting spending were shared for those of you who want to decrease your spending in any of the categories. As you create your Conscious Spending Plan, refer back to those chapters to find ways to better align your spending in each category with your values, or to decrease spending so that you can find money to use for something that gives you more pleasure.

In this section, I show you how to use the Conscious Spending Model to create a spending plan that fits you and your family's values. Chapter 12 shows you how to create your spending plan.

Chapter 13 focuses on the structures and systems that make Conscious Spending easier to implement, as well as some everyday habits that will help to make your interactions with money more conscious. After this you are good to go . . . unless you have one or two special challenges to deal with. Chapter 14 looks at the challenge of digging out from debt. If you are starting out weighed down with debt, you can use Chapter 14 to develop a short-term plan to pay the debt down and a long-term goal for how you will use your money once you have eliminated your debt or cut it to a more manageable size. Finally, Chapter 15 is a resource if you want to increase your earnings. If, after developing your Conscious Spending Plan, you realize you need to earn more to really have the life you want, this chapter is full of strategies to increase your earnings.

CHAPTER 12

....

Starting Out

Creating a Conscious Spending Plan

THIS CHAPTER IS WHERE YOU TAKE ALL THAT YOU WANT, NEED, and habitually spend money on, mix in a good dose of reality, sprinkle in a little simple mathematics, and align your financial life with your values. No single recipe exists for how you should spend your money—this is all about your choices. However, there probably are many ways you can use your money to get more of what you want compared to how you are using it today. Your recipe may look completely different from that of people who have a similar income or situation. Your recipe may even look different from someone with similar values as yours. But that's the whole idea: Your values and desires are a unique combination that reflects your personality. Your Conscious Spending Plan reflects that unique combination.

The goal is to create a plan with enough money for all your basic costs to make your plan comfortable, with enough things that you really enjoy to make it compelling, and enough flexibility that you will not fall off the track the first time a large unexpected expense arises or desire tempts you. The goal is not to create a rigid, static plan that you must force yourself to follow for years to come.

Your Conscious Spending Plan is like a road map. It doesn't give turn-by-turn directions, but it keeps you heading in the direction you choose. If you really want to use your plan to drill down into a level of detail that helps you understand where every penny has been going and where it will go, you can do that. However, for most people that becomes tedious and does not add enough additional information to justify the extra effort. If you want to create your plan with estimates that help you with a general direction, you can do that too. The easiest way to do the exercises in this chapter is to look at your spending on an annual basis, which makes it easier to track and plan irregular payments, such as a bonus that may come once a year or an insurance premium that is paid every 6 months. Once you have developed your annual plan, you can divide by 12 to create a monthly plan or by 52 to create a weekly plan, depending on how you decide to implement your plan.

In Chapter 13 you will create the structures, systems, and habits that will turn your plan into reality. Remember, if this starts to feel difficult or restrictive, focus back on Rule 3: You want to manage your money better so you can maximize your pleasure. At the same time, you understand (perhaps begrudgingly!) the need to also respect Rule 1 and Rule 2, so the plan is based on living within your means and taking care of your future.

Let's get started on your plan. There are five steps described in this chapter:

1. Size your pyramid.

2. Work out where your money is currently going.

3. Clarify how you want to reflect your values.

4. Allocate your basic costs.

5. Allocate your optional spending.

First you work out how much money you have to play with. I use the word "play" deliberately because I want you to remember that the aim of the game is to end up with more money to use for the things that make you smile, whatever they may be. Next, you begin to explore where your money currently goes, knowing that the aim is not to find an exact answer, but to identify how aware you are of where the money is used. Then you touch back on the exercises that you did earlier in the book and get clear on what your priorities and values are in relation to how you spend your money. In the fourth step you allocate money for your basic costs, including Security, starting from the bottom of the model and working your way up. Finally, in step five, you allocate the remaining amounts based on your personal values.

Step One: Size Your Pyramid

The first step in creating a Conscious Spending Plan is to work out how much you have at your disposal, known as your disposable income. I call this sizing the pyramid because the amount that you determine is the size of your pyramid will be the total amount that you can allocate to the seven categories of your Conscious Spending Plan.

To simplify the process, look at all the money that you have choices about, which means every cent that comes in the door in the form of after-tax income, commissions, tips, bonuses, interest and dividend income, and all other payments such as financial gifts from parents, unemployment payments, pension withdrawals, and so forth. Exclude income tax, as well as mandatory government payments to Social Security and Medicare.

We simplify the math by mixing tax-deductible and nontax-deductible items. As you plan how to spend your money in a later step, some of the choices you make will have tax implications. Some items in your Conscious Spending Plan are paid for with pretax dollars (employer-deducted health care, retirement savings) or are tax deductible (mortgage interest, charitable spending). In these cases, a dollar is not really a dollar. For example, if you are currently not contributing to a retirement plan, and you start putting away $5,000 in a plan, it will lower your taxable income and decrease your taxes by $5,000 times your marginal tax rate. The tax impact is reflected in the amount of income tax withheld from your paycheck, and you should adjust your withholdings after major events in your life such as buying a home so that you do not overpay taxes.* The reason you don't want to overpay your income taxes is that you don't want to give Uncle Sam or your state government an interest-free loan. When your taxes change, the size of your pyramid will need to be recalculated as well.

For the sake of simplicity, we ignore these effects as we create a plan; however, when you revisit your plan every year or after any major decisions; such as buying a house, remember to resize your pyramid to reflect the change in the amount of state and federal taxes you pay. The good news is that most of your decisions are likely to have an impact on the positive side, that is, to lower your taxes. For example, increasing the amount you put aside in a tax-sheltered retirement plan or buying a house will lead to lower taxes. Only a few decisions will lead to higher taxes, but that doesn't mean they are bad decisions. For example, if you have not

---

*Ask your employer's benefits coordinator to get you the IRS form and state government forms that are used to calculate your withholding. Use the worksheet on the form to determine how much you need to have withheld for federal and state income taxes.

had a cash cushion in the past, you will find that creating one may lead to a small amount of taxable interest income (although a lot of banks and investment firms offer tax-exempt money market funds).

What if, after doing the next exercise, you find you have only a small amount of disposable income that really is not compatible with your dreams and aspirations? First, wait until you have completed the planning process in this chapter before arriving at such a conclusion. If you still feel the same then, know that you are able to plan to change that, too. When we looked at the money flow in Chapter 2, we saw that there are two transactions that you can impact: earning and spending. Whereas most of this book is about spending because that is where you have the power to change today, Chapter 15 looks at how to begin to increase your earnings. That process generally takes place over a longer time frame; however, you will see that there may be some short-term strategies that you can use to increase earnings.

Exercise: Size Your Pyramid
. . . .

To determine the size of your pyramid, take the most recent pay stub of each member of your household who will be included in your Conscious Spending Plan and fill in the following:

Annual salary of all household members   _____

Plus bonuses, commissions, and tips   _____

Plus interest, dividends, and other
    investment income   _____

Plus other payments   _____

Equals total pretax income   _____

Using the pretax income, calculate the size of your pyramid by working out how much of that income you have absolute control over. You get this amount in the following way:

Total pretax income (from preceding listing)   _____

Less federal, state, and local taxes   _____

Less Social Security and Medicare payments   _____

Plus average tax refund*   _____

Equals total disposable income   _____

. . . .

Step Two: Work Out Where Your Money Is Currently Going

Step two gives you insight into where your money is currently going, which may help you find where there is the most leakage or unconscious spending. You can skip this step if you feel you already have a very good understanding of how you spend your money; however, most people who complete this step find enough information that surprises them that I challenge you to do it anyway, even if you think you have a good sense of where your money goes.

Sometimes, people find that they cannot account for thousands of dollars that they spend. This unaccounted for spending may be money that is spent in cash (lunches, public transportation fares, restaurants with friends, small purchases), or it may be for items that can only be worked out by going through a year's credit card

---

*If this is more than a couple of hundred dollars, adjust your withholdings so that you are not giving Uncle Sam a free loan.

charges and bank statements (clothes, vacations, unscheduled costs for car repairs, or unreimbursed medical expenses). If you want more insight into where all the money goes, keep a spending diary for a couple of weeks or a month to begin to fill in the blanks. However, the more important lesson may be to find out just how much of your spending you have little or no insight into.

Sometimes just beginning to work out where money goes can be enough to shock you into action.

. . . .

"I have always perceived myself as someone who did not spend a lot of money, probably because I'm tight when it comes to my social life," Sandra said. "Yet I never had quite enough to put away for retirement, and it was only when I sat down and looked at where my money went over a year that I realized how a couple of items were a whole lot higher than I ever would have guessed."

Single and earning $35,000 a year in public relations, Sandra has been able to live within her means fairly easily. "I simply wouldn't consider going into debt for everyday expenses, but it wasn't until I saw exactly how much I spend on clothes and my car that I realized just how unconscious I have been around money. I now realize that I could cut back on clothes and easily find money for more social spending as well as some retirement savings." Reflecting on her closet, Sandra observed: "If I had realized that I spend a couple of thousand a year on clothes, I'd probably buy fewer things, but get better quality. When I think of how full my closets are, I just want to use that money for something else."

Her car is also a target. "I had just assumed I'd get a new car when my lease is up, but now—well, I'd simply get more satisfaction from beginning to save for retirement. I don't spend that much time in my car, but I will be retired for decades."

. . . .

When we talk in Chapter 13 about structures and systems that support you, you may choose to use a software program to begin tracking your spending, if you don't already use one, so that you get more insight into how you spend your money on an ongoing basis. Being able to see where your money actually goes will help you be a Conscious Spender.

Exercise: Work Out Where Your Money Is Currently Going

Table 12.1 includes every category and subcategory of the Conscious Spending Model. You can use this table or a spreadsheet to work through this chapter and create your Conscious Spending Plan.

Take the table of all the categories and subcategories and begin putting your current spending on an annual basis into each section. Use the column marked "current." Start with the figures that are easy: your rent or mortgage, car payment, insurance and other expenses that do not vary from month to month. Multiply these monthly payments by 12 to get your annual spending. Then take a look at past bills or checking account records to add in approximate amounts for bills that you pay every month, which may include your utility bills, groceries, and gasoline. It is fine to approximate. After this point, it may get more difficult, depending on how well you keep records, how much you spend in cash, and how predictable your spending patterns are. Continue until you have accounted for every cent you spent, which is the sum of your total disposable income as well as any debt you ran up over the year. If you cannot account for a sum and cannot guess what the money was spent on, place that amount in a row that you label "unrecorded."

Step Three: Clarify How You Want to Reflect Your Values

Before deciding how to use the money that you have at your disposal, let's revisit your values and priorities. The aim here is to get clear about your household's most important underlying values. What I don't want is for you to create a long list of wants that are so far out of your reach that you will feel unmotivated or constantly dissatisfied. For example, connecting with friends might be a very important value to you, yet the list of wants that might arise from that value could extend to everything from entertaining more often to having a weekend home to entertain in. Focus on the key values that most define you and your household members and a few ways to express those values that are within reach.

. . . .

"More than anything, I think that I am family-oriented," Hugh said. "Especially since having a child, I really connect strongly with my family. Another top priority is peace. If I don't have peace in my life, I cannot function well in the hustle of my work life." An options trader on the floor of one of Chicago's hectic exchanges, peace seems the antithesis of his everyday life. "I'd rather call it an antidote. I would go mad if I had peace all the time, so perhaps it is not peace that I value so much as balance." Working with family connections and balance as his two most important priorities, Hugh set out to create a list of how he could reflect those values with his spending. "Family is easy: It's about taking my family home to visit my parents or my wife's parents at least twice a year, and also about having a home large enough that we can easily have my parents or one of my brothers and his family over to visit." He quickly fell into listing home improvements he could make, but realized they were not as critical as simply being with his family more often.

Table 12.1   Conscious Spending Model

Category	Spending		
	Current	Planned	Gap
Soul			
Travel and vacation home			
Cable, books, periodicals, and music			
Hobbies, classes, sports, and toys			
Electronic equipment			
All the rest			
Body indulgences (e.g., massages, manicures, a personal trainer)			
Jewelry			
Art and collectibles			
Other			
Soul subtotal			
Society			
Charitable contributions			
Helping gifts			
Donated goods and services			
Society subtotal			
Social			
Outings, events, and restaurants			
Group and team activities			
Communication			
Gifts			
Social subtotal			
Self and Family			
Transportation			
Vehicle			
Auto insurance			
Gasoline			
Maintenance			
Taxis and public transport			
Clothing			
Personal care			
Haircuts			
Personal care products			
Dry cleaning			
Education and work-related costs			
Allowances			

Table 12.1   (continued)

	Spending		
Category	Current	Planned	Gap
Other household costs			
Tax preparer			
Bank charges			
Other			
Self and Family subtotal			
Sustenance			
Groceries and household supplies			
Takeout and nonsocial meals out			
Health care			
Health insurance			
Unreimbursed health expenses			
Dietary supplements			
Fitness			
Gym membership			
Fitness equipment			
Pet food and pet health care			
Sustenance subtotal			
Shelter			
Mortgage or rent payments			
Property tax and home-owner fees			
Home and mortgage insurance			
Household running costs			
Utilities			
House maintenance			
Mowing/gardening services			
Cleaning services			
Shelter subtotal			
Security			
Cash cushion			
Retirement savings			
Life insurance			
Disability insurance			
Umbrella liability insurance			
Consumer debt repayment			
Security subtotal			
Unrecorded			
TOTAL			

"Balance? That's not so easy. I want to say that a weekend home in the country would be great, but it would stress our finances and create a whole lot more chores to do. This is more about time than money, but the things that I could buy to support my having more balance in my life would be services, like a lawn service so I can reclaim my weekends, and a cleaning service so that my time with my family is spent interacting, not doing chores. Cutting caffeine from my diet would save at least $5 a day and help me feel more balanced too."

. . . .

You will find some of the items on your list are an on/off switch—you either spend a certain amount or you spend nothing. For example, having someone else handle the hassle of your taxes may cost $500, but there is no option of having someone half handle them. Others are a sliding scale. For example, travel is on many people's list, and $1,000 of travel may be a trip within the country to see friends or a whitewater rafting trip in an area you can drive to, whereas $3,000 may be a trip overseas with a friend or a sea kayaking adventure on the other side of the country.

Exercise: Select Your Top Priorities
. . . .

Whether or not you completed the exercises earlier in the book, take 10 minutes now to list your top values, leaving several blank lines on the page between each one. Reorder them until you feel you have the most important five values identified. If you are in a relationship or have children still at home, make sure that the top values of the whole household are reflected.

Once you have created the list, go back to each value and find at least three ways to help satisfy this value that feel within reach financially, even if you are not sure exactly what they cost or where the money would come from. Don't include items that are so expensive that you feel they are impossible on your current salary, even if you manage your money a whole lot better. For example, for a couple who value their romantic connection and earn $50,000 annually, the list might include a romantic vacation together each year, dinner out every month, and installing a gas fireplace. It probably would not include buying a weekend home. Although they may not be able to do all three activities in the same year, or may need to limit themselves on how much each costs, some or all of the items may be achievable.

By now, you should have a list of at least 15 ways that you could use your money to reflect your values. You may not be able to afford all of them while still living within your means and taking care of your future. Prioritize the list, with the single most important item being ranked number one and so on down the list. As you do this, ask yourself: If I could afford only one of these items, which one would give me the greatest pleasure and satisfaction? Note that sometimes the biggest and best items don't make it to the top of the list. One client started with a rather expensive vacation at the top of her list, until she realized that she was able to get four or five smaller items on the list for the cost of one vacation. Keep this list with you as you develop your plan.

Step Four: Allocate Your Basic Costs

Before you can start planning on spending your money on more trips, a larger house, or a charity of your choice, you have to make sure your basic costs are covered. The reality of most people's personal finances is that most of the money goes toward basic bills—a house, car, work clothes, tuition, and so on. Although you make choices about all of these costs, they are not completely optional.

When the Conscious Spending Model was introduced back in Chapter 3, it was likened to two models that inspired it: Maslow's Hierarchy of Needs and the food pyramid. Both of those models start with the most basic needs at the bottom of the pyramid and build up to the least necessary but most fulfilling needs. In Maslow's model, you won't crave to fulfill your needs to express yourself or have social interactions until you have secured a roof over your head and food in your belly. If you're hungry or cold, your priorities simply don't extend very far. In the food pyramid, you need a balance of all the categories; however, you need a lot of the basics such as grains, fruits, and vegetables and only a little of the fats, oils, and sweets at the top of the food pyramid to have a balanced diet.

The Conscious Spending Plan you are creating to reflect your own wants and needs has the same underlying principles. The most basic costs required to meet your fundamental needs of security, shelter, and sustenance are at the base of the pyramid, and the more optional costs that fulfill social and self-esteem needs are higher up in the chart. The first step in creating your plan is to allocate your baseline expenses from the bottom up to ensure that your most basic needs are met.

. . . .

"I was feeling very stressed about money because it felt like there was never enough, and certainly not enough for nice extras," Liz said. "It was only when we were doing the baseline costs that we realized how out of line our spending was with our income. I left work a couple of years ago to take care of the kids and do some part-time nursing, but we were still living like a two-income couple with no kids." After doing the math, Liz and Kevin found they were spending nearly half of their income on their home and another large slice on their transportation. "We still bring in a good amount by many people's stan-

dards, but of the $6,000 a month after tax, we spend $2,700 on our mortgage and property tax, $200 on utilities, $1,000 on cars and car insurance, and at least $200 on food, $160 on communications, $100 on Kevin's lunches, and $90 on gas. Take out $500 a month for child care and $500 for retirement and college savings, and we're down to $550 for all the other costs," Liz said as she ran down their list. "That sounds like a lot, but factor in kids clothes and toys, Thanksgiving at my parents, maintenance on the house, and health-care bills, and we're often at zero before having anything left that's purely for fun."

Liz and Kevin sat down with their calculator and bills and decided to make some changes. "The plan will take some time to kick in. The first decision we made was to keep our car after we finish paying off the loan next year. And we have shelved our plans to renovate the kids' bathroom—just a coat of paint will be enough for now. We won't consider moving, though, because the schools here are great," Kevin explained.

Liz chimed in, "We are also going to play with our work schedules to see if we can lower our child-care costs. I need the mental stimulation of being out of the home, but if we can do it on nights that Kevin can commit to being home by 6.30 P.M., then we won't need a babysitter to bridge the gap."

. . . .

The key is to set your baseline spending at the minimum that you feel is comfortable and possible. This minimum is not about imagining how low you can go, but about first making room for your basic costs. Try to set your baseline below today's spending, whether that is 5 percent lower, 50 percent lower, or more. Leave blank all categories that are purely optional unless choosing not to put money in them would start World War III in your household. One client said that she considered her cable bill completely optional, but knew that with two teenagers whose social interactions depend on watching the "in" shows, it would create too much disharmony to cut back on the cable spending at all. It went into the baseline.

Security is the one area where your baseline spending may be higher than today's spending. Given the three rules, taking care of your future is a baseline necessity—you must pay yourself first—and means that you take care of your Security needs before you start funding some of the more optional parts of your plan. Believe me, it is less painful to assume that you have to do it and allocate the money up front than to go back at the end and try to squeeze it in.

Exercise: Allocate Your Basic Costs

Take the table that you used to assess your current spending, and start entering in your baseline costs in the column labeled "planned." Use annual figures and, if you are doing this on paper rather than on computer, do this step in pencil.

Starting at the base of the model, at Security, enter the costs that you face that are necessary. If, for example, you would not move to lower-cost housing, then your current spending on your mortgage or rent is your baseline. However, you may see that other costs in the Shelter category can be lowered, for example, that you could cut your electricity bills by not leaving lights on when leaving a room and adjusting your air-conditioning thermostat to a higher temperature setting. Enter the amount to which you think you could easily cut costs.

Your baseline should include Security spending so that Rule 2 is honored. While the amount is up to you, I like to see clients put away at least 10 percent of their income in retirement savings plus build a cash cushion, unless they are carrying debt. If you are in debt, make sure to add a reasonable amount for debt repayment so that you can move toward being free of consumer debt as soon as possible, though still contributing to your retirement fund, if possible.

Once you have filled in your baseline costs, look at the total compared to your available income. Do you have anything left for optional spending? How much of your income goes toward the basic bills? Are your basic bills exceeding your earnings? If your answer to the last question is yes, then you need to reassess all the areas where your money is currently going to determine where you can cut back. Look at the big ticket items such as housing and transportation. Which are significantly out of line with your earnings? Which other expenses that you regard as basic are actually optional?

· ·

Step Five: Allocate Your Optional Spending

The last step is where the fun comes in. Now that all the basics have been taken care of, you can choose what to do with the rest of your disposable income. Add up all that you allocated in the last step and deduct it from the total amount you have to play with. Unless you are really scraping to make ends meet, there should be some money left. Now the playing begins. Keeping the list that you developed in step three in mind, look at all the other subcategories: What other spending do you want to do that was not baseline spending but is really aligned with your values?

Throughout this book, you have been looking at where you spend money in a way that is most aligned with your personal values. Some of your most aligned spending may be the clearly fun stuff: vacations, hobbies, or social life. Other aligned spending may be in parts of the pyramid that everyone spends on, but not everyone gets a sense of deep satisfaction from. For example, Shelter may be just a comfortable roof over your head, or it may be a reflection of your connection to your family, or your love of comfort and self-nurturing, or even your desire to show the world that you have made it. Now choose how much of your money will go toward things that you really appreciate.

Often people find areas for which they did not allocate much baseline money, yet they still feel are important in the overall plan. For example, clothing may have a low baseline amount, but you choose to spend more than the baseline amount even though it didn't make the list in step three. Similarly, cable subscription is usually not a baseline need but may still be something that you choose to spend money on. For such items, ask yourself: What value am I honoring if I spend money on this? Will I really get more pleasure out of this spending than out of the spending on my list?

The process of filling up the categories that are aligned with your values will shine a bright spotlight on the trade-offs that you choose. If you have been an Unconscious Spender in the past, it may be quite an eye-opener to actively choose between spending on two different things that you like. Most people find a number of areas where they have habitually spent money that are a lot less important to them when looked at in the larger picture of their values. Others feel that the process helps them really focus in on their values in a way that the theoretical self-analysis failed to do. Choosing between, say, driving a top of the line car and having more expensive family vacations may be a cut-and-dried decision for some, but an agonizing wrench for others. Some choose based on which item or activitiy appeals to the strongest value. Others choose based on which item or activity brings pleasure over a longer period. Most people choose based on a subjective feel for what combination will fit them best at this time in their lives.

Once in a while, I come across people who don't want to plan for fear that it removes spontaneity. For those people, we create a category called "spontaneous fun" and allocate a good-sized amount into that bucket, knowing that as the year progresses, it may be spent on travel, or classes, or a stereo upgrade, or a fashion statement. The "what" of the spending is less important to them than the "how." By having an unallocated bucket, they retain the feeling of flexibility and abundance. The important thing with that approach is to allocate a certain amount to the spontaneity bucket and keep it to one side. Keep this money as a tool for self-expression and make sure that it doesn't just fade into your everyday spending. One way to do this may be to define a quality or two that makes an item qualify for funds from your spontaneity bucket. And while the spontaneity is not planned, the total amount available for the spontaneity is clearly defined in your plan. After all, even spontaneous people have to pay the rent!

Although your Conscious Spending Plan involves spreadsheets or tables, creating it is an art, not a science. The answer that seems right today may change for any number of reasons tomorrow. The key is to get a directional plan and not to feel locked in by it. If your desires or circumstances change, then alter your plan. If you find you are consistently spending a lot more than you expected on one category, either look at how to manage the spending in that category (refer back to the chapters in Part Two for ideas), or realize that your spending will be higher and you will need to trim in another area to find the space for this extra amount.

Exercise: Allocate Your Optional Spending

First, calculate how much money has yet to be allocated. That is the amount that you will be allocating in step five.

Look through the list you created in step three. There may be some items that are important but cost very little, and others that are just as important but come with a high price.

Choose where to begin. I like to set aside first the money for the items where I get a lot of enjoyment for a small amount spent. For example, I love magazines, and my habit of subscribing to a whole pile of them probably costs only $20 a month, yet I get hours of pleasure reading them. That item gets money first.

Others like to start where there is a very strong alignment with their values. One client started with her kids' education, because of all the areas she valued, that was the one where she felt most strongly aligned with her values around being a good parent.

Start by scanning all the subcategories and seeing which of the items on your list calls most strongly to you. Rather than working through the list in a methodical top-down or bottom-up fashion, stop and scan the whole list each time.

If you are doing this exercise on paper, keep a running tab of how much you have left to allocate. You may find as you get close to the end of the exercise that you start going back to rework the numbers because you realize you didn't leave enough space in your plan for something very important. Also, as you scan the columns after filling in a few of the items on your list from step three, you may also want to look at the other categories where you have just assigned a baseline amount. Once some of the items on your wish list are taken care of, increasing the amount allocated to some of your other categories may be more important to you than getting more of the items on your list.

. . . .

The Whole Plan: Looking at Your Bigger Vision

So it's all there on paper: a spending plan that reflects your personal values and the choices you want to make among all the different things that require your money. Some tough choices probably had to be made if your desires cost more than your income. However, if the planning process really did get to the core of your personal values, there's a strong chance that this spending plan will feel a lot more fulfilling than your current spending habits.

After developing your whole plan, stop and ask a few questions. Am I comfortable with the percentages I plan to spend in each of the seven categories? What does this plan say about who I am and what I value? Does this plan allow for the personal values of everyone in the household? Is there enough fun stuff to make this plan compelling and easy to follow through on? If I had to cut further in one category, which one would I choose? If I had additional income, what would I plan to spend it on?

There is no objective right or wrong in your planning, as long as it is meeting the three rules: Do you plan to live within your means, take care of your future and maximize your pleasure? If it sounds like you and feels good at gut level, you have it right.

Some of my clients choose to make radical changes as they go through their planning. Once a radio host/entrepreneur interviewing me commented that she valued having money to plow into her multifaceted new business ventures. Even with a brief look at the model, she was able to realize quickly that her largest expense—an apartment in one of the most costly markets in the United States—was very low on her scale of enjoyment. To her, the apartment was simply a place to sleep, store her clothes, and change. She rarely ate there, never entertained there, and would have been happy with a closet, bathroom, and bed. Her 2-minute back-of-envelope Conscious Spending Plan resulted in a commitment to find a smaller place that was more aligned with her needs.

Others have found the plan really confirms the path they are already on. One client, a divorcee whose kids had recently all left the nest, was spending a substantial amount on personal growth each year. She commented that it was great to validate that her spending really was in line with her values. If anything, the planning process helped her realize that her personal growth journey at that time was such a strong green light that she was happy to scale down on some other areas in order to find even more for the classes she felt were adding so much to her life.

Your Conscious Spending Plan is a living document. When your life circumstances change, you will want to revisit the plan and see where you need to tweak it. Having a child, getting into a relationship, getting a pay raise, launching your own business, and other events that have a significant impact on your spending or earnings are all triggers for revisiting your plan. Sometimes one financial choice may trigger a whole readjustment of your plan on a short- or long-term basis. When I bought my current house, I knew there wasn't much that needed to be done to make it a little more attractive. It was already livable, and a coat of paint and weatherproofing a built-in porch was all that was needed. However, 6 months into living there, my head was full of plans about fixing up the garden, renovating the kitchen, and perhaps putting in a second bathroom. Suddenly the adventure vacation planned for that year felt less important than a start at improving the house. Did I fail to figure the Lifetime Cost of my decision? Not really. What I failed to figure was that having a house that really felt like a haven would bring my values pertaining to Soul to the forefront and create a different way of expressing those values. In the past, I expressed Soul values by traveling adventurously. Now, I'm expressing it by creating a peaceful sanctuary with a bird-filled garden and lovely sunny study.

Filling the Gaps: Moving from Current to Planned

A plan, even a detailed plan such as the one you have just developed, is no more valuable than a New Year's resolution if you don't follow through on it. In Chapter 13 I share some specific tactics to implement your plan. But before we finish the Conscious Spending Plan, let's take a look at the *gap*.

The *gap* is the difference between current and planned spending. If you take the planned spending and subtract the current spending, you will get a number that reflects how much you plan your spending to change. Let's say, for example, that you currently spend $1,000 a year on car insurance, but you know that if you shopped around for an hour on the phone or the Web, you could cut it to about $800. Your gap is –$200, meaning you plan to decrease your spending by $200. The negative numbers are where you plan to decrease your spending, and the positive numbers are where you plan to increase spending. If you add all the gaps together, it should net out to zero as the total amount you outlay has not changed, unless you were running up debt in the past.

As you calculate the gap for each subcategory, be on the lookout for any that are very large compared to the original amount. Stop for a minute and check whether the new level of spending that you plan feels possible, and work out exactly what it will take to change it. There may even be some categories where you cut spending to zero. Again, check in with yourself to make sure that you really want to choose to stop all spending in that area. If you have made some cutbacks in your plan that you know you really won't implement, your whole plan will fail as it falls into the too-hard basket. You are still you. A plan does not mean that you suddenly find a depth of self-control or an ability to brown bag every day if that is really against your nature. Make sure that your Conscious Spending Plan strikes the right balance between moving you to where you want to be and allowing for the reality of being human. Some big gaps may be easy for you because the Conscious Spending Model has helped you realize that you simply want to let go of some unaligned spending. However, if you are expecting yourself to be frugal when you never have been before, think again. Does your plan feel doable? Is there a way of making your plan workable and compelling? Does your excitement about having more of what you want outweigh your concern about needing to decrease spending in areas where you have chosen to cut back? If you answer no to any of these questions, revisit your dreams and values, and rework the plan until you can make room for at least one very compelling item. Your vision needs to excite you enough that you will take action on it. Remember, this plan is not only about your money, but also about your *life*. Spend it like you mean it!

CHAPTER 13

....

Keeping Conscious

Designing a New Hip-Pocket Habit

A PLAN WITHOUT ACTION IS WORTHLESS; JUST ANOTHER DISTRAC-tion in your life. This chapter helps you take your Conscious Spending Plan from the realm of wishes to the solid landscape of actuality. This chapter helps you choose new behaviors to integrate your Conscious Spending Plan into everyday money management. We look at how to motivate yourself to move forward; long-run versus short-run plans; and the structures, systems, and habits you can integrate into your everyday life to become a Conscious Spender.

Planning to Succeed

Have you ever started the year out with great resolutions and a heart full of hope that *this* time will be different, this time you will follow through? Join the club! There's a reason why all the diet and fitness companies advertise in January and stop around March—by March most of us have spent more time pushing the remote control buttons than pumping iron, and the resolutions are shelved for another year.

Creating a Conscious Spending Plan is different. The plan is naturally compelling because it focuses you on what you *want*, not what you think you *should* do. The difference between a "want" and a "should" is night and day. Wants are motivating by nature. Shoulds feel like hard work. As we go through this chapter, you will find ways of remaining in touch with the compelling parts of your plan. Of course, the plan is not should-free. It is based on the three rules, two of which may feel like great big shoulds to you. However, the third rule is all about what you want, and those dreams should be compelling enough that you view the first two rules as doing what you need to do to get what you want. Another way that the plan might feel as if it is full of shoulds is if your list of wants are much greater than your available funds. This situation is a tough one. How do you put your other wants on the back burner until you can either increase your earnings or wait until they reach the top of the pile? The good news is that having more on your want list than you can easily afford means that you have plenty of incentive to keep ratcheting back your expenses in the areas that are not at the top of your list. (To improve your earnings in the long run, take a look at the ideas in Chapter 15.) The key to staying motivated toward changing your spending is to remember that the shoulds are self-imposed. They come from your desire to get more of what you want from your money, while still choosing to live within your means and take care of your future.

Your Conscious Spending Plan defines how you want to use your money. For some of you, only small tweaks are needed to get on track with your Conscious Spending Plan. For others, there is a significant challenge: It's not simply a redirection, it is a whole change of course. Your plan reflects your unique set of values and how you want to express those values. Implementing the plan and managing your money day-to-day requires the same level of personalization.

In the introduction to this book, I talked about the difference between simple and easy. Changing your pattern of spending may sound simple; however, it may not be easy to do because you have years and years of habits to break. My aim is to make it easier. Some books have thousands of ideas about how to cut back expenses and live within your means. They might tell you that you should freeze your credit card in a block of ice to make it inaccessible, or that you should carry only $20 with you at any one time, or that you should have only one bank account. The underlying assumption in those rules—those shoulds—is that your way of behaving around money fits some kind of formula. If you have some of those books, don't throw them away. Look through them for ideas that appeal to you. Some ideas may be useful to many people, but the way that you move your plan into action will be different from anyone else's. The best way for *you* to live within your means, take care of your future, and maximize your pleasure is probably very different than the best way for someone else. In this chapter, you can learn how to create a personalized set of structures, systems, and habits.

Getting Your Subconscious on Your Side

I talked earlier about how a Conscious Spending Plan is naturally compelling because it draws you to it by focusing on what you want. However, habits are hard to break, and sometimes it takes more than a dream of getting what you want to change your behavior.

There are two types of motivation: one that I call *racehorse* and one that I call *greyhound*. Both types of motivation move you forward but in very different ways. A greyhound is compelled to run because he sees a hare racing ahead and instinct pulls him forward to try to catch it. There's the sheer joy of going for what he wants in a greyhound's racing. The racehorse is compelled to run because he has a jockey on his back goading him forward with a whip. It's hard work for the horse and hard work for the jockey.*

The part of the Conscious Spending Model that is naturally compelling, that has the greyhound's "pulling-forward" energy, is the part that taps into what you want and promises more good stuff. For some people, however, it may also be necessary to use the racehorse's "pushing-through" energy.

Pushing through requires a strong enough incentive to keep you driving forward. As I wrote this book and got to the tough task of just getting it done, I found I needed to resort to this pushing-through energy. Greyhound energy drove me forward in the beginning, with excitement about the book leading me to write a proposal and sample chapters and the first very rough draft of my book. That phase was fueled by the positive images of having a book published, helping people with the concepts in it, and publicizing it. When I got to the final stretch and all the fun thinking and planning had been done, I had to move into racehorse mode (although at the pace I was going, I'd have been horsemeat). I was pushing through, running from unpleasant images such as a disappointed agent, an angry publisher, and the embarrassment of letting my friends and family know that I just couldn't get the book written. The fact that you're reading this means that the racehorse crossed the finish line—eventually!

To harness the greyhound energy, get a clear, compelling picture of what you want. You may want to get creative about how

---

*I'm not saying it is bad or unpleasant for the horse; it is simply a good metaphor for the different motivational styles.

you do this. Clients have done everything from writing a detailed description to collecting pictures that motivate them. One client carries a picture of his dream boat (literally a boat, not that other type of dreamboat!) in his wallet. It's easier to say no to little expenses when he knows such spending is keeping him away from his big dream. Another has images from magazines, photos, cards, and so on that she has crafted into a collage. Really harnessing that greyhound energy means keeping a vivid and compelling image of why you are choosing to make this change to become a Conscious Spender.

The process of harnessing the racehorse energy is similar, but this time you are turning up the volume on a negative picture. If you are more motivated to move away from something that is uncomfortable, create a strong picture in your mind of the cost of not taking action. Imagine a life where you cannot have anything that you want, any of those items that you put at the top of your priority list. For example, if you find you resist saving for retirement, paint a vivid and scary picture about how uncomfortable your life will be if you retire with little in the way of savings. Picture your friends all going off to enjoy an active retirement while you are stuck at home without the resources you need. Picture begrudgingly working part time to simply keep your mortgage paid. Keep painting a bleaker and bleaker picture until you find a way to motivate yourself to take action. A famous editor, who probably is very comfortably off, wrote an article a few years back on how she had a deep-seated fear of ending up as an impoverished bag lady. She knew it was an irrational fear, but that deep-seated fear drives her to be successful and make some smart financial decisions.

. . . .

Jackie, a businesswoman in Las Vegas, knows the value of having a negative image to provide an incentive for positive action. As she looks back, Jackie recalls that impulse spending was her weakest point: "I would just go out and see [what I wanted] and say 'You just got to get it, can't wait, have to do it now'." She slowly got into financial trouble: "You know, the kind of trouble where you don't answer the phone." She eventually paid down the debt, partly helped by a lump sum from a tax return and a family gift, and swore never to get in the same situation again. "I have one credit card, and it has a small limit," she says. "I never want to have the bill collectors calling again." That negative memory alone provides enough motivation to keep her on track with her new financial program.

. . . .

Would it be nicer to find a positive way to motivate yourself? Sure, whipping yourself into shape is never fun and takes a whole lot of energy. However, if you have or need to use a whip to move yourself into action, use it!

From Here to There

Look at your plan and how it varies from where you are today. How many of the changes that you plan to make involve major decisions versus minor tweaks? Choosing to change where you live is a much more momentous decision than choosing to cut back on lunches. Can the changes happen overnight or will they take some time? You can change your cable subscription with a single phone call, but to change your Shelter expense may take time: waiting out a lease, moving your household, or doing a few weekends worth of delayed maintenance. Are there some major steps that have to take place before you can settle into an ongoing plan? You may be facing a mountain of debt and may not be able to think about building Security until you move the debt out of your way. Another reason that a short-term plan may differ from a long-term one is that you may choose to have an intense period of building toward a goal: a comfortable cash cushion, the down payment on a house, a kick-start to your retirement fund.

If the changes will take some time, look at your plan from both short-term and long-term perspectives. In the short term, you may have a steep hill to climb or may be trapped with higher costs based on your current patterns. If your short-term plan requires some pretty heavy spending cuts, find a balance between moving quickly toward your goal and giving yourself enough slack so that you don't quickly give up and revert to past habits.

Your long-term plan may feel a lot more doable than your short-term plan, because some of the money that you initially focus on those key goals is freed up for what you really enjoy. While the long-term plan may reflect how you want your spending plan to look eventually, recognize that your plan may evolve as you move toward it. Changes in your life situation, the way you want to express your values, and your financial situation mean that your plan will evolve as your life evolves. Reassess it at least once a year, as well as any time that you experience a major shift in your life that is likely to change your spending patterns.

Even with a strong and compelling plan, it is very easy to slip back into your old money management ways. Success requires having structures and habits that support you in your quest to align spending with values.

Structures and Systems

Just as a city's infrastructure is a network of roads, pipes, and wires that help its residents connect, your financial structure is a series of accounts and tools that support your financial journey. You can create a tangled web (oh, what a tangled web your wallet weaves . . .) or a simple structure. The systems are the transactions that link the structures and also may be complex or simple. Your structure consists of all the accounts you have, including savings, checking, investment and retirement accounts, and credit cards, and your system consists of the transactions that you make in order to use the accounts.

There is no one structure or system that works for everyone because we all behave differently with our money. I once saw a TV segment on customs dogs being trained to find drugs. When the dogs uncovered the drug bait used in training, they were rewarded and praised so highly that they quickly transformed from working dogs into incredibly excited puppies. There are some people who react the same way if you put a credit card in their hand. Their mind goes blank, the future is erased, and a world of instant possibilities open up. At the other end of the scale, there are those who interact with their money like a three-year-old child who is determined not to share his or her toy. They only part with their money after it has been pried from their clenched hands. The structures and systems that work for you may depend a lot on whether you are a Spender or a Saver by nature. A Spender who gets into binge buying won't be supported by the same structures as a Saver who thinks that skipping one contribution to his or her retirement account is living on the edge.

. . . .

Once a week, Tracy and Brendan get their "allowance." "At the beginning of the week, my husband and I both get a certain amount of cash out of the bank, and that's it, unless something really big comes up." The stores that they own and run are close to a variety of restaurants, and convenience eating used to make up a substantial part of their everyday spending. Now, they use cash for all lunches, snacks, and random expenses such as tolls and parking fees. This structure is supporting their aim to decrease spending on nonsocial meals. "I *like that using cash makes me conscious," Tracy tells me. "When I am using a credit card, I don't care what I order at a restaurant. However, I like caring about what I order. I think 'I can have this, but this other thing that costs $5 less tastes just as good to me. I would get just as much enjoyment out of it.' I find that paying with cash brings me to think that through."*

. . . .

Structures and systems can range from very simple to complex. A simple structure may include one account with savings, checking, and investments integrated into it, one debit or credit card, and that's it. A complex structure may include numerous accounts, multitudes of credit cards and store cards, several loans, and so on. A simple system may include all savings and major bills being on autopay, and all other bills being paid once a month by check. A complex system may include transferring cash between various accounts, paying bills as they arrive, or filing them and having a last minute scramble, and using various checking accounts to pay different bills. Among my clients, I've had some who are supported by having a single account, and others who have set up what looks like a complex set of accounts, but a set that really works for them. One woman deliberately had a number of accounts because she knew that if she saw the money in one place, she was likely to feel affluent and spend it. She had an everyday spending account, a cash-cushion account, a vacation and holiday savings account, an account for annual expenses such as insurance, and so on. Another person in one of my classes skipped the accounts for everyday spending altogether and set up a series of envelopes labeled "groceries," "lunch," "clothes," "personal care," "gas," and so on, depositing the month's planned spending in each envelope at the start of each month. When the money ran out, she stopped spending or made a conscious transfer between the envelopes. If there was some left over at the end of the month, it was used for a treat.

....

Steve redesigned all his financial structures and systems after taking a Conscious Spending class. "Before, even if I had the money, I was not keeping up with my bill payments," he said. "The bills would sit in a pile on my desk, and when it finally bothered me enough, I'd pay them and then have to pay late fees." A 40-year-old computer engineer for a high-tech government agency, the move to on-line banking was an obvious step. "I now do my banking and all my bill paying on-line, I have been up to date on all my bills," he said. "Simplifying the structure feels awesome. It has enabled me to do other things too: keep track of what's going on, know what my balance is, know how much I have on credit, and what's getting paid for."

"I'm more conscious of my money in a friendlier way. Before it was something I dreaded doing—the check just went in the account and then I spent it. Now I can plan what's going on. I have all my debts on a list and I can knock them out. If I pay that debt completely off, I can scrub that name off the list. Like Space Invaders . . . 'take that!' "

....

My financial structure and system used to be bare bones. I had one account that was an investment account with checks and a debit card, which I used for all cash withdrawals, I had one credit card, and I had my retirement accounts with one investment firm. My systems were on autopilot. My pay was directly deposited, with my retirement contribution automatically taken out. My credit card, which I used for every transaction over $10, was paid off in full by direct debit every month. My utility bills and mortgages were also on automatic payment systems. If I were hit by a truck, my financial life (except for the income!) would have gone on smoothly without me. This simplicity worked well for me; however, I had to change my structure and system once I became self-employed. Now I keep business and personal money separate and have more than doubled the paperwork. I miss the old days, but my accountant is happier. While this simplicity worked for me, some clients are horrified, knowing that in their hands, the investment account would be run down to zero every month. The point is to create a system that works for you, without taking up the one resource that feels scarcer than money: time.

One quick aside about bill paying: I'm a huge fan of setting up automatic payments (electronic funds transfers). I have friends who pay their bills using the Internet or the telephone; however, the great thing about automatic payments is that you don't have to do a thing—not log on, not make a call, not write a check, nothing, *nada*—once the system is set up. With any direct payment, you can still call up and challenge any bill if you think there is an error or need to override it for a month. Note that automatic payments are usually set up with the company that bills you, not your bank. And there is rarely a charge for it (once I had a mortgage company charge $1 a month to process my payment). Your bank should not charge you because to them it is just a normal check. If they charge you, change banks. Electronic funds transfers *save* the bank money, so you shouldn't be asked to pay for them. The transfers may also save you money: You will never again pay a late fee because of a forgotten payment. There's nothing to lose, and time to save. Another useful system: Some utility companies offer a plan to smooth your costs over the year. For example, my gas company lets me pay the same amount each month rather than a high amount in winter and very low amount in summer.

Another part of your structure is how you track your spending and saving. Computers have taken the sting out of balancing checkbooks, tracking your annual spending, and seeing how you are going against your plan. With the Internet allowing information from most bank, investment, and credit accounts to be downloaded directly into software, tracking where all your money goes is easier than ever. Software such as Quicken and Microsoft Money are great, although I have some clients who are very happy with a monthly handwritten table, or who only track areas where they know there is a big potential for variation. Again, there is no right answer, so find what works for you.

Exercise: Spring Clean Your Structures and Systems

Take one morning to edit the structures and systems in your financial life. First, find all your credit and debit cards, including all those store cards and gasoline cards that have found their way to the bottom of your junk drawer. Separate the credit and debit cards into those that you use regularly and those that you never use. For the unused ones, phone or write a letter to cancel each one, and once signed and sealed, cut them up. For the cards you use: If you have more than one, ask yourself if that is supporting your life or complicating it? Is there one card with a high enough credit limit to support all your monthly spending? If not, can you request an increased limit so that you only need one card? Do you have an outstanding balance on any cards? How much can you pay off today? Is there a way to consolidate your loans on one card with a low interest rate? Call each company whose card you choose to keep and set up automatic payment of the full amount each month or as much as you can afford. While you are on the phone, ask them to lower their interest rate (they may not say yes, but it is worth a try).

Then, pull out one copy of each of the bills and loans you pay on a monthly or quarterly basis. Call the customer service number of each entity and request a form to set up automatic payment, or arrange to have your payment paid by credit card every month, if (and only if!) you pay your card off in full each month. The day you receive a form, fill it out, attach a voided check, and return it.

Finally, take one statement of each of the investment, savings, checking, and retirement accounts that you have. What is the smallest number of accounts that can serve your needs? Are there any that can be consolidated? Does your bank or brokerage firm offer a combined checking and savings/investment account? Do you have retirement accounts with past employers that can be rolled into a single retirement account? Will an automatic investment plan help you save? Call your financial institutions and arrange to take any steps that you need to create a structure that supports you.

. . . .

Habits

While your structures and systems describe how you manage your money over the month or year, habits are how you interact with money on a daily basis. You may have habits that really support you, and you may have some that are hurting your finances.

Changing habits is more difficult that changing your structures and systems. Changing habits requires changing your behavior, and it may take time to integrate new habits. Changing habits is like trying to drive down a dirt road with deep ruts. Even though you intend to keep out of the ruts, your tires may slip back into the path of least resistance—the ruts.

The key to creating habits that support your financial goals is to create habits that you want (if you think you *should* have them, you'll stop them soon), that address your spending stress points, and that you find easy to implement. So keep it simple and relevant, and try to create motivating habits.

. . . .

Peter spoke up in the Conscious Spending class, excited to have found a small but significant financial leak. "If I have cash, I spend it, so I try to spend less by only ever getting $20 from an ATM at a time. The ATM near work is not part of my bank, so I pay not only $1 to my bank, but also $1.50 to the bank whose ATM I use—which means I pay more than 10 percent in fees every time I get cash," he told the group. "The really bad part is that I get cash probably once a day. Twice sometimes. I'm probably spending $20 a week on bank fees, all because I habitually use ATMs like most people use their wallet," he said. I jumped on the calculator. Over 10 years, that would add up to more than $16,000 if it were invested with a 10 percent return. He chose to play with new cash habits: He now gets $200 cash at a time, puts all but $20 in a safe place at home and each day, he takes $20 and puts it in his wallet. "The only tough part is the few hours that I have the full $200 cash in my hands. It's tempting to just spend it."

. . . .

Many of your habits probably have to do with how you interact with cash or a credit card. Habits may involve what you carry and where you go. One habit that supports many people is to be deliberately cash poor (the "deliberate self-delusion strategy"), which involves carrying only $20 or even only $5 in cash at any time to help break little "frittering-away" habits such as picking up lunch, taking trips to the vending machine, and buying things that just catch your eye. Another habit that many choose is to leave credit cards at home, or even freeze them in a chunk of ice (so that you have to take the time to thaw the ice if you want to use them) if extra control is needed. Others carry their card, but keep track of their expenditures by running a total on a slip of paper, rounding the money up to the nearest $10 each time both to make the math easier and to give the illusion of having spent more than they actually have. Some get very creative with their habits. One person carries a feather in her wallet next to the cash. This simple thing of beauty stops her for a second when she reaches for cash and reminds her that she wants to use money to align with her values of simplicity and beauty.

One habit that I began consciously but have now integrated into my everyday thinking is to run through a series of questions before I buy anything unplanned that is more than about $20. I call the questions my *Safe Spending* questions and have them printed on a credit card sleeve that I slip over my credit card.* The questions remind me to stop and think before I spend; they are:

- Can I afford this without borrowing money?
- What else would be more aligned with my values?
- Will I be glad I bought this 1 year from now?
- Who am I trying to impress? (Tip: I know I'm on the right track if the answer is: "No one. I can afford it and I want it for my own enjoyment.")

. . . .

Tracy slips her Palm Pilot out as we talk and starts scrawling quickly in the graffiti that the machine reads. She uses her Palm for everything from note taking to reminders. "I keep the Safe Spending questions and a list of the financial habits that I chose when I took your Conscious Spending class on my Palm Pilot," she said. "And I just read them a couple of times a week or when I go to record an expense. It keeps me focused on my goals and makes me think twice about whether what I am buying really aligns with my values." She uses the ritual of looking at the questions as a way of stopping and thinking. "When the feeling of really wanting something comes over me, be it

---

*I give out preprinted sleeves at classes, book signings, media events, and so on. Grab one next time I'm in town.

dessert or something I see as I walk by a shop window, I know that it is not rational. It's a feeling like 'Oh, wouldn't it be so cool?' or 'I really want dessert.' It's an emotional thing and in that moment, I'm not remembering any of the reasons why I might not want to do that." By referring to the questions, Tracy is able to step back from the desire for a short-term high and check in with her Conscious Spending Plan. *"It's not like I want to stamp out that feeling, I just want to know that I'm really making a choice and I'm considering my values in that choice."*

. . . .

Some habits that support you concerning money may have nothing to do with money directly. For example, one client had been taking a break each afternoon to walk out for a gourmet mochalattecino (the more Italian-sounding syllables strung together, the better it sounds!). After looking at what she was spending, she asked herself what she truly valued. She realized that what she valued was a brain break—just a walk to get air into her head. She kept her habit of taking the afternoon break, but changed the destination: She filled her water bottle and wandered to the park and back. Better for her hips and hip pocket. Another client chose to meditate for 10 minutes each morning. From a more centered place, she was less likely to soothe her soul through quick fixes costing big bucks. I enjoy volunteering one night a week to play with kids at a local nonprofit agency. Even though I do it for the fun of being with the kids, I always walk away aware that my tempting spend of the day really is not important in the bigger scheme of things.

Another way to bring supportive habits into your life is to set up a Conscious Spending circle. It is easier to adopt a new way of interacting with your money when you spend time with people who have a shared goal of becoming Conscious Spenders. Find a

group of at least seven people who share your goals, and set up a time to touch base at least once a month. You don't even have to get together in person; e-mail can be a very time-efficient way of checking in with each other and having an ongoing discussion.*
Better still, set up a group on-line where you can hold live chats as well as post tips and send messages to the group.† The key is to have a level of accountability to each other so that you stay on track, as well as share tips and ideas that work for you. I help Conscious Spending circles by offering a 10-session program that provides a structure you may want to follow.‡

You can also reinforce new habits by reading publications that support your goals. Spend some time browsing the magazine stand to see what publications appeal to you. There are plenty out there, from investment publications such as *Money* and *Individual Investor*, to lifestyle publications that can help you focus on what you really want, like the *Simple Living Journal*. Also look for publications that help you stay focused on your Soul spending goals. Whether you aim to travel more, take up a craft, spend time with your family, stay on the cutting edge of fashion without going broke, or restore old cars, there's a publication (or 10) targeted at you. Browse them for ideas and inspiration.

Exercise: Habitually Yours, or Choosing Habits That Support You

Create some habits that will help you easily move toward the financial goals in your life.

---

*For people who don't want to organize a small group, I have a free monthly teleclass or a biweekly newsletter that may help you stay on track. Information is available on www.MsSpent.com.
†Try the free service at www.egroups.com.
‡Find it in the resources section of my website at www.MsSpent.com.

Take a week or two to observe how you behave around money and tempting spending situations. Is there a location or emotion that makes you most vulnerable to unplanned spending? Do you find it easier to spend using cash, checks, or credit cards? Is it small or large purchases that do you in? How do you know if you really want to buy something? Do you buy things you are not sure of, thinking that you'll return them?

Then sit down and list 10 habits you would like to have that support you with money. Be creative: A fun variation of string around your finger might be the reminder that you need. Cut the list down to five, and choose some way of tracking how you do against the list for at least 3 weeks. If any one of the habits doesn't work for you, stop it and find another. Check the list every couple of weeks until you really have integrated the habits into your life.

. . . .

One Last Thought

You already have structures, systems, and habits that impact the way you interact with money. Most were probably chosen unconsciously. Whether you have a little money or plenty, moving to conscious structures, systems, and habits can pay big dividends by helping you to remain in charge and to move toward your Conscious Spending Plan. Where possible, create structures, system, and habits that are inherently motivating. Find your rabbit—your dream, your goal—and chase it with a greyhound's glee!

SEVEN WAYS TO STOP THE URGE TO SPLURGE

1. Start with your plan. Make space in your Conscious Spending Plan for at least one big dream a year. Put a dollar tag on your big dream so that you know what you are aiming for.

2. Carry a picture of your big dream in your wallet. The unplanned splurge will look less attractive when you know it keeps you $50 further away from the vacation of your dreams or the education you want to give your kids.

3. Leave your credit cards at home. If you must go on a social shopping trip to the mall, make social shopping purely about knowing what's out there.

4. Make your purchases pass the wish-list test. Only buy items over a certain dollar amount ($50? $100?) if they have been on your wish list for at least 2 weeks.

5. Never buy something the first time you see it. Even if you just walk out of the store for 10 minutes, you will have time to think twice before you purchase.

6. Ask yourself some Safe Spending questions as you open your wallet:

   - Can I afford this without borrowing money?
   - What else would be more aligned with my values?
   - Will I be glad I bought this 1 year from now?
   - Who am I trying to impress?

7. Be prepared. Keep some money aside for spontaneous fun and unplanned crises. Sticking to a strict spending plan is unrealistic for most and not much fun for anyone. Make room in your plan for splurges that add fun to life and crises that can knock you off track.

....

CHAPTER 14

Iceberg Ahead

When You're Weighed Down by Debt

DEBT. NOW THERE'S A FOUR-LETTER WORD MOTHER NEVER WARNED you about. Debt used to carry a social stigma, a whispering behind hands if your dirty secret got out. Before bankruptcy was created, people who got in over their heads financially were sent to debtors' prison, where they usually were forced to work to pay off their debts. After that, it was considered a sign of poor self-control, just as unacceptable as the women who "let themselves go."

Today, having debt has become socially acceptable and barely raises an eyebrow, unless a person is really out of control. It's easier to get a credit card or store card than it is to get a driver's license, temptation to purchase is everywhere, people accept higher levels of risk, and our culture supports instant gratification.

People get into debt for a lot of reasons. Most people who default on loans have both a low income and a low net worth. Simply struggling to get by on a low income can be the start of trouble for many people. For some people, getting into debt is a case of bad planning combined with bad luck. By not taking care of Se-

curity, they do not have a cushion to protect them from the blows
life occasionally throws. An accident, divorce, illness, or retrench-
ment can put under someone with no savings, even if they don't
have much debt. Many of the people who file for bankruptcy cite
a specific incident that set the ball rolling.* However, the National
Bankruptcy Review Commission pointed out that when households are in debt, these "ordinary and not-so-ordinary troubles
that families weathered a generation ago may become unmanage-
able for a family that has already committed several paychecks to
meet monthly bills."† For many more people, getting into debt is a
gradual journey, like slowly walking into the ocean and suddenly
realizing that you're up to your neck. It happens by consistently
putting today's wants and whims ahead of tomorrow's needs. The
desire to have something now outweighs what it costs. Finally,
there are also people who buy into spending patterns without understanding the Lifetime Cost that they are taking on; for example, they buy a house with an affordable mortgage but then find
that utility bills, taxes, and maintenance costs drag them under.

Whether it was bad luck, bad planning, or plain bad self-control that got you into debt, now is not the time for self-flagellation.
Beating yourself up, analyzing the whys, or railing against the bad
turn of events is not going to get you out of the situation. All you
can do today is change the way you choose to spend your money
from here on out. Now the only important thing is how to get out
and stay out, of debt.

Although debt may arise from being out of control with money,
debt itself has a way of controlling you. Whether you are actively

_____

*Consumer Bankruptcy: Causes and Implications, VISA Consumer Bankruptcy Re-
ports 13, Visa U.S.A. Inc., July 1996.
†Bankruptcy: The Next Twenty Years, National Bankruptcy Review Commission
Final Report, October 20, 1997, p. 86.

paying down debt or attempting not to notice it, it's there as a background noise that prevents you from spending your money on what you really want. I don't know of one kid who has sat on Santa's knee and asked for more interest to pay.

....

The phone rang, and Donna ignored it. "The answering machine will get it," she explained, not wanting to break off our discussion. But the interruption derailed her train of thought and led her to an earlier time. "You know, it wasn't that long ago that I would ignore the phone out of fear that it was a credit card company." She explained that this was in the days before caller ID. "I just never knew if it was a credit card company calling to harass me. Those calls were so hard to take, because they'd pretend to be caring, but would turn and start implying that I was stupid or lazy or lying. If I had had the money, I would have been paying them back. The whole time was really unpleasant."

Her debt had grown out of a small but consistent habit of overspending. "It's hard when you are a parent not to give your kids what they want. I know the pain of being the poor kid at school, and I didn't want them to know that." But over the years, the debt had grown to be equal to almost a year's after-tax income. "Once it got too big, it felt like I could never get back in control. Up until 3 or 4 years ago, sticking my head in the sand was the only way I knew how to deal with it. I dealt with the crises as they came along. Pleading with the water company not to turn the water off and then scurrying around with all sorts of acrobatics to get the money together." Donna eventually climbed out of debt, getting a job that paid more, learning to say no to her kids, and seeking the help of a consumer credit group that negotiated lower payments and helped her create a plan. "The irony is that now I can afford to buy my kids some nice stuff because I'm not spending hundreds of dollars a month on interest," she mused.

. . . .

If you are in deep debt, know that you are not alone, if that is any consolation. In fact, if your only debt is a mortgage, student loans, or car loans, you are better off than most. The amount of household debt is rising, and almost three-quarters of all families have some kind of debt and almost half have credit card debt.* At the same time as households have been getting into more and more debt, many lenders have lowered the minimum monthly payment on revolving debt such as credit cards to only 2 percent of the total. This means that people who are deeply in debt, say, with $20,000 on their credit cards, may still feel that they are getting by because they can afford the monthly payment of $400. All it takes is one trip-up in income flow to realize just how heavy the burden of that $20,000 debt is. When you look at extreme cases— those that end in bankruptcy—you'll find there's plenty of company there, too. More than 1.2 million households declared bankruptcy in 1999, showing a trend down from the record levels of the year before but still a very high number.†

Debt Versus Obligation

A debt is something you owe someone else. I find that word has been sanitized; just another accounting term that has lost the true weight of its meaning. I prefer the word *obligation*, because it carries with it the heaviness of having to do something that you

---

*Survey of Consumer Finances, Federal Reserve Board.
†Consumer Federation of America, January 18, 2000, press release.

would otherwise rather not do. Obligation is visiting your crotchety old relative. Obligation is listening to your boss's husband recount his dull sailing stories again. Obligation is paying back some money you owe that you'd really rather walk away from. Obligation is no fun, but you have to do it, which is why I like the word in this context.

Another reason why I like the word *obligation* is that it has commitment written all over it. Remember being young and unencumbered? No debt, no large pieces of furniture; you could pick up and leave town for a job (or a partner) of your dreams without putting too much on the line. I remember the day I bought my first bed. I was about 22 and had a roommate who owned the couch, TV, dining room table, and so on. All I contributed was a chest of drawers that my mother had given me, a bedside table I had scrounged, and a couple of lamps. That bed felt like my first dose of adult responsibility. With both the joy of growing up and the sadness of clipped wings, I realized that I no longer could fit all of my possessions into my little car. Debt is a burden far larger than a queen size bed. If you have debt, it is harder to walk away from a job you don't like or run toward a dream you have always held in your heart. It is harder to leave a relationship that doesn't support you or to drive into a new sunset in a new town. Obligation means that you are stuck. And stuck means you have less freedom to go for a life that you would really love.

Is Debt a Problem?

. . . .

"I always strongly believed that if I could afford to pay my monthly payments, I was doing fine," Brad told me one day. He earned a reasonable amount in a steady job, and could meet his monthly obliga-

tions of his mortgage, car loan, and $10,000 of credit card debt. "I mean, it was not like I was living extravagantly; it was just a couple of thousand a year more than I earned. My credit card payment had grown, but it was only $250 a month, which didn't feel like much compared to my mortgage and car." After a while, however, Brad realized that the debt had a cost much larger than just the interest. "Suddenly I had this boss whom I hated, and my best buddy moved to California. I wanted to do that, too; you know, just uproot and run away. But I couldn't afford the couple of months of transition that he had, and it's next to impossible to job hunt from a distance."

Looking back, he philosophizes about the time. "If I had had the money, I may still not have moved, but it was like the debt was a ball and chain that limited my ability to make my own choices. When I lost my job 2 months later, I really felt the debt's weight and was very lucky that I landed an okay position within a month. It's okay, but I don't love it." While he is sticking out the job, he has made a commitment to paying off his debt. "Nowadays, I just can't stomach having so few choices."

. . . .

Brad's starting philosophy isn't unusual; even the federal government operates from a place of focusing on whether it can afford monthly payments for its debt. (It even claims to have a surplus in months when its inflows are a little larger than the outflows plus debt repayment. If I were sitting on an equivalent amount of debt, I'd hardly claim to have a surplus!*)

Debt is a problem for several reasons. First, debt makes what you buy a lot more expensive. If you pay cash or pay your credit

---

*At the time of writing, that debt amount was about $90,000 per household. Check the national debt clock at http://www.toptips.com/debtclock.html for the current total, and, of course, add in some for state and local government debt.

card off in full each month, your $200 jacket costs $200 (plus tax). When you use a credit card and pay only the minimum amount due, it may cost 20 percent or so more, depending on your interest rate and the amount of time that you roll the debt over. If you are prone to being charged late fees or overlimit fees, the cost is even greater. With a Full Cost such as that, would you still think the jacket is a good buy? In addition, the interest expense eats up money. If your consumer debt payments are zero, there's a lot more room in your Conscious Spending Plan for the things you enjoy.

As Brad found out, debt makes you vulnerable to unplanned events and limits you from going for the life you really want. I've had a varied career (that's a nice way of saying I've jumped around a lot), and often when I've made more radical changes, such as quitting a fairly lucrative job in banking in order to become a reporter, friends have told me that I'm lucky. Luck has had nothing to do with it. Sure, I possess an unusually high willingness to change, but the only way I have been able to afford the changes has been by never feeling weighed down by past decisions. Brad's story is the opposite. His spending habits in the past are dictating his current situation and preventing him from trying for a life he really loves.

But for me, the biggest problem with debt is philosophical: How can you really live your life in the present if you are spending your future earnings?

How Bad Is It?

The first step to getting out of debt is to know how far in debt you are. Start by taking a look at all of your financial obligations. In the following exercise you will add up the total burden, so you can begin to plan how to get out from under it.

Not all debt is bad. Debt can either be secured (linked to an underlying asset, such as a house or a bank account) or unsecured (without an underlying asset that can be drawn upon in case of default). A mortgage is generally considered good debt: The interest is tax deductible, it is secured with an underlying asset that it is hoped will appreciate in value, and the money is used to purchase something that few of us could ever afford if we had to pay cash. It is still an obligation—if you don't pay, you lose your house—but it is an obligation that most of us embrace in one of those nesting urges. A student loan is also arguably good debt, because it is a necessity for many people who aim to get a job in a field that has good earning potential.

As we look at your total obligations, we start by including all debt so that you get a full picture, and then removing your mortgage. Because all debt means you are spending money on interest rather than on other things that are closer to your values, we will include your student loans and auto loans in the look at debt.

Exercise: How Big Is Your Iceberg?

Your personal finances are less likely to sink you if you fully understand the size of the debt. Depending on how organized your financial records are, getting a handle on your debt may take half an hour or half a day. If your record keeping is really poor, you may need to gather the mail you receive over a month to double check that you recorded every debt. On a spreadsheet or a piece of paper, make columns for each of the following: priority, amount of debt, interest rate, monthly payment (or minimum monthly payment), description of debt (student, automobile, consumer), and what you received for the money spent (see Table 14.1). Then, starting with the big debts and working down, list all of your debts. Don't forget store credit cards, items being purchased under a layaway plan, and home-equity loans that are in addition to your base mortgage. Exclude any cards that you pay off in full every month. Take a deep breath and add up the amount of debt column. If it is big, don't expect this exercise to be easy; it can be very difficult to admit just how deeply in debt you are. This first step shows your total obligations. How many months or years of work does that total debt represent? What proportion of your monthly after-tax income goes to debt repayment?

If you have a mortgage, the good news is that you can now take that line away, and create a second total line that excludes the mortgage. Ask yourself the same questions as before.

Table 14.1

			Sample Debt Analysis		
Priority	Total Amount Owed	Interest Rate (APR%)	Monthly Payment ($)	Description of Debt	What I Got for It
Lowest	150,000	8.25	1,126.90	Fannie Mae mortgage	A home
3	10,500	6.92	121.48	Sallie Mae student	An education
2	6,255	9.25	64.38	HomeEqqus home equity	Trip to Europe, furniture
1	3,500	18.90	(min.)58.65	CrediCorp credit card	Social life, clothes, car repairs, repairs on home, gifts
Total	170,255		1,371.41		
Excluding mortgage	20,255		244.51		

Notes: For example, the household has a $50,000 income, mortgage, student loan, home-equity loan, credit cards, and no car loan.

Years of income = 3.40 years with mortgage, 0.41 years excluding mortgage.

Percent of pretax income = 32.9 percent with mortgage, 5.7 percent excluding mortgage.

Now fill in the last column. Some will be easy, some hard. Is your credit card debt due to the purchase of clothing or food? If you only charge clothing on your credit card, that's easy. If you put both clothing and food on the credit card but don't pay the balance in full, assume that the debt is related to the nonessential parts of your spending. So for a credit card balance that includes clothing, food from supermarkets, and restaurant meals, assume that it is the cost of clothes and restaurant meals that are carried over. In retrospect, was it worth getting into debt for those things? Would you feel more comfortable if you had trimmed some corners then and been out of debt now?

Finally, fill in the first column. Put your mortgage at the lowest priority—it makes no sense to repay a mortgage early. Put any other loans with tax deductible interest next. Finally, rank the loans by the interest rate charged, with the highest interest rate loans being the number-one priority. This priority listing is the order in which you want to repay the debt. Of course, you need to keep up the monthly payments on all obligations, but the number-one priority debt will be the first focus of additional repayment.

. . . .

Kick-Starting Debt Repayment

Now that you have a good understanding of how much debt you have and know which debts you aim to repay first, I provide five strategies that can make repayment easier or provide a kick-start to your repayment plan.

Digging out from debt, like eating an elephant, has to be done one bite at a time. Too many people try to get out of debt the way they got into it, with a feast-and-famine approach. As their debt built up, they tried to stop all spending to cut their debt, only to fail and go on a spending spree that just put them deeper in debt.

Just as a crash diet leads to weight that yo-yos between "Ugh" and "I'm never being seen in public again," crash debt repayment leads to finances that yo-yo between "Help" and "Maybe bankruptcy is the only way out." There is a better way. As for bankruptcy, I get to that later.

So what is crash debt repayment? It is the cold turkey approach: cutting up all credit cards, swearing off any spending beyond the absolute basics, and committing to brown-bagging every day, pasta and marinara sauce every night, and absolutely no fun that costs anything. For most of you, a crash approach will leave you feeling deprived, overwhelmed, and more likely to break out with debt-inducing "retail therapy." Is the crash approach doomed to failure? Not always. Mary Hunt, publisher of *Cheapskate Monthly*, dug herself out of over $100,000 in consumer debt by using radical scrimping and saving. She's a cheapskate and proud of it. Her newsletter is full of penny-saving tips from reheeling worn-out shoes to stretching ground beef with oatmeal.* If you have that level of discipline, great; you can hit your debt on the head quickly. But most of us don't. If we try to cut spending to the quick, it hurts and we stop doing it.

A kick-start is a little less aggressive than a crash. Kick-starting debt repayment involves taking a strong action toward paying down your debt, but not so strong that the effort is unsustainable. It means accepting some short-term pain for long-term gain by looking closely at your plan to make sure you are really being as aggressive as you comfortably can be. So as you create your Conscious Spending Plan, work out what an aggressive, but *comfortable*, amount of debt repayment every month is. Okay, perhaps slightly uncomfortable.

---

*Many of her newsletter tips were gathered into a book: Mary Hunt, *The Complete Cheapskate: How to Get Out of Debt, Stay Out, and Break Free from Money Worries Forever* (Nashville, Tenn.: Broadman and Holman Publishers, 1998).

How much is enough? A good number to aim for is 20 percent of your income so you can afford at least 10 percent for Security and some for fun when the debt repayment is done. However, you are more likely to succeed in cutting debt if you plan for some fun money today. A balanced diet has room for a little chocolate, and a balanced spending plan—even for someone in debt—has room for a little Soul. So find one or two things that you enjoy spending money on for which you still want to make room. For example, you might see that you can put 15 percent of your income toward debt repayment if you really cut back on your lunch spending, social life, and long distance calls. However, a *comfortable* (or almost) plan might be only 12 percent of income, allowing for a couple of video-and-popcorn nights with friends and a bought lunch every Friday.

As you look at how much you can repay each month, consider the following five strategies.

1. Consolidate Debt at a Lower Interest Rate

If you have more than a couple of outstanding debts, you can make your debt easier to manage by consolidating your loans. It is easier to track and repay one larger debt than a whole lot of smaller ones, and you are less likely to be hit with late fees and other expenses from a number of different lenders. Shop around for the best rate as you look to roll most of your debts into one loan. If you own a house or even if your bank owns most of it, you may be in luck. Often it is possible to consolidate a number of high-interest loans into a single home-equity loan. Home-equity loans have two advantages: They may have a lower interest rate because an asset secures them, and the interest may be tax deductible. Of course, a home-equity loan also means that if you default, the lender has your house as security. I have one big concern about this strategy:

Once your consumer debt has been transformed into a home-equity loan, it is easy to fall into the trap of considering it *good* debt. Don't! A home-equity loan can be a great tool for managing your debt, but if the debt was incurred to buy consumer goods rather than to improve your home, always think of it as consumer debt and aim to repay it as soon as possible.

2. Find Fast Cash

When you were filling in the last column of your debt table, you probably listed some items that you went into debt to buy that now just gather dust. Think of the gym equipment that you bought the last time you went on a workout kick, the strollers that were bought for kids one and two and you now know number three is not going to happen, the WizMo SuperThingo that looked so good on late-night TV, the really great pots you bought to replace the old ones even though your cooking skills consist of heating ready-prepared food. Yard Sale! eBay! Yep. Cash it in, return it (if purchased in recent history), donate it (tax deduction, so keep the receipt), or give it to your favorite cousin instead of buying him that CD for his birthday. Use every cent of the cash raised and the tax deduction that you will receive to gnaw away at your biggest debt.

Another way to find fast cash is around tax time. If you are owed a tax refund, discipline yourself to put it all toward your outstanding debt. Treat it like a bonus that can work for you, rather than another form of income to get frittered away.

3. Think Creatively about Trade-offs

By kick-starting, rather than crashing, debt repayment, you are committing to get your debt down as quickly as you can *without* cutting off all fun. Question everything you want to spend money on; see if it is something you can do without for a while, or at least substitute a lower-priced item for. Can you skip takeout and restaurant meals on the go and eat ready-prepared or home-cooked meals instead? Can you get a roommate to help pay the mortgage or rent? Can you freeze your spending on your wardrobe for a season or two? Can you prepare your meals differently? Can you eat in more often? Can you skip the gourmet coffee 3 days a week? Then ask yourself which one or two lower-cost splurges you need to keep to make this stage sustainable. Will subscribing to a movie cable channel make it easier to cut back on other entertainment costs? Will seeing a band perform at a local bar once a week make it possible to cut back on other social spending? Will having a manicure once a month make it bearable to skip the pedicures and highlighting?

4. Arrange Automatic Payments

If you did not have enough self-discipline to keep your spending in control, assume that you will also run low on the self-discipline to repay your debt consistently. That's okay; you can outsource self-discipline. Set up an automatic payment plan that takes the payments out of your bank account on the day that your salary goes in. If your bank or credit card companies don't let you do that, sit down and write out the next 6 months' worth of checks. Put them in envelopes and write the date that you want to mail them where the stamp will go. Just writing the checks creates a higher level of commitment to paying off the debts.

5. Remove the Source of Temptation

If you were aiming to lose weight, you would not fill your refrigerator with your favorite foods. If you are aiming to cut debt, remove temptation. As you begin to pay down your debt, watch out for people and places that make your debt repayment goal difficult. This strategy may include avoiding malls when you don't have a specific item to shop for, destroying or hiding credit cards, only using a debit card, or throwing away catalogs before you look through them. The less you rub your nose in the fact that you cannot have every whim satisfied, the easier it will be to stick to your debt repayment plan.

. . . .

When John and Patricia started pulling themselves out of debt that had taken them close to bankruptcy, they cut back on most non-necessities in order to speed their way back to solvency. Today, there is a light at the end of the tunnel: Most of their debt has been repaid and their income is increasing. "As the money comes in, the first thing that we are applying it toward is paying down all of our debt, which isn't very much anymore, so that our monthly expenses are minimal. That's important to me because I want to know that as long as we are making $4,000 a month, all of our expenses will be paid," Patricia explains. She has found that repaying debt is not only about Security, but also about simplicity. "It is so much easier not having the hassle of lots of bills coming in, not having large volumes of mail. Even if you can pay all the bills, it takes time and thought. Getting rid of all of the clutter has been very, very important to us."

They are surprised to find that their wants are waning as they get used to living within their means. "Even 6 months ago, going through a catalog I would have thought 'Oh, that'd be great to have and that'd be great to have, as soon as we get the money coming in, that'd be great to have.' Now that we have the money coming in and our credit card debt is getting paid off, I think 'I don't need that, I don't even want that' and they're the exact same things," Patricia said. "I just don't feel the same need for material things as when I was in a period of lack."

. . . .

One of the more difficult challenges is being around friends who are not on a similar path. Some of your friends may be big spenders, so find nonmoney-related activities to share with them. If your best friends think a fun time involves drinks at a nice bar and a meal at a great restaurant, see if you can steer them to a different activity, perhaps entering a competitive sports league that meets after work or going for a run so you can get fit and keep costs down. If they are not the sort of people you can mention your money issues to, tell them you are trying to get fit. Most of us would rather be accused of being a fitness freak than a cheapskate. Another alternative is to participate only partially; join them for drinks, but not the restaurant, for example.

Another tough challenge is recreational shopping. Whether its mall cruising or checking out the latest car show, placing yourself in temples of consumerism is just unfair. Even someone like me who doesn't enjoy shopping much can find 10 things that I want if I spend time aimlessly in a mall. You're only human, so be kind to yourself and avoid the places that make your debt repayment plan seem really hard to follow. And if you are in places of deep temptation, repeat the mantra, "When I get out of debt, I would like to save for a [insert dream purchase here]." You will make your goal of being debt-free more enticing and reinforce your commitment to having the money before making a purchase.

Circling the Wagons

Getting from plan to reality is tough. You wouldn't be in debt if managing your money was easy and life was always fair. No matter how you got into debt, acknowledge that you are taking on a big (maybe huge) challenge to get out of debt. To the degree that you can set up support systems to help you, you can make the task easier. Some support systems may be structural—such as setting up an automatic payment that is deducted from your bank account every payday—or emotional—such as telling your closest friends what you are doing and asking for their encouragement.

I'm a big believer in getting all the help I can to take on tough challenges. One of the best ways to take on any challenge is to do it with a group of friends or acquaintances that have the same goal in mind. One way to connect with people who are practicing Conscious Spending is to talk to friends and find any that are on a like mission. As with having a workout partner, having a buddy to compare notes with and to provide emotional support for each other can make the difference between success and failure. One great resource is Debtors Anonymous, a support group for people who have serious debt problems.* Through them, you can meet a group of people who connect regularly to share their goals, plan their debt reduction, and celebrate their victories. The great thing about a group such as Debtors Anonymous is that you not only will feel you are not alone in this struggle, but you also will build bonds with others who are focused on having more fun with less money. Other great resources are the consumer credit counseling services that offer free or low cost credit counseling in most areas.† They can help you develop a plan and negotiate manageable repayment schemes.

A Word about Bankruptcy

Over the years the bankruptcy rate has climbed substantially. Even with a recent decline, the numbers are still well above where they were only 10 years ago. Bankruptcy was created as a safety net for those who had very tough life circumstances. It still plays a

---

*On the Internet at www.debtorsanonymous.org.
†Find a credit counseling service at the United States National Foundation for Credit Counseling at www.nfcc.org.

useful role in that way; however, more and more people are using bankruptcy as an escape valve to get away from problems of their own making.

Let me get up on my soapbox for a minute. I'm not into telling other people what's right and wrong, but I think it's an ethical issue in those instances where one person's decision creates a cost for everyone else. An increasing number of middle-income people are declaring bankruptcy. People who have deep financial problems because they have *chosen* to live beyond their means for years do not, in my opinion, have a right to clear the decks by filing for bankruptcy. These are folks who wouldn't dream of walking around their neighborhood asking every person they meet for a dollar so that they could buy a large screen TV, yet, in effect, that is what bankruptcy involves. If overspenders declare bankruptcy, everyone pays. Our interest rates are higher to make up for defaults, stores have to charge more to cover the bad debts and bounced checks, and bank fees are higher to make up for a few customers' poor credit practices. By declaring bankruptcy, financially irresponsible people are asking society to pay for their past decisions. They don't hurt the big, impersonal institutions that they owe money to; they hurt the hundreds of everyday customers of those institutions, most of whom would never consider spending thousands of dollars they don't have. Their irresponsibility hurts you and me. Not everyone who declares bankruptcy is irresponsible, of course. Many people who declare bankruptcy are low-income people who have never managed their money in a way to give themselves enough Security to weather a financial storm.

So, what if you are in so deep that you do not know how to get out? Call a consumer credit counseling service in your area and make a plan to pay it back. They can help you get more manageable terms and avoid being another statistic. Bankruptcy should be the absolute last resort.

I'm not saying that you should never declare bankruptcy. Bankruptcy is a critical safety net for those who really need it—those who have been wiped out by illness or an accident, whose business goes belly up despite their best efforts, who find themselves unemployed, or who get sued and are unable to cover the legal costs or settlement. Of course, a cash cushion and appropriate insurance can prevent many of these circumstances from becoming financially devastating. Sometimes, however, even those Security tools are not enough. Consider bankruptcy if you have to, but only after you explore every other avenue.

CHAPTER 15

....

The Big Squeeze

When Your Means
Are Not Enough

IN THE FIRST SECTION OF THIS BOOK, I DESCRIBED THE FLOW OF money in your life as a waterfall: The energy and talents you have are converted into money by a transaction called earning and then the money that you bring in is converted to goods and services by a transaction called spending. The bulk of this book focuses on the second transaction—spending. The great thing about spending is that, in the short run, it is largely within your control and you can impact it immediately with the choices you make. The not so great thing is that you are starting from a place of finite resources—what you earn today. As you become a Conscious Spender, you may find that you already have enough money. However, if you find that living within your means equals doing without what you really want, then read on. In this chapter, we look at ways that you can increase your income.

If you have developed a Conscious Spending Plan that reflects your values, yet still don't have room for your dreams, you may want to start looking at the earnings side of the equation.

How Much Is Enough?

Before I start to share some strategies for increasing your earnings, I'd like to explore how much is enough for a moment.

I see people take two very important journeys in their relationship with money. One is the journey to the place where money becomes a tool of self-expression, a way to really align with what they value. The one thing that most aligned people share is a real understanding of themselves and a desire to follow the beat of their own drum—no matter how arrhythmic or unusual that beat may be. A certain level of self-confidence and willingness are required to make such a course possible. People who use money for self-expression make selective choices and seem perfectly comfortable with them. Have you ever met the person in your neighborhood whose car is substantially worse or substantially better than everyone else's on the street? What about the person who is rumored to have quite a lot of money, yet still lives in an area with people who earn a lot less? Or the person who travels the world in comfort every year but rarely spends a dime on nice luggage?

The journey to self expression is often followed by the journey to the place of having enough. It is an internal journey to a place where people feel that they have enough and simply do not want more stuff. They don't spend from a sense of needing to satisfy anyone outside their household, and they don't keep striving for more. As people become aligned with their values, they often let go of many of their unaligned wants and begin to define what *enough* is to them. *More* is simply not important to them. The interesting thing is that most people who feel they have enough have spending patterns that are aligned with their individual set of values. They have hit the stop button and stepped off the consumption treadmill that could have kept them running for the rest of their lives. It doesn't necessarily mean downshifting; it just means halting the ever-aspiring upshifting.

"Enough." How's that for a nebulous concept? *Enough* is an elusive and ill-defined term. It boils down to a gut feeling. Are you happy with the stuff—not the people or circumstances, but the material possessions—in your life? I rarely meet people who are happy with the stuff yet unhappy with the people and circumstances; usually being happy with the people and circumstances paves the way to being happy with the stuff. The stuff in and of itself cannot make you happy, but dissatisfaction lays between where you are now and where you deeply aspire to be. For many people, *enough* is that tempting place just over the horizon. At a $30,000 income, $35,000 might seem like enough, but as soon as you get there, *enough* has moved ahead and remains out of reach. By boiling it down to your values, you can take some of the dollar signs away and focus on what it is you really want in life. Who do you want to be? What to you want to do? What would you like to have? From that place, define *enough* and start working toward it. Once you get there, you may want to move the bar to *abundance* or you may be happy with a very well-aligned *enough*.

Having enough does not depend on your income; it depends on your expectations and your inner awareness of what really counts to you. For some, a $40,000 income and a modest home feel like enough. Could they spend more if they had it? Sure, but they get enough of what they value to feel a deeper satisfaction. However, for others, $400,000 may not feel like enough. At a higher income level, they may also have higher expectations about the type of home they own, clubs they belong to, clothes they wear, and cars they drive. Reaching that place of financial satisfaction feels very far off for some people at all income levels, and it may always remain elusive.

Feeling as though you don't have enough does not mean that you aren't spending in an aligned way. It is possible to spend the money you have in a way that is very aligned with what you value, but you may still aspire to have more. More to build Security. More to get a lifestyle that is easier and more comfortable. More to have more fun. Wanting more is okay, even if you have plenty by other people's standards. It's your life and you get to choose what is enough and what more is worth aiming for. If you feel that you don't have enough or have enough but want more, the good thing is that, to a large degree, you can change your situation. If you have reached a point in your journey where you realize that your income simply will not pay for the life that you desire, this is the chapter for you.

Exercise: How Much Is Enough?

Take a piece of paper and divide it into three columns or start a new document on your computer and create a table that is three columns wide and eight rows deep. Label the three columns "Category," "Enough," and "Abundance." In the left column of the next row, write Security. In the middle column, write a description of what you would need to have to feel that you have enough Security. Don't limit yourself to financial answers. For example, you may need to have a good understanding of investing, or comfort that your parents have handled their estate planning needs appropriately. In the third column, write a description of what you would need to have to feel that you have abundant Security. Again, write both financial and nonfinancial items. Repeat for each category: Shelter, Sustenance, Self and Family, Social, Society, and Soul. Take the time you need to flesh out a vivid picture.

How much does enough differ from your current Conscious Spending Plan? What additional income do you need to have enough? Are there areas where you are already experiencing enough? What is more important to you, the financial items or the others? Which nonfinancial items can you begin to get today without increasing your income? When you look at the list, what income do you think you need to feel that you have enough? That you have abundance?

· ·

A Few Words about Simplicity

Some people have very strong opinions about what is enough. That's great when they are judging what is enough for them and living in a way that is congruent with their standards. At times, though, you may meet people who feel that their own idea of enough is "right," and all who live with different standards are wasteful, shallow, or not too smart. It may come from a genuine lack of understanding of what drives other people. Or it may come from a judgmental place where they want to impose their values on the whole world. For example, if you have a large house, you may meet people who simply don't understand what drives people to have huge houses. It's not just that they can't afford a large house or don't choose it for themselves; they simply can't imagine aspiring to it. The problem arises when they don't shrug off the interesting differences between people's values, but instead judge others' values as worse than their own. They may think your choice is wrong: It takes up more resources than you need, it is an external display of wealth, and kids are starving in Africa. Their judgment may come from their religious beliefs, life experience, or belief that the world would be a better place if everyone had *their* values. Unfortunately, the last reason is wrong. If everyone stepped off the consumption treadmill simultaneously, the economy would go into freefall.

Is a simple life more affordable? Absolutely. Is it better? Not from any objective standpoint.

The "simplicity" movement, which grew out of the well-known personal finance book *Your Money or Your Life*, espouses, sometimes self-righteously, a life of few material possessions, a lot of homemade goods, and a degree of cutting corners that is simply not comfortable or desirable to many people.* This movement is a strong counterreaction to the commercial messages we receive daily from advertising and the popular culture. However, I believe that the book's message is off track for many people, because the choices that the authors believe are right from an environmental and ethical standpoint reflect their own values and do not allow room for very different value sets. If the simplicity movement approach appeals to you, that's great. You may even think that its value set provides a higher ethical standard. If so, it sounds as if you have found a way to practice Conscious Spending that works with your value set.

Many of us, however, really enjoy some of the material pleasures that money can buy. You may even have a dream that goes the whole nine yards: big house, vacation home, boat, overseas trips, and so on. That's great. If you have a clear picture of what you are aiming for, it is likely to motivate you to get it. Let's look at how. This chapter is for those who want more of the goods or experiences that money *can* buy but don't yet have the means to buy them.

We look at seven strategies to increase your resources:

1. Cashless creativity
2. Leapfrogging

---

*Joe Dominguez and Vicki Robin, *Your Money or Your Life* (New York: Penguin Books, 1992).

3. Smartening up

4. Trend spotting

5. Getting a bit on the side

6. Cashing in on your passion

7. Taking a leap

Cashless Creativity: Cost-Free Ways of Getting More for Your Money

You want more. You can either get more for the money you have or get more money. Let's look at some ways to get more for what you have, because that is an easier strategy in the short term than increasing your earnings.

Again, I do not preach cutting corners and clipping coupons unless you enjoy it or feel it brings you more gain than pain. However, there may be cost-cutting strategies that are aligned with your values that really can get you more of what you want with the money you have.

Cashless creativity involves getting clever about getting the stuff you want. It starts with the question: What do I want? Whatever the answers are, you can then start brainstorming. How can I get someone to give this to me for free or for a discounted price? The answers you come up with may range from setting up a barter arrangement to organizing an event. Some of the great ideas I have seen include:

- A theater buff volunteers as an usher every couple of weeks at the Shakespeare Theater to get to see the live performances he could not otherwise afford.

- A friend in the massage business is great at bartering. She wanted a personal coach, so she bartered down the price by working a monthly massage into the agreement.

- A vacation with his sister and parents was an affordable way for a man in his early twenties to see the other side of the world. The parents picked up the travel cost for their adult children, who could not have afforded the trip any other way, and enjoyed spending time with them.

- An avid amateur photographer teaches a beginners' class in return for use of the great darkroom facilities.

- A woman who knows her way around a sailboat is in great demand among the sailing friends she has met in a town on the Chesapeake. They own the expensive boats and always need well-trained crew to help them on weekends.

- A man on a quest for personal growth reinforces the lessons learned in the classes he has taken by assisting teachers as they run other classes.

- A college student works part time in a ski company restaurant throughout winter in return for lunches, all the skiing he wants off hours, and a basic salary. He is fast-tracking his way through college by taking the winter semester off and loading up on lower-priced summer school classes with the money he earns.

- A writer does promotional materials for a local restaurant in exchange for a few nights of great wining and dining.

- A responsible man of few possessions acts as a caretaker and house sitter for families of much property. He gets to live and write in beautiful surroundings for free and enjoys the variety and solitude that it offers. They get a quiet writer to take care of their homes while they travel and are happy to recommend him to other friends.

The key to cashless creativity is to focus on things that you enjoy. For example, if you are the one in your group of friends who is most inclined to organize events and outings, find things that you can do where the tenth person goes for free, and be that tenth person. Make sure that your cashless creativity does not step over the bounds and become mooching. I remember backpacking around the world when I was in my early twenties and inviting many of the interesting travelers I met to come to visit if their travels brought them to my hometown. One or two dropped in, but no one had the audacity that one of my friends endured when foreign backpackers visited, with friends in tow, and overstayed their welcome for a couple of weeks before their painfully polite host was forced to ask them to leave.

If you fear that your cashless creativity looks like mooching to others, you may find it is more comfortable to be up front about it than to have your friends discover it later. Just lay your plan out there and let them choose: "I am happy to organize the vacation/outing/tickets for the group if you are comfortable with me having the free ticket. It'll save you time and effort, and it would be great to be able to join you." "I'd love to spend the weekend at your beach house. I won't be able to return the favor unless I win the lottery, but if the pleasure of my company is enough reward, I'd be delighted to go." They know exactly what they are getting into, and you get to have more of what you want with the money you already have.

One final note. Cashless creativity should be easy and fun. If you are suddenly finding yourself creating situations where you have to do a lot of work to get what you want, rethink it. Would you be better off getting a part-time job or using your time and energy to increase your earnings than to do this?

Leapfrogging: Getting More Money in the Field You Are In

Remember the good old days when you stayed with a company for years and trusted that they would keep your salary rising at a fair pace so that you would keep abreast of your peers and people in comparable positions at other companies? In most industries, those days are over. I am not saying that you need to change employers, or even that your employer is paying a less than fair salary if you have been in the same place for a while. I am just saying don't assume it.

You have probably seen leapfrogging at work. A colleague leaves and lands a higher-paying job at a competitor's company, one that she would have had to wait 3 years for in your company. Sometimes you even see internal leapfrogging when a colleague takes some assignment out of the regular path to broaden his experience base, and later returns to your area a few notches above his colleagues who sat on the same lily pad the whole time. Don't sit there and croak about it. Join the game.

How can you know what your market price is? One source is the newspaper classifieds; however, it is not always clear what salaries are offered for the positions and whether you would qualify for the jobs that sound comparable, but it is a great place to start. Some of the job-listing sites on the Internet* can also give you leads, and some can be a great place to begin research for

---

*Try www.careermosaic.com, www.monsterboard.com, www.careerbuilder.com, or the jobs in the on-line classified section of your city's major newspaper.

higher-level positions.* You can find government research documents on-line or in the library,† but as with most government statistics, they can be too general to provide a good measuring stick. Magazines and job fairs also can be a good source of current data. Some magazines have articles on what people earn, or highlight one type of job and the salary ranges within it. Job fairs will give you plenty of information about the employers in the area, but often there is little specific information on salaries offered. Similarly, the grapevine at work may be a source to get an idea of what the new employees at your level are coming in at, though it can be an inaccurate source. Finally, you can ask the experts. Depending on your level, you may be able to talk with headhunters or career advisors about your value on the open market. With all of these sources, just by being curious, your radar will be up and you may pick up all sorts of information.

Of course, even if you know exactly what a new colleague earns or what a competitor of your firm would pay for your talents, you do not know your value to your employer. Do an audit of what you bring to your employer that is worth something to him or her. Do you have a knowledge set that the company has invested heavily in? Do you have an understanding of a complex system that it would take months for someone else to understand? Does your internal network mean that you get your work done more efficiently than your colleagues? It could be that your value is

---

*Take a look at www.futurestep.com for a quiz that will tell you what your market price is. It focuses primarily on executives in the $50,000 to $150,000 range, so it doesn't have an answer for everyone.
†The Bureau of Labor and Statistics has some data, which you can find in the jobs section of www.yahoo.com and in several of the other sites mentioned in previous footnotes.

highest by staying where you are, as long as your employer is paying you a market or above-market rate.

Once you've done a bit of homework, you can think about what you would like to do. You can arm yourself with data and with a list of how you have added value to your current employer, and ask for a raise. You can go shopping internally for a position that will add to your internal and market value. You can interview with other firms to find out your real worth, although I have an ethical issue with interviewing around just to feel out your salary potential if you have no intention of actually changing jobs. You also can choose to stop and regroup—perhaps build a key skill, create a long-term plan, or seek a mentor to advise you—before doing anything.

As you make a decision regarding future employment, ask yourself what you value. If the collegiality or familiarity of your current employer means a lot to you, then take that value into account. If changing jobs means moving your home or commuting a longer distance, question whether it would be worth it to you. If you are having the best time of your life in your position and simply don't want to think about changing, trust your gut. If you are with a firm that has stock options, get clear on what they are worth to you and when they vest. Just don't accept being paid a below-market salary for the sole reason of your loyalty to your employer. Your employer will not be loyal to you if the company hits a bad patch and needs to lay off people, although I believe most employers want to be fair and really do value people who embody a level of corporate knowledge.

If you decide that your first course of action should be to try to get a pay raise, find out what your company's usual approach is. Many larger firms have review processes that are the ideal time to present your case for a significant catch-up in pay if you are lagging behind the market. Finesse your pitch before you go in to the review, and make sure you are asking for the raise from a place of showing your employer your strength and your value. Too often, people ask for raises because their own financial obligations are rising, which is not your employer's problem. However, if you ask for a raise based on your skill and responsibilities, the potential you show, and the market value for what you do, you should make a strong case.

If you do decide to explore the next lily pond, use due diligence. Ask all the questions that you wish you had asked your current employer. Get a sense of the career progression, if that is important to you, and the company's internal culture. Interview them as much as they interview you. It's like dating: If you seem too eager before you fully understand what is on offer, you are not as attractive to them. There's a qualitative difference between being excited about an opportunity and being desperate for acceptance, more money, or a bigger title.

The fun part about leapfrogging is that you may get to live happily ever after without having to kiss any toads.

Smartening Up: Back to School for You

As you look at increasing your earnings, you may find you hit a brick wall because of your skill or education level. Going back to school to improve your skills or retrain is a long-term investment, particularly if you take time out of the workforce in order to do it. You may choose to advance your education in order to increase your long-term earnings potential, or you may go back to school so you can improve your mind, find more deeply satisfying work, explore a curiosity, or get an external stamp of approval. All such reasons are fine and valid; however, if you make the choice from a perspective other than your personal finances, be clear on why you are spending the time and money before setting foot in the classroom. Note that if your education is about increasing earnings, count it in Self and Family. If it is for any other reason, count it in Soul.

Going back to school may be a large step or a small one. When I left my job as a reporter to go back to school full time for 2 years, I knew that the decision would quickly pay for itself because I was in the rare situation of leaving a very low-paying industry and hoped to be hired into a very well-paying industry afterward. For many of my schoolmates who were already earning big bucks, taking 2 years away from earning was a much more difficult financial decision. It may have taken them years to get a financial payback, however, most looked to move into the most senior ranks of companies and realized that an investment in their younger years would pay off over their lifetime employment. Others have gone back to school in smaller ways that have very fast paybacks.

. . . .

Judith, a therapist in her 50s, was simply tired of battling with managed-care organizations to get reimbursed for the work she does, having to wait months and months for payment, and ending up with a small slice of the cake at the end of the struggle. "I was getting really jaded and angry. Psychotherapy with managed care felt hard. After all my training, I was getting less than the telephone repairman. It was a real burn-out situation," she said. She trained part time to be a personal coach, taking classes that built on her therapy skills and translated them into the personal-coaching field. The transition seemed natural: She could build a coaching practice while still practicing therapy, and she could get the training without spending an enormous amount of time or money. She cut back on her client load as she began the transition. "I'm purposely cutting back to create the space to refocus. You can't do it if you are working yourself to death. In the transition, I'm poorer but happier." Ultimately she will probably have a mix of therapy and coaching clients, and she is partnering to run some groups with a colleague where their coaching skills will combine with their therapy skills. Additionally, more of her therapy clients will come to her directly as she moves away from depending on managed-care organizations by changing her marketing. Although she expects eventually to earn much more than when she was only dealing with managed-care clients, she has realized that her transition is no longer about money. "Even if I'm poor, I want to be living my values."

. . . .

If you choose to go back to school to increase your earnings potential, take a look several rungs up the career ladder and see what sort of education is valued. Find a couple of people with the education you are thinking of getting and spend some time with each one, talking about what is important to look for in the training, where they recommend getting it, and how it has improved their prospects. You are not only getting advice, you are showing your get up and go and perhaps finding a mentor in the process. If you want to use the extra education to change fields, talk to people in the field you are interested in about what training they have and the schools they recommend. Even complete strangers may be flattered or happy to share their knowledge with you, and you will be taking the first step toward building a network that may land you the right job when you finish your training.

There is a cost to getting more education. Your employer may offset some of the financial cost, or you may qualify for scholarships and awards. Talk to the school's financial aid people to see if there are other sources of funding, and how to finance the balance if you don't have enough savings to cover the tuition.

Trend Spotting: Finding the Hot Fields

The work force is evolving faster than you can say "dot.com." Another way to boost your earnings is to go where there are money, jobs, and room to climb. Just as the last of the buggy wheelmakers slowly went broke, the first of the car tiremakers probably retired fat and happy. Trend spotting means getting into a field where the opportunities are going to grow at a pace faster than the workforce as a whole. Someone with 5 years of experience in the Internet field may earn substantially more than someone with 20 years experience in the electric utility field, simply because there are fewer people in the job market with that much Internet experience. Finding an emerging trend can be the key to raising your earnings.

For some people, trend spotting can be particularly important. Some sectors are in decline, such as manufacturing, where companies are moving their operations offshore or automating them. And some cities are having a tough time attracting the industries they need to stay vital. If you are in a sector or city that has fallen down and can't get up, then trend spotting, combined with some retraining or some repositioning by moving to another location, might be needed.

Recently, I was listening to a radio talk show where the guests were computer experts. A young woman phoned in and asked how she could make money in high tech without being technically inclined. The great thing about trend spotting is that there are so many ways to cash in on a trend. If we look at the Internet field, for example, we see that the companies that are employing all the high-tech geeks are also employing human resource managers, payroll clerks, public relations staff, administrators, graphic designers, writers, and so on. Those growing companies are served by businesses that include caterers, printers, service technicians, plumbers, and so on. And the employees need the services of home builders, manicurists, pet sitters, nannies, shop assistants, gardeners, and so on. So many of the skills you have today can probably be applied in some way, shape, or form to the new economy.

For business owners, trend spotting may merely involve marketing your business toward the emerging industry of your choice. If you own a small printing house, perhaps you can now own a small printing house that specializes in serving the dot.com startups in your area. If you are a pet sitter, perhaps you can open a doggie day care in the area of your town where the new businesses are sprouting up.

The key with trend spotting is to find the place where your skills or interests coincide with an emerging-market demand. If you can see the demand but don't have the skills, you may need to combine trend spotting with going back to school. The earlier you get in on a trend, the more likely you are to be carried along with it to a high degree of success. But be careful to separate the trends from the fads. Fads fade as quickly as they rise, and are more highly targeted. For example, the increasing number of high-income earners who dote on their pets is a trend, but doggie bakeries may be a fad.

Getting a Bit on the Side: Selling Your Spare Time

Taking on a part-time income-producing activity can add bucks to your bottom line, whether you are a homemaker who wants an income source of your own or a full-time worker looking to add to your income. I'm not talking about answering those ads you see tacked to streetlights proclaiming "Earn $3,000/month part time from home." They may be advertising a legitimate business, but if it is such a great deal, why do they have to advertise that way?

Selling your spare time can involve anything from teaching a class one night a week at a local college to investing in rental real estate that you manage yourself. There are a lot of opportunities out there; the tough part is to find one that fits with your interests and is lucrative enough to make it worth your while to have less time. It's tough to work two jobs. I did it for a couple of years when I became a reporter. I had been working in a more lucrative field but followed my heart and took a (temporary) vow of poverty by becoming a financial reporter at a daily newspaper. I ended up taking a part-time position at a weekend paper and doing the occasional catering job so that I could both save for graduate school and keep reheeling the expensive shoes I had bought as a banker. If you already have a job, try to increase your earnings in your current position or change to a higher-paying, full-time position before you think of adding a second job.

. . . .

Stacey has an eye for quality. When she walks up Fifth Avenue on her way to her job as a publisher's assistant, she gazes in shop windows laden with temptations well beyond her reach. For the past five holiday seasons, Stacey has taken on a weekend position for about 6 weeks, working behind the counter at Tiffany & Co. Working Friday afternoon and Saturday, she doesn't get much rest for those few weeks before Christmas, but in addition to the money she earns, she gets to buy small gifts for her family and friends at a staff discount, and she works in an environment she enjoys. "It's not my money that is being spent most of the time, but I get a huge amount of pleasure out of finding the perfect piece for customers and knowing that my taste helped them give a better gift. It's like being one of Santa's helpers—but in the nicest workshop I could imagine." She admits that working part time is not her top choice. "Yet I'd rather have a job that I love that doesn't pay a lot and supplement it with a part-

time job, than do something I didn't enjoy 52 weeks a year. This is the best of both worlds, although one day I hope to earn enough in publishing to be able to skip the holiday job."

. . . .

There are a lot of ways to get extra cash. The first option is to work part time for someone else. It is a myth that part-time work is mainly for the lower-skilled positions or is poorly paid. I know consultants who pick up projects with billing rates of $250 an hour and higher, and professionals who are part-time professors and teach a class or two at night to get extra cash and panache. As the workforce gets more flexible, you can find a part-time version of nearly any full-time position, whether you are a partner in a law firm or a salesperson in a store. Your part-time position may be in the field you already work in, in a related field, or, like Stacey's, in one that is a complete break from what you do the rest of your working time. You can take a part-time job that involves regular hours, periodic work, or seasonal stints where you fill in at heavy times. If you already have a full-time position, there may be ways to add a part-time position involving weekend or evening work with regular hours that don't overlap with your full-time commitment. Periodic work ranges from picking up occasional training or consulting projects in your field of expertise to working as a market research interviewer when you have a spare evening. Seasonal positions range from sorting packages at a shipping company in December to preparing tax returns in April.

The second option is to work part time at building a business you start yourself or that you buy into. First, let me throw up a warning flag about multilevel marketing companies. A lot of people have tried to get extra income by becoming involved in a multilevel marketing scheme, but it is very possible to take on a part-time business for extra cash and find it ends up costing you

money. The companies themselves may be legitimate and their products good; however, the business model is such that the newcomers on the bottom rungs of the sales chain often come out poorer and wiser. The distributors above them in the chain can make money from the people below them in two ways: earning a commission on the sales that the new people make, and selling the new people training, motivational events, and starter kits. Some people in these organizations recruit salespeople with a message of entrepreneurial freedom and self-determined wealth, and then sell them the classes that they need to make the dream come true. Often the cost of the classes outweighs the earnings from sales, and the new recruit finds that he or she is quickly going backward. I have met people who have become very wealthy from multilevel marketing, and I have met people who have lost their shirts. I put forward the same warning about companies that train you in anything that sounds too good to be true. Sometimes the slick marketers on the infomercials pushing their system to make a fortune in stocks, real estate, or other investment products are only wealthy because they sell training and newsletters. If you are interested in the opportunities, do some research and put on a cloak of skepticism to shield yourself from their charming sales pitches.*
And never, ever, borrow money to take just one more course if your gut tells you it does not add up.

That said, there are some good opportunities out there to build or buy into a business. In terms of buying into another business opportunity, there are publications that have ideas for people who

---

*A quick check for horror stories can be done on the Internet by doing a search using the name of the organization that you are thinking of becoming involved with and the word "scam." You may come across some interesting information from disgruntled people. Their stories may be colored by sour grapes, but it's a good way to see if there are angry people left in the wake of the organization.

want to build a business. Browse a magazine stand to find a publication that has ads for the sort of opportunities that appeal to you, and then research the companies that catch your eye. Again, it's investor beware!

Building a business from scratch is no easy thing. To succeed, you need to understand some marketing and finance principles, have a product or service that is attractive, and be prepared to put in a lot of time and energy. Later I talk about building a business based on a hobby you already have, but here I am talking about businesses that are deliberately created because you see a need in the market or feel you have a great idea. More small businesses fail than succeed. Take some classes in running a business before you start plowing money into your idea. After all, the idea is to get more money, not less!

Cashing In on Your Passion: Getting Some Money from Fun

Turning a hobby into a business is more fun, though often less lucrative, than a part time job or business.

. . . .

John enjoys tinkering around in his tool shed, his "cave" as he calls it. With woodworking tools of all sorts, leftover doors, trim, and other random items from his old Victorian and his imagination, he has been creating interesting objects for years. Once some old door handles and a piece of trim were turned into a rustic and beautiful rack of coat hooks. Another time, an old leadlight window was transformed into a lamp within his bookshelf. He received so many comments from his friends, and a request from his wife not to put any more objects into their small home, that he contacted a local craft gallery. His weekend tinkering still gives him great joy, and his hand-icraft objects bring in a good bit of extra money. Better still, now he can get a tax break on all the money he spends on supplies and equipment. Even his "cave" is a tax writeoff.

. . . .

Although John doesn't expect ever to make more than a couple of thousand a year from his woodcrafts, some hobbies grow into major businesses. Pierre and his wife were talking one night about her collection of Pez dispensers. He picked up on her need to be able to trade with other collectors around the world and started a company in 1995. The company that they started is now a household name: eBay. Now *that's* cashing in on a hobby!

Plenty of hobbies can make money with just a little extra work, from arts and crafts to heavy labor (I'd love a part-time job in demolition—what a way to get rid of excess energy). The interesting thing is to see how a business born out of a passion for your hobby may grow into being a tremendous source of joy and perhaps one day your primary source of income. Among the many things my friends have done for extra dollars are: beekeeping and selling honey, painting and selling the art in a local artists' cooperative, doing masonry jobs for neighbors, designing and landscaping gardens, playing the piano at events, photographing weddings, performing psychic readings. Most of them have a passion for their interest and have cashed in on the passion at times. Sometimes they are motivated by the need for extra income, sometimes by the joy of doing what they do and a recognition that it is fair to be paid for it.

Just as with cashless creativity, the key to cashing in on your hobby is to make sure that it remains fun. If making a business out of your hobby removes the joy, find another way to get extra cash and keep your passion alive.

Taking a Leap: Going for the Big Goal

All of the strategies we just looked at are incremental: changing jobs, following trends, adding skills, and finding additional sources of income. Your desire to increase your income toward your definition of *enough* may call for a more radical approach. Taking a leap involves a level of risk that the other strategies do not offer. This strategy may have very high returns, or it may fail. If the desire to make it big means that you are willing to take the risk of ending up back where you are or even behind where you are, consider taking a leap.

Taking a leap involves letting go of some of your certainty today in the hope of getting a big payback. One way to do this would be to quit your job and start up or buy into a business. I'm not advocating stupidity here: You will want to have researched it thoroughly first, have a good business plan, and have a source of funds to see you through the start-up period.

Another way of taking a leap that may be less scary is to join an entrepreneurial company. Many newly formed firms offer positions that have a relatively low base salary and a potentially lucrative stock option plan. The decision to join the firm is a decision to bet on the firm's ultimate success. The stock market has been very volatile, and I read daily about how the net worth of well-known high-tech industry players moves by tens of millions each day. For every person who is experiencing swings from extremely rich to merely very rich and back again in a day, there are hundreds of people lower down in their organizations watching their dreams of having *enough* wax and wane by the hour. All of the uncertainty may pay very large dividends. Companies such as Microsoft, AOL, and Qualcomm have made thousands of their employees, from receptionists to technology gurus, into millionaires. And for every millionaire that a firm has made, there are dozens of friends sitting around lamenting, "I wish I had followed John's lead . . ." The risk is, of course, that the company you tie your future to may fizzle. The stock options may end up worthless and you may end up poorer and not all that wiser. The key is to really research any company that you are considering joining, especially if your income is tied to its success. Do you think the business idea is sound? Do you respect the management? Do the media and stock analysts who track the industry think that the company seems sound? Can you explain to your next door neighbor what they do? Taking a leap is great if you feel comfortable about the company, can afford to risk the downside, and have an adventurous streak.

Finally, some people take a leap by betting on their own skills. Whether you are an investor who thinks your stock-picking skills are above the norm, or a writer who has a gut feeling that the great book idea you have might just make it, going full steam ahead to reach the dream involves taking a leap. And like the entrepreneurs whose ideas fail and the employees whose stock options are worthless, people who bet on their own skills may find they don't win the golden egg. If that scares you, then find another tactic.

Getting Down to Getting More

Increasing your income may not happen overnight. Even in a strong economy, it takes time and persistence to find the right job, gain additional skills, find a way to cash in on a trend, build a path to a new business, or turn a hobby into a moneymaking venture. Even taking a leap may sound like a fast fix, but will probably take some time until it pays dividends. One of the reasons that this book focuses primarily on managing spending is that you can begin doing that today. Increasing your means takes time and takes planning.

All of these options require research and planning, but an even more important first step is to clarify the reasons for your decisions. Focus back on your values and how you want to express them. Find the right balance between honoring the values and buying into an ever-increasing list of wants. There is often an assumption that people should aim for abundance. However, abundance doesn't always mean a lot of money or stuff. The most crucial abundance is an abundance of what you value. And remember, if you do want to increase your means, you have all the tools available to you. Even uneducated, poor, and otherwise disadvantaged people have built fortunes. The one thing that they had was determination—and that's something money can't buy.

Bibliography

Books

Cook, Philip J., and Charles T. Clotfelter. *Selling Hope: State Lotteries in America*. Cambridge, MA: Harvard University Press, 1991.

Dominguez, Joe, and Vicki Robin. *Your Money or Your Life*. New York: Penguin Books, 1992.

Edelman, Ric. *The New Rules of Money: 88 Simple Strategies for Financial Success Today*. New York: HarperCollins, 1998.

Edelman, Ric. *Ordinary People, Extraordinary Wealth*. New York: HarperResouce, 2000.

Frank, Robert H. *Luxury Fever: Why Money Fails to Satisfy in an Era of Excess*. New York: The Free Press, 1999.

Hendricks, Gay. *Conscious Living: Finding Joy in the Real World*. San Francisco: HarperSanFrancisco, 2000.

Hunt, Mary. *The Complete Cheapskate: How to Get Out of Debt, Stay Out, and Break Free from Money Worries Forever*. Nashville, TN: Broadman and Holman Publishers, 1998.

Schor, Juliet B. *The Overspent American: Upscaling, Downshifting and the New Consumer*. New York: Basic Books, 1998.

Stanley, Thomas J. *The Millionaire Mind*. Kansas City, MO: Andrews McMeel, 2000.

Underhill, Paco. *Why We Buy: The Science of Shopping.* New York: Simon & Schuster, 1999.

Weiss, Michael J. *The Clustered World: How We Live, What We Buy, and What It All Means About Who We Are.* Boston, MA: Little, Brown, 2000.

Studies/Articles

Bankruptcy: The Next Twenty Years, National Bankruptcy Review Commission Final Report, October 1997.

Hitt, Jack, "The Broke Millionaire," *GQ* (April 1999): 196–203, 234.

Jacobs, Eva, and Stephanie Shipp. *How Family Spending Has Changed in the U.S.,* Monthly Labor Review, Department of Labor, March 1990.

Recent Changes in U.S. Family Finances: Results from the 1998 Survey of Consumer Finances, Federal Reserve Board Bulletin, January 2000.

....

Conscious Spending

Next Steps

Log on to my website, www.MsSpent.com, where you will find a lot of great resources, including the following freebies:

- *Read Ms. Spent's advice column and bulletin board.* Access the original financial advice column on the Web. Submit questions and read past columns. Post comments on the bulletin board.

- *Access Web resources.* Follow the links to find a debt counselor and more, such as news from the IRS and Social Security Administration.

- *Subscribe to Ms. Spent's Money Mastery.* This free, biweekly e-mail newsletter will support you in taking action to improve your financial life. It is my gift to you to help you get more out of life and your money, more of what you are passionate about. Each newsletter has tips and ideas that help you align your self and spending to get more fun for your money. Subscribe to it on line.

- *Take Ms. Spent's Introduction to Conscious Spending.* This free telephone-based class is run biweekly at varying times. Jump-start what you learn in *The Ms. Spent Money Guide* and ask me questions. There is limited space available. All you pay for is the long distance call. Find and register for current classes on the website.

- *Join the Conscious Spending Community Call.* This free monthly forum enables you to connect with other Conscious Spenders to share ideas and inspiration. Limited space available. All you pay for is the long distance call. Times and phone numbers are listed on the website.

In addition, you can take the *Ms. Spent's Money Mastery Coaching Class.* This four-week telephone-based coaching group is held for small groups to take participants from planning their spending to implementing money management strategies. Students develop their own spending plan, based on current income and obligations. A follow-up call one month later reinforces the learning and helps create real change. Students learn:

- What money is and the two transactions that influence its flow.
- The three rules of personal finance.
- The difference between Conscious Spending and Unconscious Spending.
- The seven categories of spending.
- Tactics to move from planning to realizing financial goals.
- Strategies and structures that support money management.
- Conscious Spending habits.

Dates and costs are listed on the website.

For the personal touch, you can invite me to speak at your next conference, keynote address, or workshop. Log on to my website at www.MsSpent.com for more information about booking me for your next event.

Index

Printed and bound by CPI Group (UK) Ltd, Croydon, CR0 4YY

09/06/2025

14685913-0002